TOWER OF THE SUN

Michael J. Totten

Michael J. Totten is a foreign correspondent and foreign policy analyst who has reported from the Middle East, the Balkans and the former Soviet Union.

He's a contributing editor at *World Affairs* and *City Journal*. His work has also appeared in the *New York Times*, the *Wall Street Journal*, the *New Republic* and numerous other publications.

His first book, *The Road to Fatima Gate*, won the Washington Institute Book Prize in 2011, and his second novel, *Resurrection*, was optioned for film in 2014. He won the 2007 Weblog Award for Best Middle East or Africa Blog, he won it again in 2008 and was named Blogger of the Year in 2006 by *The Week* magazine for his dispatches from the Middle East. He lives with his wife in Oregon and is a former resident of Beirut.

Visit his blog at www.MichaelTotten.com

ALSO BY MICHAEL J. TOTTEN

The Road to Fatima Gate
In the Wake of the Surge
Where the West Ends
Taken: A Novel
Resurrection: A Zombie Novel

TOWER OF THE SUN

MICHAEL J. TOTTEN

First American edition published in 2014 by Belmont Estate Books

Cover design by Kathleen Lynch
Edited by Elissa Englund

Manufactured in the United States on acid-free paper

FIRST AMERICAN EDITION

Totten, Michael J.
Tower of the Sun
ISBN-13: 978-0692297537
ISBN-10: 0692297537

In memory of Christopher Hitchens

Contents

One

In the Land of the Brother Leader

Libya, 2004

When you visit another country, it's hard to get a feel for what it's actually like until you leave your hotel room, go for a walk, take a look around and hang out while soaking it in. Not so in Libya. All you have to do is show up. It will impose itself on you at once.

My flight touched down on the runway next to a junkyard of filthy, gutted and broken-down aircraft in an airport otherwise empty of planes. When I stepped out of the hatch into the Jetway, I came face-to-face with three uniformed military goons who scrutinized me and everyone else from behind oversize reflective sunglasses.

Colonel Muammar Qaddafi, mastermind of the 1969 al-Fateh Revolution (a euphemism for his military coup), Brother Leader of the Great Socialist People's Libyan Arab Jamahiriya, greeted arrivals in the passport-control room from a menacing, almost snarling gold-gilded portrait. A translated overhead sign (rare in Libya) said, "Partners Not Wage Earners." In other words: Don't expect to be paid.

A bored official glanced at my visa, rubbed his face, stamped my passport and pointed me toward my first Libyan checkpoint. A man in an untucked button-up shirt, with a cigarette jutting out the side of his mouth, waved me toward a metal detector. He hadn't shaved in two days. I walked through. The alarm screamed, and I braced for a pat-down. He just stood there, took a long drag on his cigarette and stared bleary-eyed into space over my shoulder. I guessed that meant I could go. So I did.

There were no other planes coming or going, so it was easy to find my ride. His name was Abdul. He wore a snazzy black leather jacket and a Western-style goatee.

"Welcome to Libya!" he said as he led me into a parking lot the size of an Applebee's.

"We're really busy right now. This is Libya's high season." They must shut down the airport entirely during the low season.

The capital city of Tripoli was an asteroid belt of monolithic apartment towers. The streets were mostly empty of cars, the sidewalks empty of people. I saw no restaurants, no cafés, no clubs, no bars and no malls. Nor did I see anywhere else to hang out. Libya, so far, looked depopulated.

We drove past a shattered former government compound surrounded by a lagoon of pulverized concrete that once was a parking lot. It was obvious when that thing was built. The 1970s were the 1970s everywhere, even in Libya.

Only as we approached the center of Tripoli did traffic pick up. Hardly anyone walked around, and it was no wonder: a mile-long pit on the side of the road appeared to be the place to give juice bottles, plastic wrappers, garbage bags and worn-out tires the heave-ho.

I saw no corporate advertising: no Pepsi signs, no movie posters and no cute girls flashing milk-mustache smiles for the dairy industry. I did, however, see one hysterical propaganda billboard after another. They were socialist-realist cartoons from the Soviet era, the same kinds of living museum pieces still on display in North Korea and other wonderful places where starving proles live in glorious jackbooted paradise.

The happy-worker theme was a common one; smiling construction workers wore hard hats, and Bedouins turned widgetmakers basked in the glory of assembly-line work. One poster showed two hands chained together at the wrist below an image of Qaddafi's sinister *Green Book* descending from heaven.

At the hotel I ran into my second Libyan checkpoint. A metal detector was set up at the entrance. A young security agent sat at a metal desk and showed off his open copy of the *Green Book*. He propped it at such an angle that I could read the cover, but he couldn't possibly read what was inside.

I stepped through. The alarm screamed, detecting (perhaps) my dental fillings or zipper. He looked up, gave me a nodding "What's up, dude" smile and went back to pretending to read.

I poked around the lobby while Abdul checked me in at the desk.

The gift shop offered a wide range of totalitarian propaganda books and pamphlets in multiple languages. A fantastic selection of Qaddafi watches ranged in price from \$25 to \$600. I bought one for \$25. Qaddafi is shown wearing his military uniform, officer's hat and sunglasses like a swaggering Latin American generalissimo. It was busted right out of the box, the hour hand stuck forever at nine o'clock.

The lobby was plastered with portraits of the boss in various poses. He wore shades in most of them, but in some pictures from his early days, he wore a buffoonish 1970s haircut instead.

I had to suck down my giggles. God, was this guy for real? His inexportable Third Universal Theory was internationalist insofar as it obliterated any sense that Tripoli was Middle Eastern or African—at least from the point of view of the backseat of the car. I could have been in any Soviet-era republic, or even in some parts of the Bronx. But look at those portraits! Now there was something exotic.

Most of the other men in the lobby (I hadn't seen any women since I landed) looked like Arab businessmen who bought their suits from Turkish remainder bins. The only expensively dressed man sat at a shiny wooden desk, the kind you'd expect to see at a law firm. He had no work in front of him, not even papers to shuffle. His job was to stare holes through everyone who stepped into and out of the elevator.

There were no towels in my room. The bathroom was, however, generously stocked with products, all of them packaged in green—the color of Islam and Qaddafi's so-called revolution. The hotel gave me green shampoo, green soap, green bath gel, green toothpaste and even a green shoehorn and comb. All were clearly (and, I must say, unnecessarily) marked "Made in the Great Socialist People's Libyan Arab Jamahiriya." There was no booze (it's banned), no soda, no water, no juice in the minibar. A burn the size and shape of a deflated basketball was seared into the carpet.

I switched on the TV: nothing but hysterical state-run propaganda. I couldn't lower the volume (the knob was broken), but at least I could change the channel and choose whether I wanted to be droned at or screeched at in Arabic.

My window overlooked the Mediterranean Sea and, closer in, a drained and stained swimming pool. There was a forlorn rocky beach down there, cut off from the hotel and everything else by a blank gray slab of a wall. The cold wind whistling into the room from the patio sounded like moaning ghosts trapped in a well.

U ntil the middle of 2004, Americans were banned from Libya, not by Qaddafi but by our own government. The travel ban was lifted, but tourists were still required to book their trip through a Libyan agency. The regime wouldn't tolerate tourists running around loose on their own. You could make your own trip—you didn't have to be a part of a tour group—but you'd still be babysat by a guide.

I didn't go to Libya to see the sights, such as they are. I wanted to see a once forbidden country as it really was. So I set out on foot on my own while I had a brief chance.

It was a jarring experience.

The main drag along the sea into the city was one straw short of a freeway. There were no houses, businesses, restaurants or shops along the way—only clusters of vertical human-storage units surrounded by empty lots the size of a Walmart.

Trash was smeared on the sidewalks. It clogged all the street gutters. Almost every available blank space (and, oh, were there plenty of those) was a dump site.

I felt agoraphobic walking around. The streets were too wide, the buildings too far apart, the landscape barren.

The traffic was too fast, too close and too hectic. I was pinned on a thin ribbon of sidewalk between the Mediterranean and the freeway.

There was no way I could cross that river of mayhem and steel unless I found a traffic light and a crosswalk—an unlikely event, from the look of the place. There wasn't much worth seeing on the other side anyway. Those towers and the empty lots strewn with soda cans, candy-bar wrappers and billowing plastic bags didn't get any prettier as they got closer.

The sea was all but boarded up behind blank white walls and a decayed postindustrial concrete catastrophe of a "waterfront." In the few places I could get a glimpse of the shoreline, it didn't have the look and feel of the familiar Mediterranean but rather of an inland sea in a Central Asian republic. The city felt harsh and jagged, and the close but unreachable sea could not take the edge off.

Three young boys crouched next to the dry side of the seawall. They ran up when they saw me and asked for cigarettes. Those kids could not have been older than 10. I had two choices—corrupt Libya's youth or be a stuffy, uptight naysaying American. I chose to corrupt the children. When I handed over the smokes, each slapped his fist on his heart and cried, *"Allahu akbar!"*

The freeway continued as far as I could see without any way for me to cross it. Traffic was relentless, and I didn't dare wade into it without knowing the rules. I could have just bolted in front of the cars and they would have stopped. But I hadn't been in the country for even two hours. I didn't know how anything worked yet. So I went back to the hotel and ordered some dinner.

I'd say that was my mistake, but I did have to eat.

At the restaurant, there was no sign that said "Please Wait to Be Seated." Should I seat myself? Who knew? I felt ridiculous just standing at the entrance. So I found a table.

A waiter finally came over.

"Are you a tourist?" he said.

"Yes," I lied. Libya was a total-surveillance police state. One person in six worked for the secret police. Best, I thought, to keep my journalistic intentions to myself.

"For tourists we have fish," he said. He did not give me a menu. I didn't see a single menu anywhere in the country. In Libyan restaurants, you sit down and eat whatever they give you.

"What kind of fish?"

"Eh," he said, taken aback by the question. "Fish. Fish. You know, fish."

"Great," I said. "I'll have the fish."

He brought me two small fish the size of my hand, each fried in a pan. Heads, fins and eyeballs were still attached. Bones and guts were inside. They tasted bad and smelled worse. The businessmen at the tables around me drank nonalcoholic Beck's "beer." But all I got was a bottle of water.

Abdul picked me up again in the morning. His job was to show me Tripoli's sights. There weren't many: Green Square, the museum and an old city smaller than downtown Boise. That's it. That's all there is.

We started with the museum. Phoenician and Roman artifacts were on the first floor. Upstairs was the "Islamic period." The top floor was entirely dedicated to the glorification of Qaddafi.

One room displayed gifts to the colonel from foreign officials and heads of state—swords, jeweled boxes, a crystal map of "Palestine" that included Tel Aviv. A living-room set upholstered with a tacky floral print was roped off in a corner. "That's where Qaddafi sits with foreign guests he wants to impress," Abdul said.

Right outside the museum was Qaddafi's Green Square—which isn't green, by the way. It's famous, but it shouldn't be. This is no Italian piazza we're talking about. It's an asphalt parking lot ringed by a six-lane urban speedway.

The nice thing about Green Square is that it's central. The Italian Quarter, built by Italy during Mussolini's fascist-imperialist period, is on one side. The old city is on the other.

The old city was the only neighborhood that looked Middle Eastern. Too bad much of it also looked like the backstreet slums of Havana. Not all of it, though. A few buildings—like the old mosques, a soaring clock tower and the Arch of Marcus Aurelius—were stunning.

It was a pleasant place, actually. Ancient buildings with handcrafted details on them are dignified even in squalor. Rotting grandeur is still grand, after all.

The streets were too narrow for cars. Not one of the shopkeepers harangued me when I walked by as they did constantly in Tunisia when I visited there a few months earlier. There were hardly any cheap tourist gimcracks for sale. I could walk the old city in peace.

Almost everything was solely for local consumption: clothes, fabrics, jewelry, shoes, batteries and so on. One of the narrower streets was lined with almost medieval metal forges, where copper pots and crescent moons for the tops of minarets were banged into shape with hammers and tongs over fires.

I didn't see theaters, clubs or any other places of diversion or entertainment. "Until two years ago," Abdul said, "there was nothing to do in Libya but sleep. Things are better now."

Things weren't much better, though. Libya's economy was still mostly socialist. There will be no fun without capitalism. Sorry. The state just isn't gonna provide it, especially not a state that can't even pick up the garbage.

"So, Abdul," I said as we walked through the souk. "How many Libyans wear a Qaddafi watch?"

"Um," he said and laughed grimly. "Not very many. There are, you know, enough pictures around." He leaned in and whispered, "I don't like him much, to be honest."

I had imagined not.

"Look over there," he said and pointed with his eyes. "You see those two?"

I saw a couple in their mid-20s chatting next to one of the gates to the old city. He wore a black leather jacket, she a long brown overcoat and a headscarf over her hair. They stood close together but didn't touch. They looked soft, comfortable and content together as if they were married.

"Five, 10 years ago I never saw anything like that. It was absolutely forbidden."

He told me to take off my shoes as he led me into a mosque. Seeing the handmade carpets, high ceilings, marbled walls, Roman columns, intricate tile work and soft lighting was like slipping into a warm bath for the soul. The heart-stopping beauty and serenity of the mosque in this harsh urban parking garage of a landscape was a strong incentive for piety, I suspected. I'm not religious, but I could see why some sought refuge from the modern in God. Modernity in this oppressive dystopian city was a spectacular galactic-size failure.

He dropped me off at my hotel before dark. Now that I knew the layout of the city, I decided to return to Green Square alone. I wanted to know what the real Tripoli, the not-touristed Tripoli, looked like.

It was worse on foot than by car and exactly what I expected: all right angles and concrete. Almost everyone in this part of town lived in a low barracks-like compound or a Stalinist tower. Landscaping didn't exist. There were no smooth edges, no soft sights, nothing to sigh at. Tripoli's aesthetic brutality hurt me.

I walked parts of the city that hardly any foreigners ever bothered to see. It looked postapocalyptic, as if it had been evacuated in war or hit with a neutron bomb. The sound of machine-gun fire off in the distance wouldn't have seemed out of place.

Less than 1 percent of the people I saw were women. All those who did go outside wore headscarves. So much for Qaddafi's being a "feminist," as he claimed. Tripoli had as many women out and about as a dust-blown village in the boondocks of Afghanistan.

The few men I did see walked or huddled together. They looked sullen, heavy, severe. I felt raw and exposed, wondering what on earth they must have thought when they saw an obvious foreigner wandering around the desolate streets.

So I did what I could to find out. I smiled at everyone who walked past. You can learn a lot about a people and a place by trying this out. In New York City, people ignore you. In Guatemala City, people will stare. In Libya, they all smiled back, every last one of them, no matter how grumpy or self-absorbed they looked two seconds before.

I never detected even a whiff of hostility, not from a single person. Libyans seemed a decent, gentle, welcoming people with terrible luck. It wasn't their fault the neighborhood stank of oppression.

Most apartment buildings were more or less equally dreary, but one did stand out. Architecturally it was just another modernist horror. But a 6-by-8-foot portrait of Qaddafi was bolted to the facade three stories up. It partially blocked the view from two of the balconies. The bastard couldn't even leave people alone when they were home.

The posters weren't funny anymore. There were too damn many of them, for one thing. And, besides, Qaddafi is ugly. He may earn a few charisma points for traveling to Brussels and pitching his Bedouin tent on the parliament lawn, but he's no Che Guevara in the *guapo* department.

I felt ashamed that I first found his portraits even slightly amusing. The novelty wore off in less than a day, and he'd been in power longer than I'd been alive.

He was an abstraction when I first got there. But after walking around his outdoor laboratory and everywhere seeing his beady eyes and that arrogant jut of his mouth, it suddenly hit me. He isn't merely Libya's tyrant. He is a man who would be god.

His Mukhabarat, the secret police, are omniscient. His visage is omnipresent. His power is omnipotent.

And he is deranged. He says he's the sun of Africa. He threatens to ban money and schools. He vanquished beauty and art. He liquidates those who oppose him. He says he can't help it if the people of Libya love him so much, they plaster his portrait up everywhere. Fuck him. I wanted to rip his face from the walls.

If you go to Libya, you simply must visit Ghadamis. Known by travelers as the jewel of the Sahara, it's worth all the money and all the hassle you have to put up with to get there.

In the early 1980s, Qaddafi's regime emptied the ancient Berber Saharan city by decree. Everyone was shepherded into the modern concrete "new town," which begins right outside the mysterious tomblike adobe gates of the old.

The old city doesn't look like a city when you're inside. It looks like a vast underground system of tunnels and caves lit by skylights. It's not underground; it was built with a roof over the top to keep the infernal summer heat out and the meager winter warmth in. Some of the streets (which really are more like passages) are pitch black even at noon. There was no need for light. The inhabitants had memorized the walls.

It is not a small town. It's an enormous weatherproofed adobe mini metropolis. There are seven quarters and seven gates, one for each resident tribe. Everything you'd expect in a city is there—streets, homes, offices, markets, public squares and mosques, all made of painted mud and sparkling gypsum. The only thing missing from the old city is people.

If Libya were a normal country—and if Ghadamis were a normal city—the old city would be packed with hotels, coffee shops, restaurants, bookstores, Internet cafés and desert-adventure tour offices. But Libya is not a normal country, and Ghadamis is an unwilling ghost town.

My travel agency replaced Abdul with a second guide for the trip to Ghadamis and into the desert. "Yasir," I said to him. "Why were the people of Ghadamis forced out of their homes?"

I knew the answer already. It was part of Qaddafi's plot to Arabize the Berbers and to construct the New Man, a ludicrous ideal hatched in the Soviet Union. (Berbers werw also forbidden to write anything publicly in their own language.) But I wanted to see if a local was permitted to say it. He couldn't—or at least didn't—answer my question.

He only shook his head and laughed nervously. There were others around who could hear.

The old city was declared a World Heritage site by UNESCO. A few engineers were inside shoring up the foundations of an old mosque.

"It's astonishing," one of them said when I chatted him up. He was an Arab who had studied engineering at a Western university and spoke masterful English in fully formed paragraphs. "The sophistication and aesthetic perfection in the old city contrasts markedly with the failures in the new."

No kidding. I've never seen anything like it anywhere else in the world. Neither have you. Because there is nothing like it anywhere else in the world. And there never will be.

"We're here to make this place livable again because someday, you know . . ." He trailed off, but I knew what he wished he could say. Someday Qaddafi would die. When his bones pushed up date palms, the people of Ghadamis could abandon their compounds of concrete and move back into the city that's rightfully theirs.

I returned to the old city at night by myself and saw a single square of light in an upstairs room of an ancient house. The owners were forbidden to stay there at night. But it was nice to know that some of them still left the lights on.

When you visit another country, it's inevitable: you are going to meet other travelers. And you'll almost certainly talk about other places you've been. Go to Costa Rica, and conversations will turn to Guatemala and Bolivia. If you hang out in Cancún, you'll meet people who like the Virgin Islands and Hawaii. In Paris you'll hear talk of London, Prague and Vienna.

So what happens when you bump into others in Libya? In Tripoli, I met a photographer who spends every summer in Darfur. Out in the dunes, I met a long-haired, goofy, bespectacled English guy named Felix. This was the first time he had ever set eyes on a desert. (He really went for it.) He had a thing for totalitarian countries. "I like to visit places based on ideas," he said. Then he checked himself. "That doesn't mean I like the ideas."

"Where to next, Felix?" I said.

"North Korea, if I can get in."

"I'd like to see North Korea," I said. "But after that, what's left?"

"Only the moon," he said and laughed. "This is great, meeting you here. It's nice to know someone else who's open to nuttiness."

You'll find nuttiness in Libya even out in the boonies. On the treacherous so-called road from Ghadamis into the dunes, someone used an enormous piece of ordnance that looked like a mini-Scud missile to mark a 3-foot chassis-busting hole in the ground.

Yasir couldn't take me on that road in his van. So we hired Bashir to come with us. He was a burly man with a turban and a beard who taught philosophy in school. We didn't hire him, though, for his brain. We wanted his Land Rover.

The three of us left Ghadamis and headed straight toward the Algerian gate only a couple of miles away.

Just beyond it, a 300-foot-tall mountain of sand was piled in layers.

"You see that sand," Bashir said and pointed. I could hardly take my eyes off it. "Two weeks ago I drove some Japanese tourists out here. The old guy asked me who built the dune." He chuckled and shook his head. "I told him, well, my grandfather worked for a while on that project, but now he's dead."

"We can't go there," Yasir said. "We must visit Libyan sand. Last month some German tourists were kidnapped right on the other side of the border."

More than 100,000 people were killed in Algeria during the 1990s and into the 2000s in a civil war between the military regime and Islamist fanatics.

"Have you ever been to Algeria?" I asked.

"No one here goes to Algeria," he said.

We drove over a hill and were surrounded on three sides by

dizzying, towering, impossibly sized dunes. We slogged our way to the top, gasping, with calves and thighs burning, not daring to look down, to watch the sunset.

The top was unreal. The desert floor was another world far below ours. If birds were in flight, I could have looked down on them. On the western horizon was the Grand Erg Oriental, a sea of dunes bigger than France that looked from the side like a distant Andes of sand. Bashir prepared bread and sticky mint tea.

I watched the sun go down and the sky go out.

By Libyan standards, this was radical freedom. Life goes on even in countries like this one. No government, no matter how oppressive, can control all the people all the time—especially not in the vast and empty Sahara.

We ran down the sand and climbed back into the Land Rover. Bashir hit the gas. He zigged us and zagged us up, down and across the 300-foot-tall dunes along the border with Algeria. At one point—and I couldn't tell if he was joking or serious—he said we had actually crossed into Algeria.

The stars came out. A full moon rose, turning the sand into silver. We laughed like boys as we rode the dunes in the moonlight.

I didn't go back to Tripoli to hang out in Tripoli. Tourists use the city as a base to visit the spectacular nearby Roman ruins of Sabratha and Leptis Magna. I'm not exactly a ruins buff, but trips to these places came with the package. So I went. And I saw. And I was nearly alone. I shared Leptis Magna with only my guide and some goats. Sabratha would have been empty if the vice president of the Philippines hadn't dropped by at the same time.

But I was glad to be back in Tripoli. This time my hotel was in the Italian Quarter, just two blocks from Green Square. Not again would I have to walk through a swath of Stalinist blocks to get to a proper neighborhood.

My new hotel was more upscale than the first. The management (or was it the state?) pretended to have tighter security. The metal detector just inside the entrance wasn't being watched by a college kid. It was staffed by the military.

Okay, I thought. Now they're gonna be serious. I stepped through and the metal detector screamed. The soldiers ignored me, joked with each other and never looked up. The same thing happened every time I walked through it.

Libya was a totalitarian police state. But it was an awfully lethargic totalitarian police state. It's been a while, I thought, since anyone there drank the Kool-Aid.

The heater in my room sounded like a chopper over the jungles of 'Nam. It was broken and stuck forever on Cold, but the maid left it on anyway. So while it was 60 degrees and cloudy outside, it was a teeth-chattering 50 degrees in my room. I opened the window, and the cold wind off the Mediterranean actually warmed the place up.

A bath could have made me feel better, but the hot-water knob came off in my hand. The hotel had the outward appearance of spiffiness, so I'm sure there was hot water somewhere in the building behind the hole where the knob had come off in my hand. I just couldn't get to any of it.

The elite were downstairs in the lobby. Slick men in suits, mostly from Arab countries, all but ignored the French delegation that was in town while Jacques Chirac cut new oil deals with Qaddafi. There were no Americans, no tourists and no women. I felt underdressed and out of place in my khakis and sandals, but what could I do? I was in a hard-line, oily-sheened Arab police state. I couldn't have blended in if I tried—except, perhaps, in one little corner of the Italian Quarter.

If you were dropped from the sky onto the main street that ran through that district, you could be forgiven if you thought you were somewhere in the West. It was strung from one end to the other with hip, cutting-edge perfume and clothing stores. These places had bright lights, colored walls and fancy displays. They piped in Western music through sophisticated sound systems. The salespeople wore snappy, stylish clothes. The customers were young and cool. There were, amazingly, hardly any portraits of Qaddafi in this part of town. (Perhaps the warehouse was out of stock and the new stores had them on back order.)

There was far less commerce in Libya than in most countries, but this little micro-corner was bustling. I found French cheese (but not prohibited wine), Japanese DVD players, Belgian chocolate and Swiss instant coffee.

At first I thought the only coffee shops in the city could be found along a single block on one of the back streets. Old men sat out front in cheap plastic chairs and grumpily smoked hookahs. That didn't look like very much fun.

But then I found an Italian-style café fronting Green Square. I ordered a double macchiato and a cheese pastry and actually found a nice dainty table. I looked around and thought, Heck, this could be Italy or even Los Angeles if it weren't for the total lack of women around. Globalization penetrates even Arab socialist rogue states these days. And what a relief, really. You'd never know you were in the beating heart of a brutal dictatorship while sitting in that little place.

Both my guides, Abdul and Yasir, took me to dinner. We could have eaten in the Italian Quarter. But no. They had to take me out to the Parking Garage Quarter, which is to say, anywhere else but the old city.

I groaned silently to myself. I liked these guys—if not their taste in dining establishments—but I hated being schlepped around all the time and never being asked when or where I wanted to eat.

The only time I truly needed a guide was on the road between Tripoli and Ghadamis.

I couldn't read the Arabic road signs. Armed soldiers demanded papers at checkpoints. I was grateful my guides had the stacks of papers prepared. But in the city, I was perfectly capable of finding a place to eat on my own. It wasn't easy, but it could be done with effort and patience.

I appreciated the hospitality, even though it was bought and paid for. Abdul and Yasir seemed to enjoy "buying" my dinner, but I felt micromanaged and babysat. Come here, look at that, sit there, eat this. They were great guys. But I lusted for solitude. If I said so, they would have been offended.

They took me to a restaurant in a neighborhood that was downright North Korean, it was so chock-full of concrete.

"We really hope you like this place," Yasir said.

It wasn't quite as bad as a parking garage, but it was a near miss. The main floor was reserved for a wedding, so we were shepherded upstairs to a huge, dimly lit room mostly empty of tables. The wedding party hadn't arrived yet. There was no one else in the building.

I didn't know what to say in this gloomy warehouse of a restaurant. I felt like we were the only people out for dinner that night in all of Libya. Abdul and Yasir hoped I would like this place? Oh, the poor dears. I was embarrassed for them and wondered what tourist in his right mind would come to Libya when he could go to Tunisia, Morocco or Turkey instead.

Worlds can't meet worlds. But people can meet people. I forget who said that, but I like it, and I thought about it as I walked around inside Libya, hanging out and talking to regular folks.

In a nation where so many reported to the secret police, where a sideways word could get you imprisoned or killed, walking around blue-eyed and pale-faced with an American accent had its advantages. I met one shopkeeper who opened right up when he and I found ourselves alone in his store.

"Do Americans know much about Libya?" he said.

"No," I said. "Not really."

He wanted to teach me something about his country, but he didn't know where to start. So he recited encyclopedia factoids.

He listed the principal resources while counting his fingers. I stifled a smirk when he named the border states. (I hardly needed a sixth-grade geography lesson.) When he told me Arabic was the official language, I wondered if he thought I was stupid or deaf.

"And Qaddafi is our president," he said. "About him, no comment." He laughed, but I don't think he thought it was funny.

"Oh, come on," I said. "Comment away. I don't live here."

He thought about that. For a long drawn-out moment, he calculated the odds and weighed the consequences. Then the dam burst.

"We hate that fucking bastard—we have nothing to do with him. Nothing. We keep our heads down and our mouths shut. We do our jobs, we go home. If I talk, they will take me out of my house in the night and put me in prison.

"Qaddafi steals," he told me. "He steals from us." He spoke rapidly now, twice as fast as before, as though he had been holding back all his life. He wiped sweat off his forehead with trembling hands. "The oil money goes to his friends. Tunisians next door are richer and they don't even have any oil."

"I know," I said. "I'm sorry."

"We get three or four hundred dinars each month to live on. Our families are huge, we have five or six children. It is a really big problem. We don't make enough to take care of them. I want to live in Lebanon. Beirut is the second Paris. It is civilized! Women and men mix freely in Lebanon."

Almost everybody I know thought I was crazy to travel to Libya. The unspoken fear was that someone might kill me.

Well, no. Nobody killed me. Nobody even looked at me funny. I knew that's how it would be before I set out. Still, it's nice to have the old adage that "people are people" proved through experience.

Libyans were fed a steady diet of anti-Americanism, but it came from a man who kicked them in the stomach and stomped on their face for more than a third of a century. If they bought it, they sure didn't act like it.

I crossed paths with a middle-aged Englishman in the hallway.

"Is this a good hotel?" he asked.

It sure beat my last place in town. At least I wasn't stranded out by the towers.

"It's a good hotel," I said, not really believing it but grateful for what I had.

"I think it's bloody awful," he said.

I laughed. "Well, yes," I said. "I was just trying to be nice. You should see the place where I stayed when I first got here."

I heard footsteps behind me, turned around and faced two Arab men wearing coats and ties and carrying briefcases. One wore glasses. The other was bald.

"It has been a long time since I heard that accent," said the man with the glasses.

I smiled. "It's been a long time since this accent was here," I said. Until just a few months earlier, any American standing on Libyan soil was committing a felony.

"We went to college together," he said, and jerked his thumb toward his friend. "In Lawrence, Kansas, during the '70s."

"Yes," his friend said as he rubbed the bald spot on his head. The two were all smiles now as they remembered. "We took a long road trip up to Seattle."

"We stayed there for two weeks!" said the first. He sighed like a man recalling his first long-lost love. I watched both their faces soften as they recalled the memories of their youth and adventures abroad in America.

"What a wonderful time we had there," said the second.

They invited me out to dinner, but I was getting ready to leave. I didn't want to say no. They looked like they wanted to hug me.

We shook hands as we departed. And as I stepped into the elevator, the first man put his hand on his heart. "Give two big kisses to Americans when you get home," he said. "From two people in Libya who miss you so much."

Two

The Slow Rot of Hosni Mubarak

Egypt, 2005

There's no way around it: your first impression of a new city and country will be powerfully influenced by whatever you see in your first 15 minutes of walking around. It's important, then, that you choose the location of your hotel very carefully.

My starting place in Egypt was the Hotel President on the island of Zamalek in the Nile River, supposedly Cairo's Beverly Hills. The place looks nothing like Beverly Hills. It's packed from one end to the other with medium-rise apartment towers, most of them knockoffs of the concrete soul-crushers that ring cities in the old Soviet bloc. I found shops, cafés and restaurants on the ground floor, but most were quiet, simple places, dimly lit on the inside, and they were spaced far apart as though Zamalek, despite its packed urban density and higher concentration of wealth per capita, could only support a thin spread of modest establishments.

The streets were remarkably quiet for the center of a metropolitan area of nearly 20 million people, though I heard blaring horns faintly in the distance across the river on the busier mainland. The sidewalks were wide and shaded by dusty green trees. A vaguely vegetable smell, presumably from the Nile, coated the air like a thin slime. A dense foglike haze enveloped the city, partly from automobile pollution but also from farmers out in the delta burning crop waste. It gave my sleepy Zamalek neighborhood a surreal, ghostly pallor that added to the dislocation I always feel when arriving in a new country.

Foreign embassies were all over the island, most of them right next to each other. They were the former mansions of rich Cairenes built in various European styles at the turn of the last century. But after Gamal Abdel Nasser and his so-called Free Officers Movement overthrew King Farouk in 1952, these magnificent homes were nationalized by the state. Nasser wrenched Egypt into the orbit of Soviet Russia with predictably disastrous results. Most of the island's residents have been living in those drab apartment buildings ever since.

Nasser was long gone, though, by the time I arrived, as was his replacement Anwar Sadat, whom Islamist army officers assassinated in 1981 for signing a peace treaty with Israel. Egypt's then-current president, Hosni Mubarak, had no interest in Nasser-style radicalism, nor was he brave enough to risk anything if he had to pay a price as Sadat had. He'd been ruling Egypt as a standard-issue status quo authoritarian for the previous quarter-century. The entire country was drowning in torpor. His regime calcified long before I got there.

At midnight I walked along the bank of the Nile. Two commercial pleasure boats—one lit up in neon and both playing Arabic music too loud—passed each other on the otherwise dark and quiet waters. International hotels skycrapered behind them. Women were allowed out of the house during the day, nearly all with their heads wrapped in scarves, but every person I passed on the street that night was a man. Cairo is more than 10 times larger than Beirut, Lebanon—where I lived at the time—but it's two or even three orders of magnitude more conservative.

I was surprised that Zamalek was considered upper-class. The sidewalks were crumbling. Almost every apartment building was coated in soot and grime. Many parked cars had been idle so long, they looked like they were covered in volcanic ash. Only the embassies were clean and well maintained.

Some of these people had money, though. Zamalek was dour on the outside, but when I saw through the front windows into the living rooms of some apartments in the older buildings, I had to revise my opinions. It's hard to feel sorry for someone who has high ceilings, color-washed walls, wedding-cake moldings and chandeliers in their living room. My house in the States is not as nice as many of these. Zamalek's problem was that the neighborhood wasn't kept up, as if civic pride didn't exist.

In the 1980s, when travel writer Douglas Kennedy visited Alexandria, the largest city on the Egyptian Mediterranean, renowned painter Sarwat el-Bahr explained a key Egyptian concept to him. "Do you know why America does not understand Egypt? Because they do not understand the meaning of the word *Maaleesh*. In English, *Maaleesh* means 'doesn't matter,' and it is the one word you need to understand Egypt. In America everything is *now, now, now*—make the money now, make the career now. But in Egypt, everybody believes in life after death, so everything in life is *Maaleesh*."

That's how much of Zamalek looked and felt. It simply didn't matter if the public spaces were dreary. Not to the locals anyway. But it mattered to me. Zamalek disappointed—considering what it was supposed to be like—and I went back to my hotel and picked up my copy of *Travels with a Tangerine* by Tim Mackintosh-Smith, a British Arabist expat who lives in Yemen.

"Few visitors have liked Cairo on first sight," he wrote. "'Uff!' exclaimed an eighth-century caliph, 'She is the mother of stenches!' Later, a geographer wondered why anyone should have wanted to build a city 'between a putrid and mephitic river, the corrupt effluvia of which cause disease and rot food, and a dry and barren mountain range devoid of greenery.' The ground teemed with rats, scorpions, fleas, and bugs, the air with miasmas. In Cairo Symon Semeon buried his companion Brother Hugo, who had succumbed to an attack of dysentery and fever 'caused by a north wind.' My guidebook, compiled a century after I.B.'s visit, was disturbingly frank about the dangers of living in a polluted high-rise city where light and air rarely penetrate the dark alleyways. Its author, al-Maqrizi, warned that 'the traveler approaching Cairo sees before him a depressing black wall beneath a dust-laden sky, from which sight his soul shrinks and flees away.'"

What I saw wasn't nearly as bad as all *that*, at least. And the next day, when I found 26 July Street and the streets adjacent to it, I changed my mind about Zamalek. (I later changed my mind again and again about not only Zamalek but also all of Cairo.)

26 July had an elevated freeway that ran right over the top of it, giving the street a dark, *Blade Runner* feel. That may sound like a complaint, but somehow it worked. It reminded me a bit of Chicago, a city I love and wish I could visit more often. You can barely see the sky from the sidewalk, but the street is brilliantly lit up at night. All the usual neighborhood goods are for sale: shoes, watches, clothing, glasses, pharmaceuticals, snacks and so on.

I found a terrific Italian restaurant called Maison Thomas. The sign in the window said *"Le Caire Fondee en 1922,"* decades before Nasser drove all the non-Arabs out of Egypt in his Arab Nationalist "revolution" from above. Maison Thomas, unlike so much of Cairo and even the quieter back streets of Zamalek, felt truly modern. Its patrons were well dressed, most of them more so than me. The waiters and waitresses dressed sharply in black and white. Women and men—and I couldn't tell if they were single or married—went there on dates. None of the women wore the hijab, the veil or the abaya. Almost everyone seemed to be in a good mood, and almost everyone smoked imported cigarettes rather than Egypt's crap Cleopatra brand. My charming and disarming waiter seemed like the happiest man alive, as if nothing in the known universe pleased him more than bringing me food and a beverage.

I had to look hard, but I did find tiny pockets of sophistication. A first-class bookstore across the street called Diwa carried some of the best titles from the West as well as from the Middle East. A whole shelf was devoted to Arabic literature translated into English and published in beautiful eye-catching trade-paperback editions. Many of the original English titles were among the finest works of literature the West has ever produced. In the History and Current Events sections, I found books by

Edward Said, David Frum, Thomas Friedman and Bernard Lewis. (No Salman Rushdie, alas.)

Cairo was ahead of bookstore-free Tripoli, then, at least in some ways, and miles behind Beirut. But Cairo is so large that you could fold Beirut and Tripoli into it five times each and have room left over.

For good or for ill, whatever happened there would have an enormous impact on the rest of the region.

E gyptian blogger Big Pharaoh gave me an insider's tour of Cairo and the ghastly political situation facing his country.

He took me down 26 July Street on foot to the bridge over the Nile connecting Zamalek to the mainland. As we walked up the entrance ramp—built for cars, not for people—he asked if I ever walked like this in Beirut. "In Egypt you can walk wherever you want," he said. "There are no rules or laws here."

Well, I thought. There were laws against involvement in politics. But I knew what he meant. The Egyptian government didn't micromanage its citizens. Good on Hosni Mubarak for that one, at least. Egypt was a police state, but at any given moment it didn't feel like one.

"There are no laws in Lebanon, either," I said. "You can do pretty much whatever you want there."

As soon as we crossed the river, the amount of traffic—both pedestrian and automobile—multiplied exponentially while the economic conditions plunged. Zamalek was hardly the most charming place in the world, but it was exquisite compared with the rest of the city. Mainland Cairo was loud, crowded and crumbling. I could see that it must have been beautiful once, and some of its architecture was strikingly European, but it looked a bit like Prague must have during the 1970s, decades before its postcommunist restoration.

Hideous concrete tower blocks stretched to the horizon in every direction from the relatively compact downtown. I thought to myself that it looked more than a little Soviet, but it wasn't until I visited 13

postcommunist countries in Eastern Europe and the former Soviet
Union and then returned to Cairo during the so-called Arab Spring that
I realized just how accurate that observation actually was.

I was surprised, but I shouldn't have been. Nasser's Egypt was a
Soviet client state, though officially "socialist" rather than communist.
In the 1950s he purged Egypt of its tolerance, its riches, its openness
and its variety. He brought in Russian advisers, ramped up the secret
police and ruthlessly smashed everyone who opposed him. He expelled
nearly all the Greeks, Jews and other minorities in his attempt to make
Egypt monolithically Arab. (Egypt before Nasser was not considered an
Arab country. Before him, Egypt was just Egypt.) His nationalization of
industry and private property turned the economy into an incompetently
micromanaged catastrophe.

"Can we talk about politics out in the open?" I said to Big Pharaoh.

"Yes," he said. "We can say whatever we want."

"Is it because we're speaking in English?"

"No," he said. "We could do it in Arabic too."

"You're not worried about the secret police?"

"Not anymore," he said. "It is a real change from last year. Last year
there was no way. But it's better now, more open. Do you know why?"

"Tell me," I said.

"Because of pressure from George W. Bush."

That was the only piece of good news I had to report from Egypt
during the time of Hosni Mubarak.

We walked underneath an overhead freeway. I had to shout so he
could hear me. The entire world looked as though it were made out of
poured concrete, and I could taste the black tang of exhaust in the air.

Big Pharaoh pointed out a set of campaign posters on a wall. It
felt good seeing campaign posters in Egypt. It was a long way from
Libya, where menacing portraits of Muammar Qaddafi and no one
else were plastered up everywhere. The main opposition to Hosni
Mubarak, however, was not a liberal coalition but the Islamist Muslim
Brotherhood.

"Do you know what that says?" he said as he pointed at the Arabic script above the portrait of a candidate's face. "It says *Islam Is the Solution.*"

We made our way to the nearest subway station and descended the steps. It was clean down there—much cleaner than the subway stations in New York City—and I said so.

"It is almost brand-new," he said.

"How old is it, exactly?" I said.

"About 10 years," he said.

I was amazed that such a miserably poor country could build a brand-new subway while American taxpayers said they couldn't afford to build any new trains. How was that even possible?

"It must have been hugely expensive," I said.

"France and Japan helped us pay for it," he said.

"Japan?" I said. "Really. Why Japan?"

"To earn some goodwill, I guess," he said.

As our train pulled into the station, I made my way toward the first car.

"Not that car," he said. "The first car is only for women."

The genders weren't segregated as in Saudi Arabia. Women could ride any car on the train. But sexual harassment and sexual assault in Egypt were so off the scale compared with almost everywhere else in the world that the government gave women their own train car so they wouldn't have their asses grabbed by aggressive, lecherous men.

"I got in that car on accident once," he said. "By the time I figured it out, the doors closed. I got out at the next stop and was fined seven pounds." Seven pounds is less than $2, but half of Egyptians earned less than $2 a day.

We got off the train in the center of downtown and emerged next to a huge, well-lit roundabout. Perhaps it was because he and I arrived after dark when the night washed the grime away, but Cairo suddenly looked like a European masterpiece. It was not at all what I was expecting after seeing the squalid condition of so much of the rest of the city. I changed my opinion of Cairo—again.

"This is amazing," I said. "What a terrific downtown. Look at these buildings!"

"They are from another era," he said. "They are just relics. They have nothing to do with what Egypt is now."

"But they're real," I said, "and you still have them. No country builds streets like this anymore anyway."

It felt like an Arab New York or, rather, an Arab Rome. Later, though, when I went downtown again by myself during the day, I understood what he meant. Downtown Cairo is all sparkle and no substance at night. Cities can't lie during the day. Even this neighborhood, which surely once was exquisite, seemed to have all the prosperity sucked out of it. Only an empty husk remained. Egypt had clearly had a rough couple of decades. In the harsh afternoon sunlight, the neighborhood looked like it had been lifted hundreds of feet into the air and dropped back on the street.

I've seen photographs of this part of town that make it look sort of okay. Their smaller-than-life size conceals the backwardness, the gloom and the depressed condition of the place since Nasser took out his blunt instruments and went to work on it.

"I am going to take you to an Egyptian bar," Big Pharaoh said. "Is that okay?"

"You mean an Egyptian bar where no tourists would ever go?"

"Exactly," he said.

"Perfect," I said. "That is exactly what I want to see."

We walked past a women's underwear store. "When the Muslim Brotherhood comes to power," he said as he swept his arm in front of female-shaped mannequins modeling panties and bras, "they will ban this."

He led me into an establishment called Cap'dor. Instead of glass windows it had wooden shutters painted red and green. The floor was laid with gray tile, the walls lined with wood paneling. There was not a single woman inside. Apparently that's how it always is in that bar.

They didn't even bother to install a women's restroom. Beer was the only beverage available.

"There are some prostitute bars around too," he said.

"Is it legal here?" I said. "Prostitution is rampant in Lebanon."

"No," he said, "but the law is lax. The bar owner just pays off the police and no one cares."

We ordered two stout bottles of Stella beer.

"Best beer in Egypt," he said. "The company was started by a Greek guy in 1897."

The bartender brought us carrots, sliced tomatoes and *ful* beans. We dug in.

I wanted to know what he thought of the Muslim Brotherhood. Many in the Western press described the organization as moderate, but compared with what? Al-Qaeda? Sure. But it was hardly moderate compared with anything in the West.

"They are moderate because they don't have guns," he said. "They don't kill people. But most of the armed terrorist groups we see now were born out of the ideology of the Muslim Brotherhood. My biggest fear is that if the Muslim Brotherhood rules Egypt, we will get Islamism-lite, that they won't be quite bad enough that people will revolt against them. Take bars, for example. Most Egyptians don't drink, so they won't mind if alcohol is illegal. The same goes for banning books. Most Egyptians don't read. So why should they care if books are banned? Most women wear a veil or a headscarf already, so if it becomes the law, hardly anyone will resist."

"How many people here think like you do?" I asked him.

"Few," he said. "Very few. Less than 10 percent probably."

We ordered more Stella beers. He practically inhaled all the *ful* beans. I didn't think they were that great. They had little taste, actually.

"There probably aren't many Muslim Brotherhood guys in this bar," I said.

He laughed. "Ha! No way. This is a secular working-class bar. Just the fact that they're here makes them liberals."

The patrons didn't look liberal. He used that word in the most elastic way possible. These men were secular, sure, since they drank beer, but there were no women around. This was a man's establishment. How many of these guys, I wondered, were responsible for the government giving women their own car on the subway?

It was odd, I suppose, to see my pale face, blue eyes and black leather jacket in Cap'dor. No one stared, but almost all the other men's eyes lingered on me a bit longer than usual. They seemed curious and slightly pleased that someone from somewhere else decided to hang out in their place.

I asked Big Pharaoh what he thought would happen if Egypt held a legitimate free and fair election instead of a rigged one staged by the government.

"The Muslim Brotherhood would win," he said. "They would beat Mubarak and the liberals."

It was obvious just from walking around that liberalism in the genuine sense of the word found little purchase in Cairo. Women wore headscarves. A large percentage of men wore robes. It was a traditional place despite its size. The vibrant culture that must have existed when the European Quarter was built had passed into history.

"I've had a theory for a while now," I said. "that some Middle East countries are going to have to live under an Islamic state for a while and get it out of their system."

Big Pharaoh laughed grimly.

"Sorry," I said. "That's just how it looks."

He buried his head in his arms.

"Take Iranians," I said. "They used to think Islamism was a fantastic idea. Now they hate it. Same goes in Afghanistan. Algerians don't think too much of Islamism either after 150,000 people were killed in the civil war. I hate to say this, but it looks like Egypt might have to learn this the hard way."

"You are right," he said. "You are right. I went to an Egyptian chat room on the Internet and asked 15 people if they fasted during

Ramadan. All of them said they fasted during at least most of it. I went to an Iranian chat room and asked the same question. Fourteen out of 15 said they did not fast for even one single day."

"Egypt didn't used to be like this," I said.

"Nasser's biggest crime was not establishing democracy when he took over," he said. "Back then, Egyptian people were liberal. It would have worked then. But not now."

Progress is a funny thing. Westerners like to think it moves in a straight line. In America that's pretty much how it is. No serious person would argue that American culture was more liberal and tolerant in the 1950s than it is now or that it was more liberal and tolerant in the 19th century than it was in the 1950s. But Egypt moved in the other direction. Why?

"When Nasser took over," he said, "people were angry at Britain and Israel. He nationalized all the industry. He banned political parties. He stifled everything. Banned the Muslim Brotherhood. Banned the Communists. Banned all. When Sadat took over in 1970, he had two enemies: the communists and the Nasser remnants. So to counter these threats, he did what the United States did in Afghanistan during the Cold War: he made an alliance with the Islamists. He brought back the Muslim Brotherhood, which had fled to Saudi Arabia when Nasser was around. He used them to destroy the left.

"That was part of it," he continued. "During the oil boom of 1973, a lot of Egyptians went to Saudi Arabia to work. Then in the 1990s, two important things happened. After the first Gulf War, Saudi Arabia began to Saudi-ize its economy and said they no longer needed Egyptian workers. Egyptians came home contaminated with Wahhabism. Egypt's economy kept getting worse. Unemployed members of the middle class either sat around and smoked or got more religious. That was when Islamism moved from the lower class to the middle class. Now it is moving even to the upper class."

"Egypt will get over it after a while," I said, "just like Iran is getting over it now."

"That will take 25 years! I don't have 25 years!"

The Iranian ayatollahs had so far been in power for 26 years.

I felt bad for Big Pharaoh. Even the Egyptian capital, despite its immensity, hardly had a place for a person like him.

The bartender came around and gave everyone a glass with a green liquid in it. Hey, I thought. Free drinks. Apparently beer wasn't the only thing they had in the bar after all.

"What is this?" I said.

"It's the water the beans were cooked in."

I stared at him.

"This is bean juice? Are you serious?"

"Yes," he said. "You will love it."

"I don't know about that," I said.

"There is a first time for everything," he said.

"Okay," I said. "Here goes."

I took a small sip.

It was horrendous.

"No," I said.

I wanted a glass of red wine. And I wanted some women around. Hanging out at a wiener roast is no fun. It reminded me of something Carsten Niebuhr wrote in 1774: "Young men who like their comforts, and a dainty table, or who wish to pass their time pleasantly in the company of women must not go to Arabia."

"A friend of mine recently went to Algeria," Big Pharaoh said. "When he came back he told me that there are far fewer veiled women there than there are here. It is much more liberal in Algeria because there they have tasted Islamism. Egypt does need to experience what happened in Iran and Algeria ... as long as I am in the U.S. or Canada when it happens."

Even though he would rather live in the United States, he was seriously looking into immigrating to Canada. It might be easier for him to qualify for an immigrant visa. "If I live in Canada, I will be in the apartment above the party."

"The apartment above the party?" I said.

"America is the party," he said. "And I will be living right above it. So I'll be in the apartment above the party. And I'll go downstairs a lot."

"I sincerely hope you can make it out of here," I said, although I partly felt bad because his leaving would only contribute to Egypt's brain drain.

"Mubarak is a horrible, horrible man," he said. "He is the reason we are in this thing. He has oppressed all the liberals."

Optimism came naturally to me at the time. Beirut, where I lived, was looking up. The Lebanese had cast off Syrian occupation without firing a shot. The city felt like I imagined Berlin did shortly after the fall of the Berlin Wall. Hezbollah had not yet ignited the war with Israel in 2006. That would happen seven months after I left Cairo. Nor had Hezbollah invaded Beirut. That wouldn't happen for another two years. Nor had the Syrian civil war erupted, which would—rather predictably—spill into Lebanon.

Beirut seemed to have a bright future ahead of it. I was wrong about that, but Cairo's bleak future was obvious.

"You want to feel good?" he said. "You want to be optimistic? Go back to Beirut."

I had to check myself. Perhaps I was wrong about the Muslim Brotherhood. Maybe they really were moderates, and Big Pharaoh, as one of the few Egyptian liberals, was being paranoid and excessively partisan. It happens.

So I called senior Muslim Brotherhood leader Essam el-Erian and asked for an interview. He was the Brotherhood's smooth media man, the go-to guy journalists liked to talk to when they need a fresh quote or wanted to know what the Brotherhood stood for and thought. He spent time in Egypt's dungeons, not because he was a terrorist (he wasn't) but because, like Egypt's liberals, he was an enemy of Hosni Mubarak.

I felt some sympathy for him even though his politics were radically different from mine. Though I couldn't say I wanted to see him in power, that didn't mean I wanted to see him repressed or in prison.

"Your campaign slogan says Islam is the solution," I said. "If Islam is the solution, why did millions of Iranians move to the United States after the 1979 revolution? Why do so many people in Afghanistan hate the Taliban?"

He laughed. Not a belly laugh, but a knowing laugh, as though he fielded a version of that question every day.

"Listen, Mr. Michael," he said. "Iran is not Egypt. Egypt is not Afghanistan. Afghanistan is not Sudan. Sudan is not Algeria. There are different models of Islamic life. We have a very long civilization here. It is ancient. We have common values here between Muslims and Christians and even Jews."

I liked his answer but could not take his word for it. I needed specifics. It's not enough to say that Egypt isn't Afghanistan. That was obvious anyway. *How* was his ideology different from that of the Taliban?

"Okay," I said. "What kind of model for Islamic life does the Muslim Brotherhood have in mind for Egypt?"

"I cannot answer specifically now," Erian said. "We are not in power. We are struggling for democracy. All people must be respected in a democratic system. It is very important to be tolerant."

Nice-sounding boilerplate, but it was a dodge. I decided to get back to this later rather than beat him over the head right at the start.

"If the Muslim Brotherhood were in power in Egypt," I said, "would you cooperate with the West against al-Qaeda?"

"From the first moment we are against al-Qaeda," he said. "We condemn all violent activities. We condemned it then. But we have doubts about the way the West fights terrorism. This way of fighting is the wrong way. We need a concrete definition of terrorism before we can cooperate."

"What's your definition of terrorism?" I said.

"We need an international meeting and conference to decide on a definition."

"Good idea," I said. "So if you attended an international conference, what definition of terrorism would you suggest?"

"I am not going to give you a definition," he said. "We need dialogue and consensus. It is not only for the Muslim Brotherhood to decide."

"But what would you say to Western governments if they agreed to a dialogue with you? What is *your* definition of terrorism? Never mind what anyone else thinks."

"I cannot give you an answer now," he said.

This guy was more useless than government ministers I've interviewed. But I had to give him credit. He was extremely well practiced in the art of saying nothing.

I decided to try another angle on the first question he'd dodged.

"Would the Muslim Brotherhood ban alcohol in Egypt?" I said. "Would you ban books?"

"We are not going to do anything without discussion. We are not in power."

"Should women be forced to wear a veil or a hijab?" I said.

"You must understand," he said. "We are outlawed. We can clarify these points after we are free."

"Why don't you clarify now?" I said.

"We need fresh air," he said. "We need fresh air before we can clarify this."

"People want to know what you stand for," I said. "My job is to help you explain yourselves to them."

"The government likes to confuse people about what we really believe," he said.

"Tell you what," I said. "You clarify your vision of an Egyptian Islamic state now and I promise to get the word out."

"We need fresh air before we can clarify anything," he said.

He went round and round like this, refusing to even hint at what their Islamist program might look like. It seemed plain enough to me that his deliberate obfuscation was a ploy to feign moderation and conceal a hidden extremism.

"Mr. Michael," he said. "It is late and I am tired. Just two more questions please."

We had only been talking for a few minutes. And he hadn't yet answered even one question.

"Okay," I said. I had plenty more questions I wanted to ask, but if I was only allowed two, I needed to ask something he couldn't dodge quite as easily. "If you could change three things about American foreign policy, what would they be?"

"Respect human rights and international law," he said.

We could have dug into that one for hours, except of course he wouldn't let me. Instead of dwelling on it, I moved straight to the last question, one that tends to be a lightning rod for Islamists.

"What do you think about the fatwa against Salman Rushdie?" I said. Since he wouldn't answer my question about whether or not he wanted to ban books in Egypt, perhaps he would give it away when discussing the world-famous "blasphemer" whom Iran's Ayatollah Khomeini sentenced to death for his novel *The Satanic Verses*.

"It was the wrong way to treat," he said. "Ignoring would have been better."

What could I say? It was a good answer, the best answer there is. He did know how to put on a moderate face when he wasn't blatantly dodging my questions.

I can only assume he had a definition of terrorism that Westerners would think is extreme. Otherwise he would have told me what it was.

I can also only assume he would like to ban booze and veil women. Otherwise he would have said that he didn't.

If I was wrong about the Brotherhood—and if Big Pharaoh was wrong—it was the Brotherhood's fault for dissembling.

I couldn't go to Egypt without seeing the pyramids, especially since they're less than an hour from the center of Cairo. So I hired a grizzled 60-year-old driver named Nabil to pick me up at my hotel in the late morning.

He and I cruised from the city center to the outskirts through miles of shabby apartment towers. I saw precious little economic activity—unsurprising since half the country earned less than $2 a day—and couldn't escape the sense that most of Cairo, despite being the Arab world's cultural capital, was actually a cultural void packed with people who spent nearly all their energy struggling just to get by. The culture produced by Egypt and consumed by the rest of the region was created by a minuscule minority.

The quality of the apartment towers was inversely proportional to their distance from downtown. The farther Nabil drove from the center, the worse everything looked. Soon the tenements were nothing more than red brick warehouses for humans, many of them without windows and no doubt without air-conditioning.

Nothing was worse than the slums on the outskirts. Streets weren't paved. Each neighborhood had its own garbage dump where children played barefoot. Lush agricultural land—tended by farmers with oxen and adorned with what presumably were date palms—was checkerboarded throughout the slum blocks. The housing was horrid, but the landscape was verdant and subtropical, and it helped take the edge off the ugliness.

I wanted to raise my camera to the window and take pictures, but I was worried it would embarrass Nabil. I imagined he wished every tourist who came through Egypt did not have to see what I was seeing. So I pretended I didn't.

"So, Nabil," I said. "What do you think of Hosni Mubarak?"

"He does many good things for people outside of Egypt," he said. "For Americans, Europeans and Israelis, he is a man of peace. I like that. But he does nothing for us. Look at these poor people."

At least Mubarak didn't plaster his picture up everywhere like Qaddafi did, at least not in Cairo. Unlike Nasser, he didn't even attempt to gin up a cult of personality. He was not a mass murderer like Saddam Hussein, not a totalitarian like Syria's Bashar al-Assad. He was just a standard-issue strongman who'd leave you alone if you stayed out of his way, though he ran Egypt like it was his private plantation.

One Egyptian, however, told me that outside Cairo, Mubarak's portraits were more common and sinister. He looked like everyone's dad in the pictures I saw. In Upper (southern) Egypt—the stronghold of the Salafists and the Muslim Brotherhood—he was supposedly decked out in sunglasses and an officer's uniform.

"Do you have any children?" Nabil said.

"No," I said. "I'm married, but I don't have any children."

"Good," he said.

Good? Middle Easterners tended to be slightly horrified and confused by Westerners who don't have children.

"Why is it good?" I said.

"Raising children is a huge responsibility," he said. "I have three, and it is so hard. I have an electrician's degree, but the government doesn't pay enough money for us to live on." Apparently, finding electrician's work in the private sector isn't much of an option. "So I drive car," he said.

I had agreed to pay him $12—his asking price—to drive me out to Giza and wait for me for two hours while I looked at the pyramids and the Sphinx. Twelve dollars for a half-day's work may be a lot in Egypt (I don't know), but it seemed like nothing to me. So I quietly decided I would pay him $20 instead if he didn't try to extract any more from me.

"What do you do for a living?" he said.

"I'm a writer," I said.

"Oh!" he said, delighted. "What do you write about Egypt? You write about pyramids?"

"Sure," I said. "I'm also interested in politics. Mubarak and the Muslim Brotherhood."

He twisted up his face.

"I not like them," he said. "I like women. And I like beer."

"Beer and women are good," I said. He grinned and gave me a high-five.

We pulled off the freeway and turned onto a dirt road between the tenements. A cart drawn by a donkey got in our way. Nabil sighed. "Cairo traffic," he said.

He stopped the car at the edge of the city of Giza. The silhouette of a pyramid towered above us in the haze, easily as high as a skyscraper but *much* wider and more imposing. Two horses were tied to a post on the sidewalk next to us.

"Do you want to ride camel or horse?" he said.

Actually, I wanted to walk. I especially didn't feel like being a dorky tourist riding a camel. I'd ridden an ass-busting camel once already, in Tunisia, and that was enough.

"A horse," I said, not wanting to be a pain by insisting on walking.

Horses are more trustworthy. Camels have been known to chase down their owners (while bellowing like Chewbacca) when they get disgruntled and are finished taking orders. I admire that about them, but I didn't need any drama from an animal that weighed hundreds of pounds more than me.

Nabil summoned a horse man who introduced himself to me as Mohammad.

Mohammad offered to help me mount the horse, but I didn't need it. He mounted his own and we set out into the street alongside automobile traffic.

This was a stupid way to travel in Cairo.

"Watch your legs!" he shouted as a filthy bus roared past.

A driver rounded a corner too quickly and clipped my foot with his mirror.

"Watch your legs!" Mohammad said again.

After riding a few blocks, we reached the gateway to the pyramids. I saw then why we needed horses. The area around the pyramids was *huge*, much larger than I had expected. And it was all sand. There was no road to drive on. It would not have been possible to walk around and see everything in under four hours, let alone two.

I paid my admission, and as we passed the gate, a policeman

carrying a horse whip and a gun walked up to us.

The officer screamed something at Mohammad in Arabic. Mohammad screamed something back at him. The policeman then cracked his horse whip on the sand and narrowed his eyes at us.

Having no idea what the problem was, I pretended to be a perfectly happy and oblivious idiot, hoping it might tone down the temperature by a degree or so.

Mohammad said something nasty to the policeman in Arabic and then led our horses away as the officer's face flushed with hatred and rage.

"Asshole," Mohammad said. I acted as though I hadn't heard that.

Mohammad led his horse and mine away from the abusive policeman and toward the base of the pyramids of Giza.

"Welcome to the beginning of the great Sahara Desert," Mohammad said.

I have climbed to the top of the Maya pyramids in the Petén Jungle of the Guatemalan Yucatán. Spectacular as they are, their life size is smaller than I had expected before I arrived. The pyramids at Giza are much bigger. They're impossibly large monuments that seemed the size of small moons. No doubt they'll still be standing thousands of years after we all are gone. Egypt one day may no longer be Egypt, but the pyramids will remain as though they belong to eternity. They will weather as slowly as great mountains.

Some of the more deranged Islamists have threatened to destroy them, as the Taliban destroyed ancient Buddha statues at Bamiyan with ack-ack guns, but now that I was looking at them in person, I had to laugh. The pharaoh's tombs at Giza aren't going anywhere unless someone detonates a nuclear weapon on top of them. Even then I wouldn't count on their being destroyed. They would probably have to be nuked a second or third time.

"Are you a Yankee?" Mohammad said. "Or are you Southern?"

"I'm a Yank," I said. From Oregon.

"Can you believe you are here?" he said.

I didn't know what he meant, and he read that on my face.

"Every day people tell me they can't believe they are here after flying thousands of miles."

"I came here from Beirut," I said.

"Ah," he said. "Okay. You live in the Middle East. You know where you are then."

He and I rode our horses at a full gallop until we reached the first pyramid, then we slowed to a trot. A man dressed in Bedouin garb ambled by selling warm bottles of Coke. I bought one for 50 cents and offered Mohammad a sip.

"Can we climb to the top?" I asked, not really sure I actually wanted to.

"No," Mohammad said. "A tourist recently tried it. He fell and lost himself. It is no longer allowed."

He led me to a lookout point where all three pyramids were visible in a line, the perfect place for a photo. I suddenly wished I had come in late afternoon, when the light was better for pictures. Glare from the afternoon sun washed out all color and left no shadows for contrast.

Mohammad had been right earlier. The pyramids really are the beginning of the great Sahara Desert. The suburb of Giza was barely visible in the haze on one side while sand stretched to the horizon in the other direction. Metropolitan Cairo had reached its absolute physical limit and could sprawl no more. I wondered where on earth jobs and food would come from as the city grew ever larger. The place would turn into a Malthusian death trap if it didn't get its economic house in order.

Two uniformed police officers rode on horseback to where we were standing. They exchanged pleasantries with Mohammad as he handed them several Egyptian pounds. Then they left. The entire meeting took less than 10 seconds.

"Why did you just do that?" I said, feeling defensive on his behalf as I narrowed my eyes at the officers' backs.

"They are poor, and good people," he said. "The state does not pay them. Look after the poor, and God will look after you."

They did seem like nice enough gents in the nine seconds I saw them in action, as long as I didn't think about the fact that Mohammad, rather than the government that ostensibly employed them, paid their salary. Since they were armed men of the law, I couldn't help but wonder what would have happened if Mohammad *hadn't* given them any money, and I remembered the shouting match he had earlier with the enraged policeman with the gun and the whip.

We got back on our horses and rode leisurely toward the Sphinx. Mohammad rode silently, but he seemed to be in a pleasant enough mood.

"What do you think of the Muslim Brotherhood?" I said.

"Those are bad words, my friend," he said.

"Bad words?" I said. "Why, exactly?"

"They are bad people who know nothing," he said. "I have no school. But I know war is terrible and that we should take care of our country." I hadn't said anything about war, but it was the first thing he thought of when I mentioned Islamists. He wore a somber look on his face now.

He was a simple man and probably charged too much money to lead me around on a horse, but he seemed a decent enough fellow, and I did not get the sense he was jerking me around and telling me only what I wanted to hear. Some Middle Easterners in the tourism business say "I love America!" in the most unconvincing voice possible. It's obvious fakery. I can tell when they do it just for form's sake. Mohammad didn't seem the type to pull that with me.

"What do you think about Hosni Mubarak then?" I said.

"He is a good man," he said.

"Hmm," I said.

"What?" he said, aware that I didn't agree. "What do you want to say? Tell me what is in your heart."

"He's a dictator," I said. *And an asshole*, I wanted to add. Mubarak had been in charge of Egypt for decades, and the place was in terrible shape. It wasn't his fault that the country was not liberal, but he was certainly to blame for persecuting the liberal minority that did exist. It guaranteed his rule, sure, but it also guaranteed that the main opposition to his rule was the Muslim Brotherhood, since they could organize in mosques no matter what the state did. The liberals had no such sanctuary and couldn't compete, couldn't even attempt to convince their neighbors and fellow Egyptians that neither Mubarak nor the Brotherhood had the answers. He did it on purpose so he could tell his supposed friends in America that he was all that stood between the Islamists and an Iranian-style regime. He may have been right, but it was partly his fault.

"I understand what you mean," Mohammad said and nodded. "In America you change presidents without fighting. Here if we change presidents we could have a war."

"Maybe," I said. "And maybe not. It's awfully convenient for him that you think that."

"Listen, my friend," he said. "If we have a president who is not from the army, we will have another war. Only the officers know how to keep us at peace." I presumed he meant only the officers know better than to humiliate Egypt by picking another losing battle with Israel. Perhaps that was true, but even Syria's Bashar al-Assad knew better than to go full tilt against Israel. He fought Israel indirectly through Hezbollah in Lebanon.

The pyramids were much bigger than I had imagined, but the Sphinx was a great deal smaller. It looked especially tiny with the gargantuan pyramids as a backdrop. Only in close-up photos does it take on much size.

As we got near the Sphinx, the angry policeman from earlier returned on foot. He cracked his whip on the sand again and stared holes through Mohammad and me with his black eyes. He didn't look like a starving policeman to me. He was fat, actually, and his rosy cheeks made him look like a boozer.

"This man will guide you to the Sphinx," Mohammad said.

Oh, for God's sake, I thought. The Sphinx was right there. Only a blind man would need a guide. Mohammad didn't want to pay this jerk off, so now I had to do it? I suddenly liked him less, but it was hard to say how much pressure he was actually under. I had witnessed some of that pressure earlier, and it was a lot. There is no legal recourse at all when you're abused by policemen in Egypt.

The menacing officer stared at me, whip in hand, with undisguised hatred as I dismounted my horse. I smiled at him as though I were the perfect American idiot, utterly clueless about what was happening and incapable of reading body language or hostile intent. What I really wanted to do was break his face with my fist. I'd be in deep shit if I didn't pay him. That came across. He was mugging me, basically, and hardly even bothered to pretend otherwise.

"Do you speak English?" I said in the most genial voice I could muster as we walked together toward the Sphinx.

He actually smiled at me and shrugged his shoulders. Playing nice was paying off. What else could I do? I seethed inside even after he decided to cool it. He didn't care at all about making a civilized impression on foreigners. I despised him for that on Egypt's behalf as well as my own. The code of Arab hospitality was completely lost on this man.

It only took two minutes or so to reach the Sphinx. Other tourists were there, snapping the shutters on their digital cameras. I took several pictures and ignored the policeman completely, refusing to look at him or acknowledge that he even existed.

I walked around to look at the Sphinx from several different vantage points and stayed much longer than I would have if the bastard weren't on my case. You want baksheesh? I thought. Then you're gonna wait for it, pal.

I kept the policeman waiting for as long as I could stand, then started walking back toward Mohammad and our horses without looking back at him. Clandestinely I pulled one Egyptian pound (less than 20 cents) out of my pocket for the baksheesh he "earned" in no way whatsoever. I didn't want him to ask for money and see me pull a big wad of cash out of my pocket and demand I give him one of my larger bills.

"Hello again, Mohammad," I said as I approached.

"Hello, Mr. Michael," he said. "How was the Sphinx?"

"Grand," I said.

The policeman walked just behind me and to my right as I fantasized about cracking him in the nose with the back of my elbow. I mounted my horse and let the man wonder if I was actually going to give him baksheesh or not. Then, not wanting to start yet another furious incident, I handed him the Egyptian equivalent of 17 cents.

"*Shukran,*" I said—thank you—in the iciest tone I could manage.

No, fuck *you,* you son of a bitch, is what I was thinking. Would you treat my mother this way if she were here instead of me? Even tourists at the pyramids, of all places, get a taste of the petty humiliations people have to put up with every day in Third World police states. Imagine living in a country so messed up that it could be your job to roam around all day with a whip and a gun angrily extorting money from everybody you come across. No wonder Mohammad was fed up with this man and had the nerve to scream at him earlier.

This is what you have to put up with thanks to your pal Mubarak, I wanted to say to Mohammad as we rode away, but I didn't. He was a nice enough man, and he knew that already. He was shaken down by the cops every day when he went to work.

I went to a cozy restaurant and pub back in Zamalek and ordered a bowl of pasta. A 20-something Western woman sat alone at the next table reading an English-language newspaper. We smiled hello to each other.

"Are you a student here?" she asked in an Australian accent.

"No," I said. "I'm a writer. You?"

"Just traveling," she said.

"By yourself?" I said.

"I've been traveling alone for four months. I started in India and I'm working my way to Spain."

"Did you go through Iran?" I said. I wanted to go to Iran but doubted they'd give me a visa. The regime didn't like my job or my passport.

"I can't go there," she said.

"They're blocking Australians, too, eh?"

"Well, not exactly. What I mean is *I* can't go there." I figured she must have been to Israel and that the Iranians wouldn't let her in if she had the Zionist Entity stamp in her passport.

She whispered, "I work for the Department of Defense."

It's a good idea to whisper that sort of thing in the Middle East. Conspiracy theories are out of control, especially in Egypt.

If she and I had some privacy, I would have asked about her job. But I couldn't expect her to tell me anything interesting where others could hear. Australia didn't have sinister designs on Egypt, but neither did the United States. That didn't stop Egyptians from hatching dark, elaborate fantasies.

The waiter brought my pasta. It was so undercooked I could barely eat it. I should have sent it back, but I didn't want to be difficult. He, like many Egyptian waiters, was so embarrassingly friendly and charming, I didn't have the heart to complain.

"What's it like traveling by yourself in Egypt?" I asked her.

"Difficult," she said. "I'm leaving tomorrow."

"Is it difficult because you're a woman?"

"This is the absolute worst place for a woman to travel alone," she said. "Men harass me constantly. They hiss, stare and make kissy noises."

"A Syrian friend told my wife if she ever goes there to carry a spare shoe in her purse. If any man gives her trouble and she whacks him with the bottom of the shoe, a mob will chase him down."

She laughed. "Syria is wonderful. I mean, it's much more oppressive than Egypt. But it's also more modern. No man ever bothered me there. No men bothered me in Lebanon, either. I was surprised. Lebanese and Syrian men are more respectful even than European men. The worst part is that Egyptian men won't back down when I tell them to leave me alone."

I remembered Cairo's subway, how the first car in the train was only for women.

"I'm having the time of my life, though," she said. "Tomorrow I'll be in Spain. It will be fun to be a single woman in Spain." She winked at me, gathered her things and got ready to leave. "Happy travels," she said. And then she was gone.

I met Blake Hounshell in the lobby of the Hotel President in Zamalek. He was an American student studying Arabic at the American University of Cairo and the founder of the group blog *American Footprints*, formerly known as *Liberals Against Terrorism*. He would later become the editor of *Foreign Policy* magazine.

"Let's go somewhere off Zamalek, shall we?" I said. "This city is huge and I need to see as much of it as I can."

"What would you like to do? Have lunch? Coffee? Smoke *shisha*?" A *shisha*, or hookah, is an Arabic water pipe, like a bong for flavored tobacco.

"How about all of the above?" I said.

"I know just the place then," he said, "in a cool neighborhood where lots of young people like to hang out."

He hailed us a cab and we hopped in the back. I had no idea where we were going, but a cool neighborhood where lots of young people like to hang out sounded perfect.

But the neighborhood he took me to looked grim and depressing, much more so than Zamalek, and was not at all what I expected from a place hip young people had colonized. But I kept my gripes to myself.

"You have to revise your expectations downward in Cairo," he said, as though he knew what I was thinking. "This probably looks Stalinist to you."

"It isn't *that* bad," I said. But it was, actually, almost that bad. Much of Cairo looked Stalinist.

"No, it's not pretty," he said. "But you get used to it."

He led me into what counts in Cairo as a nice restaurant. The floors were orange tile. The chairs were made of wicker. A mild feeling of gloom hung over the place like a cloudy day just before rain.

"Do you like living in Cairo?" I said as we sat down. A beaming waiter brought us two menus and bowed.

"Well, it's a big sprawling mess," he said. That was certainly true. "You either hate it or love it. I think I'm in the latter category. I was bored back home in the States, and I'm not bored here at all."

He and I have different personalities. I worried that I'd be bored and alienated into depression if I lived in Cairo after I saw all the sights, though I loved living in Beirut, a vastly more sophisticated and prosperous city that was also thrilling and edgy. It's impossible to be bored there for even five minutes. Going from Lebanon to Egypt was like descending into a poorly lit basement.

How far the mighty do fall. Fifty years earlier, Cairo was a relatively wealthy, liberal, cosmopolitan jewel of North Africa and the Middle East. Nasser's cultural and economic wrecking ball smashed the place as totally as the communist regimes he aligned himself with. Mubarak was no communist—that's for damn sure—but he was spectacularly uninterested in cleaning up Nasser's mess. *Wall Street Journal* reporter Stephen Glain once aptly described Egypt as a "towering dwarf." I don't think the description can be improved upon.

Hounshell and I ordered sandwiches, soft drinks and a *shisha* to share as we talked politics.

"There are 21 political parties," he said. "But 16 don't really exist. They are newspapers, not parties. Their reporters aren't really reporters. They have no handle on policy or ideas whatsoever. Some of them even sell access. If someone wants to smear a businessman, for instance, space can be bought for that in their pages."

The only real opposition to Mubarak's National Democratic Party, the Muslim Brotherhood, had been active in Egypt for 77 years at that point and had painstakingly built a formidable political machine through the mosques even while banned.

The two main liberal opposition parties, al-Wafd and al-Ghad, were tiny, disorganized and woefully unprofessional. They were fringe parties, not broad-based popular movements. It's not that the Muslim Brotherhood truly represented everyone else—they didn't. But the liberal parties had not been around for as long and hadn't been free to operate normally or build themselves up. Their ideas found little traction in Egypt anyway. The country was, for all intents and purposes, a two-party state, with Mubarak's military regime on one side and the semiunderground Islamists on the other.

Hounshell and I passed the *shisha* pipe between us. The tobacco flavor was apple, widely considered the best.

"The MB is going to win around 100 seats in parliament," he said. (As it turned out, they won 88.) "That's 100 out of 444 seats, plus another 10 appointed by Mubarak directly. That's a lot of seats considering that they only ran 120 out of fear of being smacked down by the state if they posed too much of a threat."

It *is* a big deal that the Muslim Brotherhood won more than half the seats they contested, especially since Mubarak's NDP still cheated and even opened fire with live ammunition on voters.

"All the ministers are members of parliament," he said. "So the minister of energy," for example, "has to face an election. In all the races where these big guys are running, we are seeing vote rigging, vote buying, intimidation and cheating."

During one of the early rounds of elections in Alexandria a street battle erupted between NDP guys wielding swords and Muslim Brotherhood members who came at them with chairs. The army fired tear gas at groups of voters in Brotherhood strongholds to keep them from reaching the polls.

How extreme was the Muslim Brotherhood, really? That's the argument that never ended in Egypt, in large part because the Brotherhood refused to admit where it stood. People saw what they wanted to see. Anti-Islamists feared the worst while optimists hoped the Brotherhood's self-identification as moderate was sincere.

Would they actually ban alcohol if they came to power? Who knew?

They wouldn't say. Would they force women, even foreign women and Christian Egyptians, to wear the veil? No one had any idea.

"Islam is the solution" was their rallying cry, but they said they wanted to build an Islamist state democratically.

They also claimed, at least sometimes, that they were not sectarian—a difficult thing to believe considering that they wanted an Islamist state. "I went to a Muslim Brotherhood rally," Hounshell said. They chanted Muslims and Christians, we are all Egyptians."

The problem for Egyptian Christians (who make up between 10 percent and 15 percent of the population) wasn't that the Muslim Brotherhood wouldn't recognize their right to live in Egypt and be Egyptians. The problem was that they stood a real chance of losing some of their already diminished rights and being forced to live by the code of another religion.

Mubarak's regime was secular, yet even under *him,* Christians were blatantly discriminated against when it came to government jobs. In a country where huge swaths of the economy are controlled by the government, that's a serious problem. They also had trouble building churches. Muslims could build mosques, no sweat, but Christians faced years of bureaucracy, and regime apparatchiks routinely said no. So Christians feared that if the Brotherhood ever ascended to power, the already existing discrimination from the secular state would only increase under an Islamist state. Why wouldn't it?

"The Muslim Brotherhood is run mostly by old people," Hounshell said. "The old guard is definitely less moderate and less democratic. But they are also more willing to make concessions to the regime. They really don't believe in democracy. The younger members, though, are more democratic. At least they seem to be. They talk a good game, but the way this will all play out if they ever come into power ultimately is unknowable."

To those who were easily and perhaps willingly fooled, Mubarak appeared to cry uncle after sustained U.S. pressure to open up his one-party state and hold real elections. But the reforms were a farce—and hailing his just-kidding charade as a sign of progress in the Middle East was naive and reckless.

Human-rights activists and independent politicians—most famously Saad Eddin Ibrahim and, more recently, Ayman Nour—continued to be harassed, arrested and booked on trumped-up charges. And since kicking around his opponents during "campaign season" wasn't enough to guarantee victory, Mubarak worked over the voters as well.

In early 2005 he announced that he would allow candidates other than himself to run for president. Millions of Egyptians were ecstatic. Finally they would have an actual choice in an election—a first-time experience for everybody. Yet no one who wasn't already registered to vote under the old system, in which Mubarak was the only candidate, would be allowed to vote in the supposedly real election at the end of the year.

The Egyptian government knew better than to imitate the Syrian and Iraqi Baath Parties by claiming to get 99 percent or even 100 percent of the vote. That didn't mean Mubarak actually won a normal election. It only meant he was a tad less obvious about it.

He was still pretty obvious, though. The democratic opposition parties only won 3 percent of the seats. It all went according to government plan, then. Kicked-around parties like al-Wafd and al-Ghad had no better chance of beating Mubarak at his game than the Green Party had of winning the White House in the United States.

"Rigging elections is a sport here," American political scientist and long-time Cairo resident Josh Stacher told me in his office. "There are 2,000 different ways to do it, and the methods vary by constituency and region. When all else fails, they just physically block people from voting."

All else failed in the Nile Delta during the third round of elections, including the physical blocking. Military police fired not only rubber bullets but also live ammunition at voters, killing at least eight and wounding more than 100.

Mubarak's regime didn't fail merely in politics. It spectacularly failed in every way a state can possibly fail. The economy was moribund. The habitable regions of Egypt were so overpopulated that cemeteries and garbage dumps had been transformed into slums packed with millions of people. Barely half the population could read or write. The state was a mafia with an army; its grubby paws stifled and profited from practically everything. Just walking around, I felt hopeless depression and dread like a dead weight.

Democratic and Republican administrations in Washington both described Mubarak as a moderate and an ally. They gave him $2 billion a year. To a certain extent he was "our son of a bitch." And that was precisely the problem.

Stacher explained how it looked to Egyptian eyes. "Mubarak's NDP fires tear gas at people who line up to vote. 'Made in the USA' is stamped on those canisters. When this sort of thing happens, lots of people here compare themselves to Palestinians living under foreign occupation."

The popular Egyptian notion that Mubarak was an American "puppet" is understandable to a point. The U.S. government was far too cozy with the man. At the same time, it was a bit of a stretch. His state-run media organs propagandized relentlessly and hysterically against the United States, arguably more so than any other newspapers and TV stations in the Middle East.

The U.S. was frequently compared to Nazi Germany. (At the same time, Egypt's media wallowed in Holocaust denial.) Al-Qaeda's man in Iraq, Abu Musab al-Zarqawi, was described as an American agent. Colin Powell, according to government weekly *al-Ahram al-Arabi*, accused the Sudanese government of genocide in Darfur as part of an American plot to steal oil. Just a few months earlier al-Mihwar TV had the audacity to air an interview with an Egyptian general who claimed that Vice President Dick Cheney admitted that the September 11 attacks were hatched by rogue elements in the White House. These are mere samples of what Mubarak's government-controlled media cranked out on a regular basis. No one who airs and publishes this kind of nonsense can honestly be counted as a friend or an ally, let alone a "puppet."

The Bush administration, to its credit, pushed for democratic reforms in Egypt, but it wasn't enough. Gently prodding a dictator who is otherwise treated politely and as a friend doesn't work if he's not a reformer. The Nasser-Sadat-Mubarak regime created Egypt's 21st century problems in the first place, and Mubarak turned out to be a little like Assad in Damascus. He created problems only he could solve, and he refused to deliver.

The very idea of a good autocrat is for the most part an oxymoron, but they do pop up here and there. Robert D. Kaplan defined such a rare creature as "one who makes his own removal less fraught with risk by preparing his people for representative government." Mubarak missed that mark by a couple of time zones.

Still, his government could only do so much damage to a thousand-year-old city like Cairo without physically tearing it down. I wanted to see the oldest parts of the city, places where dreary human-storage units didn't make up the skyline. I also wanted to see the blogger Big Pharaoh again. I liked the guy, and his pessimistic view of the place more or less lined up with mine. So we met at my hotel and took the subway as near as we could to Khan el-Khalili, the ancient souk near the Fatimid walls of the old city.

We got off the subway a half-mile or so from our destination and walked through a concrete catastrophe of a neighborhood on the way. Most storefronts were either closed permanently or shut behind grimy metal gates that pulled down in front of the entrances like garage doors.

"Don't eat anything from these guys," Big Pharaoh said as he gestured to a man selling food that was spread out on a rickety outdoor table. "If you eat that, you'll *die*."

"I'll *die*?" I said. "From what?"

"From a horrible disease."

I'm sure he exaggerated, but I duly noted his warning.

"We're coming up to the place where a bomb went off earlier this year," he said. "Are you okay with that?"

"I live in Beirut," I reminded him.

"Are you sure?" he said.

"Yeah, I'm sure," I said and laughed. "It's not going to explode again. Who planted it, anyway? Al-Qaeda?"

"Some guy in an extremist organization. Don't worry, everyone hates them."

He complained about how some parts of Cairo that used to be beautiful became squalid, in particular one area where derelict European-style architectural wonders were blanked out by an octopus of freeway on- and off-ramps.

"May God damn Nasser in hell all over again!" Big Pharaoh said.

"Plenty of countries built ugly crap like that after World War II," I said. "It wasn't just Nasser. I know what you mean, though. Even most Westerners have no idea how badly he ruined this place."

"Some of them love charismatic dictators," he said. "Like Castro and Qaddafi."

"Qaddafi is only charismatic if you're outside Libya," I said. "Inside he has all the charisma and charm of a serial killer."

Nasser wasn't as bad as the mad scientist ruling Tripoli. No doubt about it: Egypt was in far better shape than Libya. Egypt had people who could say what they wanted without being yanked from their beds in the night, as long as they didn't act on their opinions in public. Egypt had intellectuals. Egypt had art. Egypt had opera. Egypt had restaurants with menus. Most Egyptians didn't partake of Cairo's high culture, but at least it *existed*. In Libya it did not. Not under Qaddafi. He wouldn't allow it.

We walked past an old mosque set 15 feet below street level, built by Sharf el-Din and his brother in 1317–37 A.D. Just in front of the entrance was a courtyard of sorts created by the walls of the two buildings next to it on either side. The entrance was shut, and the lights set up to illuminate it were turned off. This mosque, unlike most, had no minarets.

I walked down the stairs and tried to open the slender wooden doors in case they were open. They weren't. Just to the right of the entrance was a plaque identifying the mosque as Monument Number 176.

You can spend a lot of time gawking at extraordinarily well-preserved monuments if that's what you're looking for in Egypt on holiday. Cairo suddenly seemed a better tourist attraction that I had so far given it credit for. The city as a whole is pretty shabby, but Beirut—which is in much better shape—is effectively only 150 years old. It lacks the sense of history and wonder that Cairo, dumpy as it is, can rightfully boast.

Big Pharaoh and I continued walking toward the old market on a busted-up sidewalk walled off from four lanes of traffic by a metal fence that looked like a 5-foot-tall, mile-long bicycle rack. Shuttered and boarded-up storefronts eventually fell away and were replaced by brilliantly illuminated shops selling all manner of oriental art, jewelry, housewares and textiles.

On our left was an 800-year-old Shia mosque built by al-Saleh Talai in 1160 A.D. (This one was Monument Number 116.) Marble Roman-style columns flanked the entrance below a classical Islamic arch. The doors of this mosque were made of tarnished hammered metal and looked original. It appeared to be in pristine condition, at least on the outside, for such an old building. I thought of an old saying about Europe and the United States, where Egypt can stand in for Europe. In Europe (and Egypt), 100 miles is a long way. In America, 100 years is a long time.

"You see those men in white robes and white hats?" Big Pharaoh said and pointed with his eyes toward two traditionally dressed men crossing the street. "They are Shias from India who moved here with Sadat's permission to live next to the Fatimid mosques and take care of them."

The Fatimids founded Cairo and built the oldest remnants in the historic center. Some parts of the ancient city walls still remain, along with an enormous metal door—impenetrable by medieval armies—at one of the gates.

"Khan el-Khalili is just up ahead," Big Pharaoh said. "You will love it. It is very exotic."

"Is it exotic to you?" I said.

"No," he said. "But it will be exotic to you."

I'd spent enough time in Arab countries by then that the exoticism had worn off, but I could still appreciate it. Khan el-Khalili is exactly, precisely, what I always imagined the Middle East would look like before I went there. Shopping—or buying things, I should say—never interested me much, but getting lost in the twisting narrow streets while gawking at gold, silver, hookahs, spices, jewelry, antiques and dramatically colored bolts of cloth reminded me that I was far from home and that I should savor my time while I could.

Some of the hustling shopkeepers could be endearing and entertaining when they weren't annoying.

"Welcome to my country!"

"How can I take your money from you?"

"I don't cheat as much as the others!"

Neither of us wanted to buy anything, though, so we set off for food.

I saw small birds the size of my fist being roasted by an ancient man at a food cart.

"Do you know what those are?" Big Pharaoh said. They looked like tiny chickens.

"Nope," I said.

"They're pigeons," he said. "They are stuffed. The cooks stuff rice—" he broke off laughing. "They stuff rice up its ass."

"Do you want a kebab?" the cart owner asked. "A pigeon kebab?"

"No, thank you," I said and walked on.

"We don't waste food in Egypt," Big Pharaoh said. "We eat every part of the cow here." That seems to be the case almost everywhere in the world except in the U.S. and Canada. "We eat the brains, the testicles and even the eyeballs. But I have *never* eaten an eyeball." Every man has his limits. "And I never will." He didn't mention testicles one way or the other.

"The brains are delicious," he said. "You would love it!"

Perhaps. But neither of us particularly wanted bovine noodle for dinner that night. So he took me instead to a restaurant called Egyptian Pancake near the entrance to Khan el-Khalili.

"This is the best pancake place in all of Egypt," he said.

Egyptian pancakes are more like slabs of thick pita bread than the breakfast fare of the United States. I ordered mine stuffed with white cheese and tomatoes. Big Pharaoh ordered his stuffed with beef. We ate at an outdoor table and talked about travel.

"I went to the Greek side of Cyprus when I was 5," he said.

"I didn't like the Greek side of Cyprus," I said. "The Turkish side is more interesting. The Greek side has no identity. It's like a gigantic outdoor frat house for British louts on a budget. It could be anywhere. If I flew all the way across the world just to go there, I would be pissed."

"I got lost on the beach," he said. "I was 5 years old. I remember screaming for my mother, and of course I was screaming in Arabic. I went up to all these Greeks asking if they had seen my mother, tears streaming down my face, and none of them understood me. I remember thinking I was going to spend the rest of my life here in Cyprus."

"Obviously your parents found you," I said.

"My father found me, and I ran up to him and hugged him like crazy."

"Where else have you been?" I said.

"Bulgaria," he said.

"I would love to visit Bulgaria," I said.

"I went there when it was communist," he said and laughed. "Communist Bulgaria! It was bad. My father didn't make as much money then as he does now. So when we wanted to go on vacation, all we could afford was a communist country."

We both thought that was funny. But, hey, I was willing to visit a communist country. I went to Libya, for God's sake, when I could have gone to Prague.

"Bulgaria is beautiful, though," he said. "The mountains, the forests, amazing. We went to a place called Butterfly Island. It is the most beautiful place I have ever seen. In the spring, the entire island is covered in butterflies." He made sweeping gestures with both his arms. "I had not even heard of it until my family went there."

I had not heard of it until he told me about it.

"What's the best trip abroad you ever took?" I said.

"My best trip ever was to Los Angeles. I was in heaven! When my family came home and the plane touched down in Egypt, my sister wept." He drew lines down his cheeks with his fingers. "She wept."

Three

The Next Iranian Revolution

Iran/Iraq Border, 2007

In a green valley nestled between snowcapped peaks in the Kurdish autonomous region of northern Iraq, an armed camp of revolutionaries prepared to overthrow the Islamic Republic of Iran. Men with automatic weapons stood watch on the roofs of the houses. Party flags snapped in the wind. Radio and satellite-TV stations beamed illegal news, commentary and music into homes and government offices across the border.

The compound resembled a small town more than a base, with corner stores, a bakery and a makeshift hospital stocked with counterfeit medicine. From there the rebels could see for miles around and get a straight-shot view toward Iran, the land they call home. They call themselves Komala, which simply means "Association."

Abdullah Mohtadi, the Komala Party's secretary general, and Abu Baker Modarresi, a member of the party's political bureau, hosted me in their meetinghouse. Sofas and chairs lined the walls, as is typical in Middle Eastern salons. Fresh fruit was provided in large bowls. A houseboy served thick Turkish coffee in shot glasses.

Both men started their revolutionary careers decades earlier, when the tyrannical Shah Mohammad Reza Pahlavi still ruled Iran. "We were a leftist organization," Mohtadi said, speaking softly with an almost flawless British accent. "It was the '60s and '70s. It was a struggle against the Shah, against oppression, dictatorship, for social justice and against—the United States." He seemed slightly embarrassed by this. "Sorry," he said.

I told him not to worry, that I hadn't expected anything else. The U.S. government had backed the dictatorship he fought to destroy. Pro-American politics had not been an option.

The Shah's secret police, the SAVAK, arrested Mohtadi and his closest comrades. He suffered three years of confinement and torture in the dictator's dungeons. Modarresi quietly sipped his coffee while Mohtadi explained this to me, interrupting only to say that he too was arrested, tortured and jailed for four years. Both were later released. And both took part in the 1979 revolution that brought down the state.

The even more tyrannical Ayatollah Ruhollah Khomeini replaced Reza Pahlavi, and the Iranian revolution, like so many others before it, devoured its children. It had been broad-based and popular at the beginning: liberals were allied with leftists, and leftists with Islamists. It didn't seem like a recipe for fascism, but that's what they got. The Islamists came out on top and smashed the liberals and leftists.

Mohtadi was still a critic of the United States, though much milder about it. "There has been lots of oppression," he said, "and killings and torture and expelling people from their land and sending them to internal exile in Iran and shelling the cities and all kinds of oppression. The problem with the policy of the United States is that for a long time, they neglected the violations of human rights in Iran. Also the European governments, the European countries, they didn't say anything about the atrocities going on in Iran. They called it a critical dialogue, but it was not a critical dialogue. It was lucrative trade with Iran."

Don't confuse the Komala Party with the Komala Party. Iraqi Kurdistan hosts two exiled leftist parties from Iranian Kurdistan, both with the same name, the same (red) flag and the same founder. Both parties have armed camps and military wings. Both built their compounds on the same road outside the city of Sulaymaniyah. They're right next to each other, in fact. Stand in the right place, and you can see one from the other. The difference is that one is liberal and the other is communist.

I didn't know there were two until I set up an appointment to meet Mohtadi, of the liberal Komala Party, and accidentally wound up unannounced inside the communist camp. The communists were good sports about my mistake. They granted me interviews, introduced me to Secretary General Hassan Rahman Panah and fed me lunch. They gave me the grand tour. They didn't tell me I was at the wrong compound. That news came from Modarresi, when he called to ask why I hadn't shown up.

On the surface the two parties are more confusingly interchangeable than the Judean People's Front and the People's Front of Judea in *Monty Python's Life of Brian*. Perhaps not coincidentally, Mohtadi says *Life of Brian* is one of his favorite movies.

Today's liberal Komala Party members belonged to the communist Komala Party and the larger Iranian Communist Party until they bitterly divorced in the 1980s.

"They were hard left to the point of Maoist at one point," says Andrew Apostolou, a Brookings Institution historian who specializes in the region and knows Komala well.

"We took part in the Communist Party of Iran," Mohtadi said, "but after some years we realized it was a mistake. We criticized that and split from them. It took some years, of course. It was not just like that." He snapped his fingers.

"You split with them over what, precisely?" I said.

"Over so many things," he said, his voice heavy with disappointment. "They have lost contact with the realities of the society. They have no sympathy for the democratic movement in Iran. We think the time for that kind of left is over." Mohtadi disagrees with Iran's communists on every point that matters: human rights, democracy, economics, the appropriate use of violence, the proper stance toward the West. Komala's economic views are still leftist, like those of small-*s* "socialists" in Europe, but Mohtadi flatly rejects systems like Cuba's. "I know they have social achievements in health care and education and all that," he said. "But in terms of political oppression and cult of personality, that's outdated. It's not acceptable for a modern civil society."

For his part, Panah, of the communist Komala, said dismissively of his wayward comrades, "We do *not* speak to each other."

Even in Iraq and Iran, left-wing parties fracture and withdraw into mutually loathing camps. The radicals always denounce the moderates as heretics, sellouts, "capitalist roaders" and neoconservatives.

Both Komala compounds were shelled and gassed with chemical weapons by Saddam Hussein. Saddam did his worst to erase the Kurds of Iraq from the face of the earth. Komala's members came from Iran, and they opposed the Islamic Republic just as he did. But they were still Kurds.

Komala was defenseless. Komala needed an army, not only to fight the Islamic Republic but also to defend itself in Iraq. So it built one.

The Iraqi Kurds called their guerrilla movement against Saddam Hussein the Peshmerga (Those Who Face Death). The contemporary Kurds' professional army, which functions as a constitutionally sanctioned regional guard in the Kurdish autonomous region, is also called the Peshmerga. And the liberal Komala called its warriors the same thing. They protected the base from Iranian infiltrators and death squads, and they crossed the border into Iran during uprisings. "When the time comes, we can organize not hundreds but thousands of Peshmergas," Mohtadi said. "It is very easy."

The most recent major Iranian Kurdish uprising was in 2005. It failed to topple the state, but it was huge and made headlines all over the world. "It swept many cities and towns and even villages," Mohtadi said. "It started from Mahabad. Young people were brutally killed by the authorities, tortured and then killed."

One of the victims, Shwane Qadiri, belonged to the Revolutionary Union of Kurdistan, which had recently changed its name to the

Kurdistan Freedom Party. "He was a member of our party," says party spokesman Zagros Yazdanpanah. "After that, all of Iranian Kurdistan rose up. Everywhere in all cities there were demonstrations against the Iranian regime. Our people inside are organized. Our people are in hiding; it is very dangerous."

"There was an uprising in Mahabad and violent clashes between people and the authorities," Mohtadi added. "That incident was spontaneous. There was no political party behind it. And from Mahabad, spreading it to other cities, we were behind it. We were the most influential political party that organized most of the demonstrations. We even organized its date and its time."

Yazdanpanah says Komala shouldn't take all the credit—his party organized demonstrations, too, as did others—but he agrees that Komala's role was substantial. It sent in its fighters, hoping to seize control of parts of Iran from the regime. The Revolutionary Guards and the police were too much for them, though, and they later had to return to Iraq.

Nadir Dawladi Abadi, a member of Komala's political bureau, gave me a tour of the training camp where Peshmergas are made. We walked unannounced into a classroom where new recruits studied weapons. Everyone in the room stood up at once and greeted us formally. They did not return to their chairs until I awkwardly gestured for them to sit. I felt like an intruder, but they ignored me as the lecture continued.

To my surprise, there were women there. None wore a hijab, the Islamic headscarf, over her hair, which is required by law in Iran. The students sat in plastic chairs with notebooks and machine guns in their laps. "They are studying RPGs [rocket-propelled grenades]," Abadi whispered to me.

Modarresi later told me new recruits also study what he calls the Komala ideology. The red Komala star, a branding remnant from the communist days, loomed like a baleful eye on the wall over the whiteboard. The idea of a red star and "ideological instruction" made me wince. Modarresi put me at ease. They aren't reading *Das Kapital* or

The Communist Manifesto, he said. They're learning about democracy, human rights, pluralism and civics, concepts that are not taught in schools by the Islamic Republic. I can't confirm Komala's classroom curriculum, but the party members are well known locally for being ex-communists despite their continued use of the red flag and star.

"What kinds of weapons do they learn how to use in their training?" I asked Abadi.

"Kalashnikovs, AK-47s, sniper rifles, grenades, RPGs and antiaircraft guns," he said.

"Can you tell me how many Peshmergas you have here?" I said.

Abadi laughed, shook his head and laughed again. "I'm sorry," he said. "I don't even know the answer to that."

We walked the grounds. Several members of the party joined us so they could listen in. I snapped pictures of everyone with my Nikon. Then, unexpectedly, they all wanted pictures of me. Out came cell-phone cameras and giddy smiles. I posed with them for 10 minutes. Apparently, they didn't receive many visitors from the West.

"How much longer do you think the Iranian regime will survive?" I asked Abadi after they put their cameras away.

"Ask your government," he said and chuckled. Big laughs all around.

"What would you think if the United States invaded Iran?" I said.

"There are many points of view about that," Abadi said. "But in general, the people of Iran are happy to see that."

"A war?" I said. "Really?"

"Invasion, yes," he said. "The people of Iran are thinking politically. The people have had many bad experiences since the 1979 revolution. They want the American people to topple the regime, not to occupy the land."

He did not only mean that the Kurds of Iran want a war, as the Kurds of Iraq wanted a war. He also meant that most Persians wanted an invasion.

This was not the official Komala line. "We are not for a military attack by the United States," Mohtadi said later. "Support the internal opposition against the regime. That's the best way to change. We are for regime change."

Abadi's claim, that Iranians as a whole would support an invasion of Iran, is a bit dubious. Some would certainly support it. But the regime points to the threat of invasion as an excuse to remain in power, and there is a danger that American intervention would merely drive potential rebels back into the government's arms. Even among the antiregime activists, there are many—including Abadi's boss, Abdulla Mohtadi—who say they want revolution and not an invasion.

The Komala Party's members, or at least its senior leaders, are among the most experienced armed revolutionaries in the world. They've already toppled one Iranian government, badly as it may have turned out for them in the end. As they plot another insurrection, they hope this won't be a rerun of the last one. "We are for democratic values," Mohtadi told me. "We are for political freedoms, religious freedoms, secularism, pluralism, federalism, equality of men and women, Kurdish rights, social justice. We are for a good labor law, labor unions. There is an element of the left in our political program."

They sounded like European-style social democrats. I asked if I could describe them that way. "We won't be angry," Modarresi replied with a laugh.

When are acts of violence against a state justified? What kind of violence is moral, and what kind is not? These are the questions Komala grappled with.

The old-school Komala Party, Hassan Panah's communist group down the road, thought any act of violence against an oppressive state was justified, including attacks on civilians who live in and visit the country. For the Kurdistan Workers' Party (PKK), the Marxist-Leninist guerrilla militia waging a terrorist war in eastern Turkey, Turkish soldiers, cops and civilians werw legitimate targets. So were Kurdish civilians opposed to the PKK's program and methods. So were foreign tourists visiting the Turkish beaches. The PKK opened a branch in Iran, where it pretended to be something else. There it called itself the Party of Free Youths in Kurdistan, or PJAK. Panah's Komala supported both the PKK and PJAK.

An ancient Middle Eastern saying holds that "the enemy of my enemy is my friend." It may seem that Panah's party subscribed to this maxim, despite the fact that its Islamist "friends" in the Iranian revolution of 1979 liquidated the left when they came to power. But Panah wouldn't even speak to Abdulla Mohtadi or anyone else in the liberal Komala Party. And Panah's party, like Mohtadi's, was heavily armed. The communists holed up in their own lonely compound were, if not terrorists themselves, at least armed supporters of terrorists. At the end of the day, this may be a distinction without much difference.

Running an ethically sound revolution requires hard moral as well as political work, and Mohtadi would have none of Panah's apologetics for scoundrels, even if it meant the Islamic Republic would last longer. "They are very fanatic in their nationalism," he said of the PKK. "They are very undemocratic in nature. They have no principles, no friendship, no contracts, no values. In the name of the Kurdish movement, they eliminate everybody."

Mohtadi and his party also stood foursquare against the Iranian Mujahideen Khalq, a small and ideologically bizarre armed group that fused Marxism, Islamism, Iranian nationalism and a personality cult around its leaders. They appear on most countries' lists of terrorist organizations, including those of both Iran and the United States. Mohtadi knew all too well what happens to revolutions with totalitarians in them. Even his old comrade Panah knew that when they worked together in the 1970s.

"We were not against revolution," Mohtadi said. "We were not against overthrowing the regime of the Shah. What we were against was violence by small groups of guerrillas who were separated from the mass movement. There were two different groups, religious and secular leftist guerrilla groups, who were influential at that time. People thought they were the way out of the dictatorship. Many, many intellectuals and students and political activists joined them. But we wrote pamphlets criticizing their methods."

These aren't academic questions in the Middle East. Opposing this or that faction or group isn't about political posturing, as it often is in the West. Dilemmas over the use of force don't apply strictly to the struggle inside Iran. The Islamic Republic sent spies into Iraq. Gunfights between government agents and party members have broken out on the roads in the province. Occasionally, Mohtadi told me, his people awkwardly ran across Tehran's men in the city markets of Iraqi Kurdistan's northeastern city of Sulaymaniyah. There they could pretend they didn't see or didn't know each other.

Most worrying is when the regime's secret police sneaked into the compound.

Nadir Abadi showed me to a small one-room building on the Peshmerga training grounds. Three men lounging inside on the floor stood up to greet us. "These people recently came out of Iran," he said. "They want to become Peshmergas. We have to investigate them first, so they have to stay here two or three months. After their identities are cleared, they will join the training courses."

"I'm curious how you investigate them," I said, "but I suppose you can't tell me."

"We have contacts with underground activists who do such kind of things," he said. "We can learn about them from them. It's not that complex."

But it did take several months. And what, I asked, do they do when they catch someone they think is a spy?

"We don't have jails here," Abadi said. "We thought about executing them. But we don't want to do that. So we make them sign a paper and confess their guilt and promise not to do it again. Then we send them back to Iran."

It may sound like a weak response in such a tough neighborhood, assuming the claim is true. But unless the regime figured out a way to evade Komala's intelligence agents, the seemingly weak response apparently worked. It had been years now, Abadi said, since they caught anyone on-site who worked for the Islamic Republic.

Some armed political parties in the region sucker gullible reporters into portraying them as more moderate and reasonable than they really are. A member of Hezbollah's political bureau tried it with me before their media-relations department threatened and blacklisted me. But Brookings' Apostolou didn't think the party was playing the fake-moderate game. "They are not linked to the PKK, PJAK or the Mujahideen Khalq," he told me.

"We were against the guerrilla-warfare movement that swept the world in the 1970s," Mohtadi said. "We had our theories against that. We believed in political work, raising awareness, organizing people."

Komala's model of the ideal guerrilla movement was Iraq's Kurdish Peshmerga. These men (and, yes, women) were and are a genuine "people's army" backed almost unanimously by civilians. (The PKK, meanwhile, car-bombed its Kurdish opponents.) The Peshmerga fought honorably against Saddam Hussein without resorting to the terrorism and authoritarianism that corrupt so many Middle Eastern militants of both the left and the right.

Komala's stance on erstwhile enemies like the United States was also complex and cautious. Mohtadi bristled when I offhandedly, without meaning offense, referred to the party's previous position as anti-American. "We were not anti-American," he said. "We were against the policies of the United States at that time."

I've heard this sort of thing before from people who don't really mean it. At least a dozen Lebanese supporters of Hezbollah have told me, a tad unconvincingly, that their "Death to America" slogan expresses merely a policy disagreement with the United States. There may be a small point in there somewhere. The Arabic language is flush with hyperbole. But if the U.S. government opened sessions of Congress by shouting "Death to Hezbollah" or, worse, "Death to Lebanon," I doubt Hezbollah would take it in stride.

Mohtadi, though, wasn't made of Hezbollah material. Instead of railing against the United States and waging war on its allies in the region, he met with State Department officials and asked for help from the American government. "We are not asking for an invasion," he told Eli Lake at the *New York Sun*. "We are saying that helping Iranian parties fight for democracy and regime change is good for us and good for America."

Mohtadi and Modarresi asked me to stay for dinner. Several other political bureau members joined us at the table. Servants brought us baked chicken, barbecued lamb, steamed rice, an enormous stuffed fish from one of Kurdistan's lakes and four bottles of red wine from Lebanon.

The 66 hostages seized at the American embassy in Tehran in 1979 finally came up in conversation. "We were against that from the very beginning," Mohtadi said. I half expected him to bang his fist on the table. Suddenly his soothing demeanor was gone. Mention of the hostage episode had riled him up. He may have been politically anti-American when the embassy workers were taken, but he said that act of anti-Americanism gravely violated his own standards of conduct.

Besides, the United States was a potential if not actual ally in Mohtadi's struggle against the Islamic Republic. Perhaps it's not surprising that Mohtadi's list of ideological foes changed over time. His enemies became precisely those with whom he aligned himself during the battle against the Shah: the totalitarian left and the Islamist right.

More encouraging than Komala's moderation and political evolution was its plausible claim—backed up by most Iranian activists, expatriates and dissidents—that Iranian society as a whole is far more sensible and mature than it was in 1979, at least at the level below the state, on the street. The aftermath of an Iranian revolution, Mohtadi said, will not resemble the postwar occupation of Iraq with its civil war, insurgency, kidnappings and car bombs.

"We have an internal opposition," he said. "We have an internal movement against the regime. Women were warned not to celebrate 8 March, Women's Day. They did. There are demonstrations in Iran. There are movements in Iran. You have the intellectuals, the political activists, the human-rights activists, then the Kurds, Arabs, Azeris, Baluchis, different nationalities. There is a movement in Iran, unlike in Iraq under Saddam Hussein, where you had Kurds and nobody else." (Iraq's Shias did rise up against Saddam in 1991, but they had been quiet since Baghdad's brutal response to that insurrection.) "It's not like that in Iran."

Iran's opposition undoubtedly had more breadth and maturity than Iraq's did under Saddam Hussein. And if Iran's government were to fall to a mass revolution rooted in civil society instead of an outside invasion, postregime chaos seemed less likely—assuming the various ethnic groups could hold it together.

Iran is commonly thought of as Persian, but ethnic Persians make up only 51 percent of the population. Twenty-five percent are Turkic Azeris, 10 percent are Kurds, and smaller numbers are Baluchis and Arabs. How are Iran's relations among its various "nationalities"? "Much better than the relations between Kurds and Arabs" in Iraq and Syria, Mohtadi said. "Historically, Persians and Kurds have been, as people say, cousins. Culturally they are closer to each other than Kurds and Arabs, who have almost nothing in common."

"The Iranian people and the Iranian Kurds are more developed," he continued. "They are more cultured; they are more organized. Even the Iraqi Kurds admit that culturally [Iranian Kurds] are higher and more developed economically. The credit doesn't go to the Islamic Republic. For a long time Iran has been a civilization. Iraq's tribal and medieval culture, the brutality, the lawlessness, revenge—Iraq was very primitive and still is, apart from Kurdistan. You look at it, and you become astonished at how undeveloped politically they are."

He had a point. Iraqi Kurds built the only safe, prosperous and politically moderate place in Iraq, yet they admire the Iranians (though not their government). The Iraqi Kurdish city of Sulaymaniyah is far more liberal and open, and noticeably less backward and tribal, than the Iraqi Kurdish cities of Erbil and Dohuk. This, according to people who live there, is partly due to Sulaymaniyah's proximity to Iran and the centuries-long liberalizing effect that Iranian Persians and Kurds have had on their culture.

Mohtadi could be wrong. Maybe he was talking about a minority that only appeared to him like a majority. Perhaps his analysis was slightly deceitful, a little self-serving. These things happen. We know how inaccurate Ahmed Chalabi's rosy predictions about post-Saddam Iraq turned out to be. There is no way to know for certain until the Islamic Republic is gone. If Mohtadi turns out to be wrong, though, he won't be alone. Most opposition groups inside and outside Iran claim the Iranian people—Persians, Kurds and Azeris alike—are far more prepared than Iraqis for civil, democratic politics.

What they didn't know—what no one could know and what may in the end matter most—is how much damage a fanatical minority can do in Iran after it's thrown out of power. It may not matter if most Iranians want a normal life in a quiet country. Most Iraqis were not insurgents, but the insurgency raged on.

We could look, though, at the behavior of the ruling fanatics. As oppressive as the Iranian government was, it was an enlightened model of restraint compared with Saddam's regime in Iraq.

Saddam destroyed the city of Halabja with air strikes, artillery, chemical weapons and napalm. He wiped out 95 percent of the villages in northern Iraq. He drained the marshes in southern Iraq and chopped down the forests of Kurdistan. He threw dissidents into industrial shredders and acid baths. The most mundane things were banned: cell phones, maps, even weather reports. The Mukhabarat, his secret police, arrested anyone who so much as looked at one of his palaces. Iraq was the North Korea of the Middle East.

Iran was harsh, but it wasn't *that* bad. Opposition to the regime was widespread, deep and open—unthinkable in Saddam's Iraq. It was impossible for the Iranian government to crack down on everyone. The police hardly even tried anymore.

"You can complain about the government," Mohtadi said. "You can insult them. But America is a red line. Khomeini himself is a red line. The Israelis are a red line, absolutely." Iranians couldn't buck the party line on certain topics, but they were brave enough, or just barely free enough, to protest the government to its face. "When [Iranian President Mahmoud] Ahmadinejad spoke to students," Mohtadi pointed out, "hundreds of students stood up and called him a fascist and burned his picture."

Sealing the rugged Iran-Iraq border is all but impossible in the north, where like-minded Kurds live on both sides of it. People, as well as goods, cross every hour. Alcohol is smuggled into Iran. Gasoline and drugs are smuggled out. Komala's location in the area made it the perfect place for a vast, sprawling safe house. Activists, underground party members and dissidents from Iran—from the Persian heartland as well as from Iranian Kurdistan—slipped through the mountains to visit every day.

I've stood on the border myself and contemplated walking undetected into Iran. Komala leaders even offered to take me across and embed me. "We can get you inside Iran and leave you for weeks, if you want, among our supporters and among our people," Mohtadi said. "It is very easy."

If I were caught in Iran without a visa or an entry stamp in my passport, I would almost surely be jailed as a spy. Tempting as the offer was, I had to pass. Anyway, I could speak to Iranian dissidents, if not necessarily ordinary Iranians, in the Komala camp just as easily as I could have inside Iran. As it happened, a famous Persian writer and dissident had arrived there just before I did.

Kianoosh Sanjari was a member of the United Student Front in Tehran. At 23, he had been been imprisoned and tortured many times. His most recent arrest was on October 7, 2006, after he wrote about clashes between the Revolutionary Guards and supporters of the liberal cleric Hossein Kazemeyni Boroujerdi. Charged with "acting against state security" and "propaganda against the system," he was released on $100,000 bail the previous December. Some months later, he fled to Iraq and moved to the Komala camp.

Unlike most Iranian visitors who used Komala as a safe house, Sanjari didn't bother to remain anonymous. He told me his real name and said I could publish his picture. "I'm just now coming out of Iran," he said. "It's a hell there. I know the sufferings. I am inclined to accept any tactic that helps overthrow this regime."

"Does that include an American invasion of Iran?" I asked.

"Maybe intellectuals who just talk about things are not in favor of that kind of military attack," he said. "But I have spoken to people in taxis, in public places. They are praying for an external outside power to do something for them and get rid of the mullahs. Personally, it's not acceptable for me if the United States crosses the Iranian border. I like the independence of Iran and respect the independence of my country. But my generation doesn't care about this."

Sanjari had fierce and intimidating eyes, the eyes not of a fanatic but of a dead-serious person who is not to be messed with. He spoke slowly and with great force. "They repress people in the name of religion," he said. "They torture people in the name of religion. They kill people in the name of religion. The young generation now wants to distance themselves from religion itself."

Islamists seem to fail wherever they succeed. Perhaps Islamic law looks good on paper to Muslims who live in oppressive secular states, but few seem to think so after they actually have to put up with it.

More than 100,000 Algerians were killed during the 1990s in a horrific civil war between religious insurgents and the secular Soviet-style police state. As a consequence, Islamists became more hated in Algeria than at any time since they rose up. Al-Qaeda tried to reignite the war there, but couldn't quite pull it off.

Iraqis turned against al-Qaeda faster and harder than Iranians turned against the Islamic Republic. Harsh as the Islamic Republic may be, al-Qaeda is worse by an order of magnitude. Its infamous warnings to street vendors in Iraq's Anbar province not to place cucumbers next to tomatoes in the market because the vegetables are "different genders" is one of myriad reasons most Sunni Arab tribes in that region flipped to the side of the hated Americans.

Islamist law became so widely detested and flouted in Iran that it's a wonder the regime even bothered to keep up the pretense. In June 2005, Christopher Hitchens wrote in *Vanity Fair* that every person he visited there, with the exception of one imam, offered him alcohol, which was banned.

Everyone I met at the Komala compound said the Iranian regime wallowed deep in the postideological torpor that inevitably follows radical revolutions. Except for the most fanatic officials, the government cared only about money and power. "Followers of the regime are not ideological anymore," Sanjari said. "They are bribed by the government. They will no longer support it in the case that it is overthrown. Even among the Iranian military and Revolutionary Guards, there are so many people dissatisfied with the policies of the regime. Fortunately there aren't religious conflicts between Shias, Sunnis and different nationalities."

Mohtadi concurred. "The next revolution and government will be explicitly antireligious," he said.

The Iranian writer Reza Zarabi says the regime has all but destroyed religion itself. "The name Iran, which used to be equated with such things as luxury, fine wine, and the arts, has become synonymous with terrorism," he wrote. "When the Islamic Republic government of Iran finally meets its demise, they will have many symbols and slogans as testaments of their rule, yet the most profound will be their genocide of Islam, the black stain that they have put on this faith for many generations to come."

It's certainly possible to be overly optimistic. Iranian dissidents have been predicting an imminent revolution for several years running. Michael Hirsh wrote in *Newsweek* that women in Tehran have "gone defiantly chic" in style and that the men are looking "less and less menacing and more and more metrosexual," which makes the place sound more like freewheeling Beirut than an Islamist theocracy. But the state, he added, could still endure for some time. "It is an old, familiar umbrella of oppression that now stays just distant enough to be tolerated, even if it is little loved," he wrote. "The success of this oppressive but subtly effective system should give the regime-change advocates in Washington some pause."

Whom to believe? Hirsh's analysis held up for years, but Iran is notoriously unpredictable even for those who are supposed to be experts. The 1979 revolution shocked even CIA agents who lived in Iran while it was brewing. They insisted the Shah was firmly entrenched and could not possibly fall.

The Middle East is so rife with conflict, factions, murky alliances, foreign interventions, multisided civil wars and wild-card variables that trying to predict its future is like trying to forecast the weather on a particular day three years in advance. There's a reason the phrase *shifting sands* has become a cliché.

If the Islamic Republic is overthrown, almost anything might happen. Iran could become a modern liberal democracy, as most East European states did after the fall of the Soviet Empire. It could revert to a milder form of authoritarian rule, as Russia has. It could, like Iraq, face chronic instability and insurgent attacks. Or its various "nationalities" could tear the country to pieces and go the way of the Yugoslavs. Optimists like Sanjari and Mohtadi may have a better sense of what to expect than those of us in the West, but they still do not know.

The only thing that seems likely is that a showdown of some kind is coming, either among factions in Iran or between Iran and the rest of the world. Predictions of the regime's imminent demise have been staples of Iranian expat and activist discourse for years, so it's hard to take the latest ones seriously. But authoritarian regimes increasingly seem to have limited shelf lives. As Francis Fukuyama's flawed but compelling book *The End of History and the Last Man* points out, there has been a worldwide explosion of liberal democracies since the 18th century, from three in 1790 to 36 in 1960 to 61 in 1990. (In 2006, Freedom House classified 148 nations as free or partly free.) History isn't over and never will be, but it hasn't been kind to dictatorships lately.

The Iranian state is soft and vulnerable compared with the worst abusers out there, and it constantly faces resistance from citizens. Something will give.

"Movements are taking shape in Iran," Sanjari said. "The Iranian regime confronts the whole world with its policies. Political developments are very rapid now. Developments in Iran aren't controllable. I hope the Iranian people overthrow this regime with no or few sacrifices. But that is a dream."

Four

Between the Green Line and the Blue Line

Jerusalem, 2011

If you were to walk the streets of Jerusalem's Old City while knowing nothing of the city's history or politics, you would have no idea that Israelis and Palestinians are officially in their seventh decade of war with each other. Here, in this ancient square kilometer, is where Arabs, Jews and the three Abrahamic faiths come together. The Western Wall of King Solomon's temple, the holiest site in all of Judaism, is mere feet from the al-Aqsa Mosque, the third holiest site in all of Islam. Both are just minutes from the Church of the Holy Sepulchre, where Jesus was said to be buried beneath the hill where he was crucified.

Arab shopkeepers in the Muslim and Christian quarters sell their merchandise not only to tourists from just about everywhere but also to their Jewish Israeli neighbors. You're as likely to hear Hebrew spoken as Arabic, and most of the time you can't tell by looking who is a Jew and who is an Arab. Most of the Old City's Arabs return to their homes at the end of the day on the east side of the city, and most Jewish Israelis retreat to houses on the west side, but the two communities mix here every day and, at least superficially, get along as well as people in any other civilized city. There is little crime and even less political violence. It certainly isn't a war zone, or at least it isn't today.

This fragile de facto peace may be the foundation for a genuine and lasting peace later, but most proponents of a two-state solution to the Israeli-Palestinian conflict would erect, for the first time, a real international border through the heart of Jerusalem. There's a chance it might work, but if it doesn't—and the odds are remote that it could work well anytime soon—the collapse of this delicate and hard-earned status quo could do serious damage to the city so close to the hearts of both peoples.

Israel has been at war since the day it was born. When the Jewish state declared independence from the British Mandate in 1948, Egypt, Jordan, Syria and Iraq invaded and vowed to destroy it. The war lasted until the following year, when separate armistice agreements were signed with each aggressor. The Jordanian-Israeli armistice line slashed right through the center of Jerusalem, with the Jordanians controlling eastern, northern and southern sectors and the Israelis controlling western Jerusalem and an enclave in the east on Mount Scopus. The line became known as the Green Line. Neither Israel nor Jordan ever declared it the border, because it was simply drawn where each army happened to be standing at the time of the cease-fire. Each side knew, or at least hoped, that it was only a temporary armistice line, that there was nothing holy about it, that the final status was still up for grabs and would be later decided by negotiation or conquest.

Israel's toehold in the western sector was surrounded on three sides and connected to the coastal plain by a narrow strip of land just a few kilometers wide. The Jordanians held the high ground overlooking that corridor, and they dug in on the tops of the hills surrounding it and the city. Despite the armistice agreement, Jordanian soldiers frequently used those positions to fire artillery shells, mortars and sniper rounds at Jewish civilians below.

Jerusalem had a Jewish majority when Israel declared independence, but Jews caught on the Jordanian side of the line were killed, expelled or taken to prison camps, their property confiscated or destroyed. Cultural and holy sites were ravaged. The Jordanians tore up an enormous 2,000-year-old cemetery on the slope of the Mount of Olives with bulldozers, razed the Jewish Quarter of the Old City to the ground and smashed its synagogues into rubble.

Abdullah el-Tell, commander of Jordan's 6th Regiment of the Arab Legion and later the military governor of Jerusalem's Old City, even boasted about it. "For the first time in 1,000 years," he said, "not a single Jew remains in the Jewish Quarter. Not a single building remains intact. This makes the Jews' return here impossible."

Jordan, Egypt and Syria launched their second war of annihilation in 1967. The Israelis handily defeated all three armies in six days and pushed the 1949 armistice lines outward. They took the Golan Heights from Syria, the Sinai Peninsula and the Gaza Strip from Egypt and the West Bank from Jordan.

Egypt and Jordan later relinquished their claims to Gaza and the West Bank and signed peace treaties. Israel returned the Sinai to Egypt. Israel never annexed these territories, because adding millions of Palestinian Arabs to its population would threaten its Jewish majority over the long term. Israel did, however, annex the formerly Jordanian-occupied parts of Jerusalem, partly because Israelis yearned to reunite their capital but also because they vowed to never again let a hostile army surround them on high ground.

One of the first things the government did after its victory in 1967 was build Jewish neighborhoods in empty places that were formerly used by the Jordanian army. About 200,000 Israeli Jews now live in areas like French Hill, Ramat Shlomo and Gilo on the other side of the Green Line. Residents can look down the dizzying heights into the heart of the city from hilltops once occupied by snipers and artillery crews. Some of the new neighborhoods went up in areas that were Jewish before the Jordanians destroyed them after Israel's declaration of independence.

"Annexing East Jerusalem was a dramatic event," said Orly Noy from the Ir Amim organization, a center-left human-rights NGO active in East Jerusalem. "That meant that, at least according to Israel, all of Jerusalem became a part of the sovereign state of Israel. That means all Israeli laws apply, including the right of the Arab residents to become citizens. Israel never annexed the West Bank, and even according to

Israeli law, the West Bank is not part of the sovereign state of Israel."

She unfolded a map of Jerusalem that her organization produced with two thick colored lines on it—the Green Line, which was the 1949–67 armistice line, and another line in blue that marks the edge of the Jerusalem municipality since annexation. This blue line is what the state of Israel now considers the border.

The Green Line is invisible in Jerusalem. You'd have no idea where it is just by looking. "After annexation," Noy said, "it became a national task to erase the Green Line. We didn't want anything to remind us that the city was ever divided." The blue line on Ir Amim's map, though, cannot be missed on the ground. The Israeli government built an imposing concrete wall there during the Second Intifada to keep Palestinian suicide bombers from the West Bank out of Israel.

"Most of us don't expect a real peace anytime soon," said Israeli historian Yaacov Lozowick, the author of the books *Hitler's Bureaucrats* and *Right to Exist*. "So we suspect that the reality of that barrier after several decades will become the border. That's why it was so important for the Palestinians to push the fence as close as they could to the Green Line."

Palestinian negotiators say they refuse to sign a peace treaty unless the eastern side of Jerusalem—the portion Jordan temporarily conquered and annexed—is ceded to them for their capital. And that can't happen if the separation barrier becomes a permanent border. Before the wall was built, the blue line hardly meant anything. It still doesn't mean anything to the international community, which never recognized either Jordanian or Israeli sovereignty over East Jerusalem, but to Israelis and Palestinians, it means everything.

The Green Line doesn't exist on maps in city hall. The only line that matters there is the expanded municipal blue line. Everything between the two is controversial. The Palestinians say the Green Line should be the border. (I'm referring here to Palestinians who at least say they're willing to recognize Israel and its right to exist. The terrorist organization Hamas and its fellow travelers insist that Israel shall cease to exist inside any borders.) The Israelis, meanwhile, say the municipal line, where the separation barrier sits, is the de facto border already, at least for now. The two sides may one day compromise with a new line, but no one knows where that line would be drawn, and no one knows for sure it will even happen. In the meantime, city hall has no choice but to govern Jerusalem as the unified city it effectively is.

"Around 200,000 Jews live in neighborhoods built on the other side of the 1967 line," Deputy Mayor Yakir Segev told me in his office. "These neighborhoods have always been considered parts of Israel that will remain under Israeli sovereignty in any agreement, whatever the agreement is. No one will dream of evacuating these big Jewish neighborhoods in the name of anything. All Israelis, and even the Palestinian Authority, understand that we're going to keep these neighborhoods and give them something else in return."

Most Israelis also want to keep the core of East Jerusalem, where about 200,000 Palestinians live. Israel offered them citizenship when it annexed their part of the city. Few accepted it, though, so Israel declared them residents of Jerusalem, issued them the same identification cards Israeli citizens use and extended to them all the legal rights of citizenship except for the eligibility to vote for members of the Knesset, the Israeli parliament.

Since then they've enjoyed all the benefits of living in Israel, which are substantial. And over the past 43 years, they've developed a political culture unique to the area. Hardly any of them participated in the Second Intifada, for instance. And after the Second Intifada, thousands finally decided to take the offer of citizenship.

"They feel threatened by the fact that they might be forced to become citizens of Palestine," Lozowick said, "so twelve to fifteen thousand of them have recently filed citizenship papers. And around 20,000 of them were already Israeli citizens. The number is growing all the time. There is tremendous social and political pressure on them from the Palestinians in the West Bank not to do that because everybody recognizes that if the number of Arabs in East Jerusalem reaches a critical mass of Israeli citizens, then Israel will not be able to divide Jerusalem. The entire city will be made up of Israeli citizens."

Hillel Cohen, author of *The Rise and Fall of Arab Jerusalem*, told me the political mainstream in Jerusalem's Palestinian neighborhoods is not one of "resistance" but rather of "passivism."

"The mainstream is against armed struggle in Jerusalem," he said. "That doesn't mean the problem will be solved soon, but I think this will continue to be the mainstream. There has also been a development of a new identity. They have a separate identity within the larger Palestinian identity. There are many sub-identities. They can be Christian, Israeli, Gazan, from the West Bank and the Diaspora. Now they have a Jerusalem-Palestinian identity."

That identity is practically defined by cognitive dissonance. They're Palestinians and loyal to their people's cause, but they have more political, civil and human rights in Israel than anyone has in the West Bank, Gaza or in any of the Arab-majority countries. Israel—despite its relentless delegitimization in Palestinian society—is an imperfect but nevertheless nice place for Arabs to live, even as alienated minorities.

Many Palestinian residents of Jerusalem are of two minds on the subject. Some almost seem to have two personalities.

"There are two different political lexicons among the Palestinians," Cohen said, "and you can hear both from the same people. A person will tell you the Jews should be killed because they're the enemies of God, they don't have any rights here and so on. But the next day he'll say we're all brothers, we're all human beings, we have to coexist here in the Holy Land. I hear both from the same people. If they say one thing to one person and something else to somebody else, I can understand that. I don't have an explanation for why I hear such different things from the same person."

I asked one Arab shopkeeper in the Old City which side of the border he'd rather live on if one were ever drawn up. "The Israeli side!" he said instantly and emphatically, as if there were no other possible answer. I couldn't imagine his saying the opposite later. "None of us want anything to do with the Palestinian Authority. They are corrupt. They are impossible. They are not straight. No one can deal with those people." He doesn't think the Israelis are "straight" either, but he insists they are better. "Which side would *you* rather live on?" he asked me rhetorically.

Another Arab shopkeeper I spoke to in the Old City said exactly the opposite. "Some want to stay in Israel because the economy is better," he said, "but not me." And like many Palestinians Cohen knows, he wildly contradicted himself. "I'll compromise on the 1967 lines even though I don't like it," he said. "If I don't compromise on the 1967 lines, I will get nothing." So he sounded at first like a moderate, but not 20 minutes later, he said he yearned for the apocalypse. " I hope Iran gets the bomb," he said. "I am ready to die. As long as Israel is destroyed, I am ready to die."

The history and details of the Israeli-Palestinian conflict are endlessly complex, and the Palestinian side is wildly contradictory and baffling to the Western mind, but the nature of the conflict is rather straightforward.

"You've got two nations that want the same land," Cohen said. "Both have strong ties to this country and strong narratives that they tell themselves and the world. And they both see Jerusalem as the center of their existence, religiously and politically. Israel was wise, strong and lucky enough to occupy the whole territory, and it tries to control it. But it's very difficult to control a population that doesn't accept your rule, so there are clashes. And some good people are trying to find a solution."

What those good people hope to do is draw a new line between the Green Line and the blue line that both sides can agree on.

President Bill Clinton suggested dividing the two countries demographically. The Jewish-majority areas would go to Israel, while the Arab-majority areas would go to Palestine. Something a lot like this was proposed at the time of Israel's founding. Areas with a Jewish majority would become a Jewish state, while areas with an Arab majority would become a Palestinian state. The Arab side in 1948 refused partition and opted for war. It happened again in 2000, when Palestinian Authority leader Yasser Arafat refused the American-Israeli partition offer at Camp David and launched the war of the suicide bombers.

One day, however, Palestinian leaders may well say yes, so an NGO called the Geneva Initiative drew up a specific proposal for the division of Jerusalem based in large part on Clinton's parameters. You can look at their maps on their website. Jewish population centers in Jerusalem on the other side of the Green Line would officially become Israeli territory once and for all, as would the geographically contiguous settlement blocs in the West Bank. Smaller and more remote Israeli settlement outposts would be evacuated and ceded to Palestine. Most Israelis would find this acceptable if a stable and enduring peace were to follow.

It makes sense on some level at least. Arab neighborhoods in East Jerusalem like Um Tuba and Sur Baher look and feel like more like clean and prosperous sections of Baghdad than anywhere else in the city. Israeli Jews don't live there, nor do they want to. The overwhelming majority of Israelis would not even notice if they lost these areas because they've never seen them in the first place.

Many parts of municipal Jerusalem are like this. The city limits go all the way up to Ramallah, where the Palestinian Authority has its offices, and all the way down to the Palestinian city of Bethlehem. These in-between places were annexed to Jerusalem in 1967, but they were sparsely populated Arab villages at the time. The residents didn't feel like they lived in Jerusalem. The only reason some feel like they do today is because they're walled off from the nearer cities of Ramallah and Bethlehem by the security barrier. These areas are only technically in Jerusalem. When I drove there in my rental car, I not only felt like I had left Jerusalem, but I also felt like I had left Israel.

The Old City and the adjacent neighborhoods are another matter entirely. This is the heart of Jerusalem. "Most Israelis are very uneager to have that area go to the Palestinians," Lozowick said.

An increasing number of Jerusalem's Arabs are also uneager to be shoved over to Palestine. Few bother asking them if they might rather remain in Israel, even though more and more of them are filing for citizenship. Even the Old City's Christian Quarter and the Armenian Quarter would be given to Palestine, according to almost every proposal for dividing the city.

Still, many Israeli officials admit both implicitly and explicitly that partition along one line or another may one day happen whether they like it or not. In the 1960s the municipality hired urban planner Israel Kimchi to plan for the eventual reunification of Jerusalem, and today he's working on plans for its eventual redivision. Like most Israelis, he hates the idea of partition, and not only because in his younger years he dedicated himself to reunification. He has visited every divided city in the world, and he does not like what he has seen. While we all know about the terrible wall dividing Berlin during the Cold War, fewer know what Nicosia on the island of Cyprus looks like today. The Turkish military controls the northern half while the (Greek) Cypriot government maintains its hold on the south. Kimchi has seen it, and so have I. A ghastly and heavily militarized dead zone cuts Nicosia in half, including the most beautiful part of the old city. Kimchi vividly recalls the years before 1967, when Jerusalem was in a similarly wretched condition. "It was terrible," he said. "We had minefields in the city."

He is especially unhappy with the idea of redividing the Old City and the rest of the Holy, or Historical, Basin, and he's trying to come up with a work-around.

"Neither side is going to give up this area," he said. "Certainly the big neighborhoods will not be given up. The focal point of the Old City and the area around it, the Historical Basin—if the two parties are unable to run it together—can be administered by a third party."

Like who, for instance?

"Like the government of New Zealand," he said. "I don't know. The Swedes. Israel won't accept the United Nations, but some kind of international force without the United Nations. France, New Zealand, Australia, the United States. We haven't made a decision, but this is the political line now among the politicians. It's one possible solution. Both sides—the Israelis and the Palestinians—want to keep the city open."

Whether the Old City and the Historical Basin are partitioned into two states or subtracted from both and turned into a third place, there will have to be a line somewhere dividing Israel from Palestine. And it's rather unlikely at this point that the Palestinians will accept anything less than full sovereignty over the Arab parts of Jerusalem, since Clinton included them in his offer to Arafat in 2000.

So Lozowick and I took a walking tour of central Jerusalem where the future border might be if that's what happens. We followed the line that the folks at the Geneva Initiative drew on a Google Earth map. It looks a lot less plausible on the ground than it does in satellite photographs, and it's hard to avoid the conclusion that dividing the Historical Basin again might not be possible.

Take the neighborhood of Abu Tor, for instance. It's on a hill just south of the Old City. The eastern side is Arab, and the western side is Jewish. The Green Line runs through its center. From 1948 to 1967, a blockwide no-man's-land separated Arabs from Jews, but the neighborhood has since been reunited.

Because Arabs still live in the eastern half and Jews still live in the western half, it would be easy enough—at least theoretically—to just make the Green Line the border. The border, however, would go right down the middle of a dead-end street where Jews live on one side and Arabs live on the other. If a wall or a fence is built on that border, residents won't be able drive down or park on their own street. And if there won't be a wall or a fence, anyone could cross the border without passing through customs or security, whether they're tourists, spies, job seekers or suicide bombers.

"If you assume," Lozowick said, "as the Geneva people do, that dividing Jerusalem will lead to everyone living happily ever after, then you can say there may be a question of who is in charge of paving the road, but otherwise it will work. But what if—for whatever reason, and despite everybody's best intentions—after the city has been divided, it doesn't work?"

A Palestinian could throw a hand grenade into Israel from inside his living room, and vice versa.

"No one here is a settler," Lozowick said. "This is the pre-1967 border. No one can say the Israelis shouldn't be here so close to the Arabs. This is where the original line was. There are a lot of places like this in Jerusalem."

What if there's peace between Israel and Palestine, but then Israel and Syria go to war? What would happen in Abu Tor? And how would the Palestinians feel if their neighbors across the street lived in a democracy with social security, health care and high wages, while they lived in a corrupt authoritarian system without any rights? And what would happen if Hamas takes over the West Bank, as it has taken the Gaza Strip, and places terrorist nests mere feet from houses in the center of Israel's capital?

Drawing a new border would be even harder inside the walls of the Old City.

On a street near the Armenian Quarter, a house that is slated for Israel is wedged between two houses that would go to Palestine. Houses in the Old City are ancient. They lean on each other. Jewish and Arab buildings lean on each other throughout. If one comes down, those next to it will also come down. It is not physically possible to weave a border between them. Only a European Union–style nonborder without a fence, wall, customs booth or security checkpoint is even possible. There's no room for anything else.

It's even stranger where the Muslim Quarter abuts the Jewish Quarter. Arabs own shops at street level while Israeli Jews own apartments upstairs. The ground floor on that street would be in Palestine, while the second floor would be in Israel.

I asked Lozowick if the people who drew this theoretical border have ever walked around in the Old City and looked at what they were proposing.

"I asked them that," he said, "and they wouldn't answer. They wave their hands."

After looking at the proposed division of Jerusalem, I drove to the already divided city of Hebron in the West Bank with talk-radio host Eve Harow. I've visited too many places in Israel and the West Bank to keep track of, and none are more ominous and disturbing than Hebron.

Five hundred Jewish settlers live in a cramped section of the city. Hundreds of Israel Defense Forces soldiers are stationed there to protect them because they're often shot at by their Palestinian neighbors. A small number of tourists occasionally drop by to visit the Tomb of the Patriarchs, the second holiest Jewish site in the world, but they understand there's a chance they'll be murdered by gunmen.

As a direct result of ethnic strife in the city, Palestinian movement is restricted or prohibited in a large swath through Arab neighborhoods immediately adjacent to the Jewish settlement area. It is completely locked down by Israeli soldiers. Shops have been forcibly closed, their doors welded shut and covered with spray paint. This is in Hebron's Old City, the part of town that would be filled with thousands of tourists and pilgrims from all over the world if it weren't a war-torn slum made ugly by hatred and security measures. The Israeli military describes this section of Hebron as the "sterile zone," but it's not an operating room in a hospital. It was once a vibrant ancient city, but today it looks like a ghost town emptied by a violent catastrophe.

This, Lozowick wrote, "is what happens when Israelis and Palestinians agree to divide a city, but can't agree to live together in peace. The blame for lack of peace is irrelevant: each side will doubtlessly say it's all the fault of the other, but the result won't be any nicer thereby. The myriads of observers, pundits, politicians, dreamers, visionaries and true believers who all know for a certainty that dividing Jerusalem is the key to peace in the Middle East need urgently to visit Hebron."

Maybe Jerusalem will be divided again and maybe it won't. Partition might solve the problem and it might not. Nobody knows, though a number of major players, including the most experienced diplomats, have convinced themselves otherwise.

"Many people still say we all know what the final settlement is going to look like," said Israeli political analyst Jonathan Spyer when I interviewed him in central Jerusalem, "so we just need to get the two sides together and work it out. To that I say, no. You don't know what the final status is going to look like. The final status you have in mind is what you came up with by negotiating with yourself."

It has been years since I've managed to find an optimist who lives in the region and believes the conflict will end anytime soon. It's possible that everybody is wrong about that, but it isn't likely. This is a part of the world where the past and the present are the most reliable guides to the future. Hillel Cohen summed it up best when I asked him what he expects for Jerusalem 50 years from now. "Some war," he said and shrugged. "Some peace. Some negotiations. The usual stuff."

The Israeli-Palestinian conflict is what happens when an irresistible force meets an immovable object. Both Israelis and Palestinians are irresistible forces, and they're both immovable objects. The White House can keep cajoling the two sides to negotiate, and the Geneva Initiative can tinker with its lines on their Google Earth maps, but they need to understand that there's a chance no progress will be made during their lifetimes and that a premature or botched partition may precipitate ruin.

Five

Tower of the Sun

Golan Heights, 2010

Before the Six-Day War in June of 1967, the Syrian army built fortified bunkers on the ridge of the Golan Heights and fired sniper rifles, mortars and artillery cannons at Israeli civilians below. The cities, farms and kibbutzim on the shore of the Sea of Galilee, and in the wider region around it, were perilous places to live or even to visit when Syria commanded those heights.

"If they saw tractors down there," Golan resident Hadar Sela said after leading me to one of the bunkers, "or anything moving at all—even a child walking to the store to get milk—they opened fire. There were bunkers like this along the entire ridge of the Golan."

Israelis have controlled the ridge since they seized it in 1967, when the combined Arab armies of Syria, Jordan and Egypt launched a war of annihilation against the Jewish state.

"Syria lost it fair and square," she said.

The bunker she showed me is just a two-minute walk from her house on kibbutz Kfar Haruv, where she and her neighbors enjoy the spectacular formerly Syrian view of the Galilee far below.

Her family is part of a small but committed Israeli movement to settle the Golan Heights, partly in order to strengthen Israeli control for security reasons but also because building and living on fresh, open, conquered land, for them, is an adventure.

"Nobody came to live on the Golan because it was comfortable or easy," Hadar said. "I came 20 years later, in 1985. It may sound corny, but in the beginning it was out of a pioneering spirit. It really was, though I know that sounds unfashionable. We remind Israelis of simpler days here."

Alongside the path to the bunker is a minefield marked off with barbed wire.

"People ask me how I could raise children in a minefield," she said. "I always say that in Tel Aviv they teach their children not to step into traffic. Here we teach them not to step into minefields."

Hadar and her significant other, Reuven, hosted me in their house and lent me their spare room for two nights. Their children have grown and built their own houses, so she and Reuven had the space. I enjoyed their company and was glad to escape Tel Aviv, Israel's largest city. The same infernal eastern-hemisphere heat wave that was setting Russian forests on fire turned the Mediterranean Sea and the Israeli lowlands into a steam bath. The coastal air felt like soup on my skin even at five o'clock in the morning. The cooler mountain air of the Golan massaged the heat out of my muscles and back.

Hadar was born and raised in Britain. Reuven is a Sabra, born and raised in Israel. "I have nowhere else to go," he said, addressing his comments not to me so much as to those who think Israelis should go "back" to Europe. His parents were ethnically cleansed from Libya.

The Golan Heights doesn't feel like Israeli-occupied Syria. At least it didn't to me, not compared with the West Bank, anyway.

Though the West Bank is technically disputed territory rather than occupied territory—it hasn't belonged to anyone, according to international law, since the British left in 1948—Area C, where the settlement blocs are located, is under Israeli control. (The Palestinian Authority controls Area A, and the two jointly control Area B.) But Hadar and Reuven's house on kibbutz Kfar Haruv felt like Israel. There are no Palestinians on the Golan. And the Israelis who settled it come from a completely different part of the Zionist movement than the settlers in the West Bank.

"I've never voted for a party to the right of Meretz," Hadar said. Meretz, in many ways, is to the left of Israel's left-wing Labor Party.

Reuven chuckled. "She's not really that far to the left," he said.

"Yes, I am," she insisted.

Aside from her love for the democratic socialism of Israel's kibbutzim, she didn't sound all that left-wing to me, either. She even sounded to the right of Reuven in some ways, though he is no hard-liner.

"Before the First Intifada we didn't think much of the Palestinians," Reuven said. "They were just low-wage workers who commuted to Tel Aviv from refugee camps in Gaza or wherever. They didn't have equal rights and we didn't care. It wasn't until after the First Intifada that we saw them as human beings. We got what we deserved, if you ask me."

Hadar agreed in principle, but she wouldn't go as far as he did. "I was nearly killed by Palestinians who threw rocks the size of small boulders at my car," she said. "So don't tell me the First Intifada was nonviolent."

Syria's and Egypt's failure in the 1973 Yom Kippur War, despite their strong performances at the beginning, finally convinced Arab governments that the Jewish state could not be destroyed by conventional means. The Israel Defense Forces had proved itself too hard a target, not just in 1973 but also in 1948 and 1967. And now that Israel was sitting on the Golan, the Syrians had no soft Israeli targets to shoot at. They couldn't even see the Galilee region, let alone fire upon it.

Later that same decade, however, Iran's Shah Reza Pahlavi was overthrown in Tehran, and Ayatollah Khomeini's Islamists came out on top in the postrevolutionary struggle for power. When Israel invaded South Lebanon in 1982 to oust Yasser Arafat's Palestine Liberation Organization from the Lebanese-Israeli border area, Khomeini redeployed 1,500 men from battlefields in the Iran-Iraq war to Lebanon's Bekaa Valley to arm, train and equip his new overseas project—Hezbollah.

Syria's then ruler Hafez al-Assad did everything he could to help the Iranians. If the Syrians couldn't fight Israel from their side of the border, Hezbollah could do it for them in and from Lebanon. So the Syrian-Israeli front line shifted from the Golan and the Galilee over to South Lebanon and the Israeli region below it.

Though the Golan physically looms over all this terrain, Hezbollah mostly left it alone during the war in 2006, when it fired thousands of Katyusha rockets into Northern Israel. Israelis on the Golan, though, take a keener interest in Lebanon than Israelis who live farther away and out of Hezbollah's rocket range—or at least Hezbollah's rocket range in 2006. According to all the latest intelligence out of Lebanon, today Hezbollah can strike not only as far as Tel Aviv and Jerusalem but all the way down to Eilat on the Red Sea in the remote south of the country.

Reuven wanted to know what I thought about Lebanon after I told him I lived there during parts of 2005 and 2006. He was interested not only because he lives a short drive from the border but also because he served there as a soldier for seven months in 1982.

He spent most of his time in the Chouf Mountains.

"Have you been to Jezzine?" he asked me.

I had.

"It is an amazing place," he said to Hadar, who has never been there. "It's like somebody lifted a village from Provence and dropped it in Lebanon."

He fell in love with the country despite all the carnage.

"For the first few months everybody was really nice!" he said. "Everyone seemed to like us." Then he laughed. I laughed. Hadar laughed.

"I can't understand that place," he said. "The Christians and Druze were shooting each other. They weren't shooting at us—they were shooting each other. Most of the time they seemed to get along perfectly fine, but then Thursday or Monday would come along and they'd fight. Why? Why did they think their lives would get better if they shot at the neighbors?" He seemed genuinely baffled. "It is a crazy country."

"I don't care if they like me," he added later, referring this time not to the Christians or Druze but to the predominantly Shia southern part of the country where Hezbollah is ensconced. "I just want them to stop trying to kill me."

Syria is only two years older than Israel. Like the Jewish state, it was forged upon the ruins of the Ottoman Empire after interim European powers withdrew from the region shortly after World War I.

What is now Israel was still under the control of the British Mandate when Syria declared independence from the French Mandate in 1946. The British had control of the Sea of Galilee and wanted to keep it. So while the Golan Heights above the sea's eastern shore went to Syria, Britain kept control of the actual shoreline. The border was set 10 meters from the edge of the water. If the sea level rose or fell and the shoreline moved, the border moved with it.

So when Israel declared independence from the British Mandate in 1948, it acquired the sea's eastern shore from Great Britain. Water is a precious resource in the Middle East, and the Syrians were not happy. They were enraged that the Jews achieved independence at all and— along with the Egyptians, the Iraqis and the Lebanese—immediately launched an aggressive war to destroy it, though Lebanon participated merely in a token manner to keep up appearances.

They lost, of course, and Israel went on existing. Israel's existence was in fact secured. Yet Syria seized control of the eastern shore of the sea by force a year later. That campaign was easy. Israel couldn't defend an isolated 10-meter-wide ribbon of land between water and cliffside. Borders like that don't work between countries at war. So the Syrians gained control of part of the Galilee even though they were not entitled to it, and they held it until Israel snapped up the entire area after Syria, Egypt and Jordan tried yet again to destroy the country in 1967.

The 1990s were supposed to be the decade that heralded peace. The Soviet Union had burst. It looked like "the end of history," such as it was, might even reach the Middle East. Yet the Oslo peace process broke down between Israelis and Palestinians, and Israel's peace talks with Syria hit the rocks.

Israeli Prime Minister Ehud Barak offered to return the Golan in exchange for peace in 2000, but Syria's Assad said no. Most Middle Eastern political analysts assume Assad never wanted a deal, that he merely went through the motions because it suited him at the time. Syria's secular, non-Muslim, Alawite-dominated government needed a permanent state of war with Israel to survive in a country with a hostile Sunni majority. Resistance temporarily lent the regime the legitimacy it would otherwise lack. Assad needed an excuse, though, to say no when the Israeli government agreed to return the Golan. And his excuse was that Israel would not give him the eastern shore of the Galilee.

Syria's internationally recognized border never included an inch of that shoreline, but Assad knew Israel would refuse to sign over the title, and he knew his own "street" would applaud him for insisting upon it. Israel can't give back the Golan unless Syria will say yes. And Syria will not say yes. So the Golan remains in Israel's hands, and Assad's son Bashar got to keep the grievance he needed to justify war.

The territory has now been in Israel's hands more than twice as long as it was in Syria's.

"The Alawite regime is the best guarantor that Israel will be able to keep the Golan," Israel Eshed, head of the Golan Tourism Association, told me. He's one of Hadar's neighbors in a village up the road, and she took me to his house to meet him.

While the nature of the Alawite regime and its interests may be the ultimate guarantor of Israeli control of the Golan, it wasn't always this way. During the Yom Kippur War in 1973, Syria almost took it back.

"They reconquered more than half the Golan for four days," Eshed said. "They sent 100 tanks up the Valley of Tears."

Egypt attacked Israel in the south at the same time, and the Israelis were entirely unprepared for it. Initially, it looked like they might actually lose, and by the end they lost more than 2,500 soldiers.

"What happened to Israeli civilians on the Golan who lived in the areas that were captured?" I asked.

"They were evacuated," Eshed said, "before the Syrians took them. Otherwise the Jews here would have been massacred. There were Jewish villages on the Golan in ancient times, and again since the 1800s, but the Syrians massacred them in 1948, and they would have done it again in 1973 if they could."

"That war was deeply traumatizing for us," Hadar said. "It still feels like a fresh wound here, like your Vietnam."

War memorials are scattered from one end of the Golan to the other.

"There are only two crossing points to the Golan from Syria," Eshed said, "in the north and in the east. Thanks to the topography, we can easily hold off the Syrians in the southern Golan. And if they can't take the Golan, they can't invade Israel."

Even so, he doesn't believe holding onto the Golan Heights matters as much for Israeli security as it used to.

"Giving up the Golan would be bad for the Zionist movement," he said. "Israelis love the Golan. We want to keep it."

Security concerns aren't entirely idle, however, not when the Golan looms so large over the vulnerable Galilee. "We can't act like Europeans in the Middle East," Eshed said. "The Arabs don't understand Yiddish."

Hadar's house on kibbutz Kfar Haruv is on the southern and all but impenetrable part of the Golan. It's wedged between sheer cliffs to the east and the west. I needed to see more, and she accompanied me in my rental car on a drive north, where we would meet Yehuda Harel, a former member of the Knesset, for lunch.

We passed a number of destroyed Syrian military bases.

"Have you heard of our famous spy Eli Cohen?" she asked me as I stepped out of the car to take pictures.

"Of course," I said.

The Israelis sent him to Syria in 1962, and he worked his way very high up in Damascus. For a while, he was the chief adviser to the minister of defense before Cohen was found out and executed.

"I'm not sure if it's true," she said, "but many say it was his idea to have the Syrians plant eucalyptus trees on their bases when he came to the Golan. They grow fast, and he said they would provide shade for the soldiers during the summer. But what they also did was mark out military targets for the Israeli air force. Our pilots could easily see the trees from the skies."

Harel has lived in Israel during its entire history as a modern nation-state, though he lived in Damascus during World War II, when his family temporarily relocated there from the British Mandate for Palestine. The pub where we met him looked, felt and operated exactly like a microbrewery in Seattle or Portland.

"I was 8 years old," he said, "and I remember it very well. My father was there with the British army, and he brought the whole family with him. It was a small town then. Only around 300,000 people lived there. Now it's more than a million."

As a young man, he lived in the Galilee region and endured shelling by the Syrians from the Golan for years. After Israel seized the area, he and a handful of others bolted up the mountain to start a kibbutz. The government had nothing to do with their decision, but the Galilee's kibbutzim gave them their blessings.

"We wanted Israel to annex the Golan," he said, "for protection."

The Golan was mostly empty when he and his seven companions arrived. All was blackened from the fires of war, and they settled in a destroyed Syrian camp.

"We weren't at all confident that Israel would keep the Golan," he said. "It seemed at the time that there was only a small chance it might happen. But in order to shape the future, you have to act."

After six months, the Israeli government allowed them to build a proper kibbutz. They lived at first in a Syrian barracks. When the kibbutz population grew larger, they moved into the ruins of the shattered garrison town of Quneitra, a city that once housed 20,000 Syrians and that was at the time half demolished and entirely empty. They lived in an old Syrian officers' neighborhood surrounded by walls.

The Israelis held the city for seven years but gave it back in 1974. The United Nations Disengagement Observer Force (UNDOF) stepped into a narrow demilitarized zone between the two sides.

The Israelis expected Syria to rebuild Quneitra. "As far as I'm aware," Hadar said, "rebuilding was one of the terms of the agreement under which it was given back." Israel wanted Damascus to have something to lose in the border area should war break out again. Instead, Assad left it in ruins—and forbade its former residents from ever returning home— as a macabre memorial to "Zionist brutality." It remains a broken ghost town to this day and has been in a state of ruin and decay longer than I've been alive.

After the Yom Kippur War and shortly before the disengagement, Yehuda and his neighbors founded a new kibbutz named Merom Golan next to a volcanic crater 3,000 feet above sea level. They grew apples, grapes and cherries there, and it's still thriving and growing.

"Tell me," I said, "is the Golan Heights still strategically important for Israel?"

"Arab armies have started wars with us again and again since 1948," he said. "They despise us, but we're stronger and we won all of them. Syria doesn't believe it can win a war against Israel with tanks or a regular army. So it's buying missiles, big missiles. And if Syria fires them at us, what can we do? We can shoot back at Damascus. A lot of Syrians would be killed, yet they'd win the war against Israel just like Hamas and Hezbollah won their wars against Israel."

He was referring to the Second Lebanon War in 2006 and Operation Cast Lead in Gaza in 2009.

"Why do you think you lost those two wars?" I said. "Because you didn't win? The way I see it, nobody won."

"We lost," he said. "We can beat them in a war face-to-face, but we can't beat them from a distance. And they know it. They are much better at missile war than we are."

"We certainly lost the war of public opinion," Hadar said.

"Sure," I said, "but that's better than actually losing."

"And we didn't finish the job," she said.

"We can't finish the job," Yehuda said. "How can we finish the job? Hezbollah now has more rockets than ever. Bigger rockets. Stronger rockets. We can't do anything about it. We can bomb Beirut. So what? It doesn't do any good. It doesn't help us at all. And it turns the world against us. Syrian rockets can reach Tel Aviv, and we don't have much of a deterrent. Rockets don't have to be very accurate if they're fired at Tel Aviv."

Most of Hezbollah's rockets are pathetically inaccurate, but the Tel Aviv metropolitan area is enormous and hard to miss.

"But we do still have a deterrent," Yehuda said. "Our tanks can reach Damascus in 48 hours from the Golan Heights. We can destroy the Alawite ruling class. We can drive right through the Valley of Tears down below. Damascus is only 60 kilometers from the border. My house is closer to Damascus than it is to Haifa. We could drive there in my car in less than an hour."

"At the end of the Yom Kippur War," Hadar said, "our army was less than 30 kilometers from Damascus."

"You know what Syria is like," Yehuda said. "Syria is a country with a strong center. Syria is Damascus just like Israel is Tel Aviv. Everything that matters is in Damascus."

"Well, what would happen if you did give the Golan back?" I said. "Do you really think the Syrians would shell the Galilee again?"

"No," Yehuda said. "They would shoot Tel Aviv."

"They'd shoot Tel Aviv from the Golan Heights?" I said.

"No," he said. "They'd shoot Tel Aviv from Damascus."

"But they can do that right now," I said. "So if you gave the Golan back to Syria, what would you lose? Okay, you'd lose the ability to get tanks into Damascus in 48 hours, but you could still get tanks into Damascus. It would just take you a bit longer. And it wouldn't be dangerous for you if they were here, would it?"

"Yes," Hadar said. "It would. We can't afford to have missiles here."

"They can already hit Tel Aviv without putting missiles on the

Golan," I said.

"But they won't without the Golan," she said. "We know they can, and they know they can. The question is, what price are they prepared to pay?"

"They are prepared to pay with the lives of thousands of people," Yehuda said, "but they are not willing to pay with Damascus or the regime."

I got the sense, however, that Yehuda Harel wasn't primarily concerned with security. He's been living on the Golan for more than 40 years, and his love for it is obvious. Like Israel Eshed, the head of Golan Tourism Association, he wants to keep it because it's his home now.

"The people of Israel love the Golan," he said. "More than a million Israelis visit here every year. They won't give it up. And Israel is a democracy. What the government wants, more than anything, is to continue being the government. What the prime minister wants most is to be the prime minister. Any prime minister who talks about giving up the Golan Heights will be afraid of the next election. So before giving up the Golan, somebody will have to convince the people of Israel."

"What do Israelis love about it?" I said. I can testify that it's a nice place. Its scenery is dramatic, its climate mild during the summer. The place reminds me in some ways of the dry side of my home state of Oregon. But few Israelis actually live on the Golan.

"I've asked many people this question," Yehuda said. "Israelis love the Golan more than they love Jerusalem."

"That's ridiculous," I said.

For more than a thousand years, Jews all over the world have said "next year in Jerusalem" at the conclusion to the Passover Seder.

"Yes," Yehuda said. "It's hard to believe. But when people are asked if they will give up the Golan or part of Jerusalem for peace, the negative answer for the Golan Heights is twice as high as the negative answer for Jerusalem."

"Why?" I said. "The Jewish people yearned to return to Jerusalem for 2,000 years. It's your cultural, historical and political capital."

"I've asked a number of people about this, some of them psychologists," he said. "And I've heard many answers. One is that the Golan is on the shore of the Sea of Galilee. Mankind knew that water gives life even before it was mankind. The Golan Heights, subconsciously, is water."

The freshwater Galilee is Israel's primary source of drinking water, and when Syria controlled the Golan, the Syrians did their damndest to take the water for themselves and dry up the sea. The lower portion of the Golan is still scarred by botched Syrian engineering projects that would have diverted or stopped the rivers that pour into the sea in the winter and spring.

Yehuda was a member of the Knesset, Israel's parliament, from 1995 to 1999. He and a handful of others started their own party solely to prevent the government from giving the Golan back to Syria.

"This was during the time of Yitzhak Rabin's government," he said. "I was one of his aides. And I made a party called the Third Way. We were a movement of people on the political left who were against withdrawing from the Golan. So many people joined that we decided to run in elections. We got four seats in the Knesset. So I found myself in the Knesset, and I didn't know what to do."

"You were the dog that caught the car," I said.

He laughed.

"Well," I said. "How did it go?"

"It was very interesting for a few years," he said. "My smallest daughter—well, my youngest daughter, she's not small anymore—was very much against my going into politics. But our movement gets stronger with every new government. Israelis don't realize how strong our democracy is. They think the government can do anything, but it can't. I know because I've seen it from the inside. The government wants to continue being the government more than anything else. People in the government are afraid of elections, as they should be. They are not good people. They are extremely selfish."

"You know these people personally," I said.

"Yes," he said. "And in order to keep their jobs, they have to satisfy people. That's the system. As Winston Churchill said, democracy is the worst system except for all the others. We don't have to create propaganda for the Golan Heights. We just have to produce the best wine and make sure tourists come here, and the people will stand with us."

Hadar and Reuven stayed on kibbutz Kfar Haruv during the 2006 war with Hezbollah. A few missiles hit the Golan. I know because I saw them strike it with my own eyes when I covered the war from the border area. Hezbollah wasted few of their precious Iranian projectiles on the Golan, however, because it's so sparsely populated. The cities of northern Israel took the brunt of the damage. So the Golan offered an almost safe front-row seat during the war.

It was even safer during the Second Intifada than it was during the Hezbollah war. Suicide bombers had no interest in going all the way up there to explode themselves in such a lightly populated and target-poor environment.

"We had so much tourism up here during the Second Intifada," Hadar said. "It was the safest place in Israel."

"It was the only safe place in Israel," Yehuda said.

"This is a marvelous place to bring up your children," Hadar said. "My kids grew up completely free here. They didn't have to worry about anything dangerous."

"A 4-year-old girl can walk at night to her friend's house," Yehuda said.

"Nobody is going to attack children here," Hadar said. "Nothing bad is going to happen. My own children know Britain well, having visited family there often and spent time there themselves after their army service. Recently they said, 'Mother, thank you, thank you for bringing us up on the Golan and not anywhere else.' When they saw what life in the U.K. is like, they knew they had the best childhood possible."

"And remember," Yehuda said, "there are no Palestinians here. More than half the people in Israel want to withdraw from the West Bank. Israelis don't want to occupy people. We are against occupation.

Today nobody believes a withdrawal will bring peace, but we are still against occupying another people. But there's no occupation here like the one in the West Bank. There is no occupation of people."

That's sort of true but not entirely true. It depends on how you look at it.

There are no Palestinians on the Golan, but there are about 20,000 Druze in the north. Unlike the Alawites who lived on the Golan before the 1967 war, the Druze didn't flee when Israel took it. Most live on the back side of Mount Hermon. Unlike the Palestinians of the West Bank and Gaza, the Druze of the Golan can take Israeli citizenship if they want it. They have the same political rights as Israeli Druze, and the same political rights as Israeli Jews.

The Druze, like the Alawites, are not Muslims. Both religions grew out of Islam—as Islam emerged in its own way from Christianity and Judaism—but then became something else.

There are only about 800,000 Druze in the entire Middle East, so they take an extremely cautious approach to politics. Everywhere they live—in Lebanon, Syria, Israel and on the Golan—they're loyal to whoever's in charge. Syrian Druze at the time were with Assad and the Baath Party. Israeli Druze side with the Zionists. Lebanese Druze adjust their alliances constantly in an ever mutating environment. The Druze of the Golan have little choice but to divide their loyalty between Jerusalem and Damascus. Most won't take Israeli citizenship even though it's available, and they won't serve in the army. They self-identify as Syrians, not Israelis. But unlike most Syrians, they say they like Israel. They obey Israeli law, and they don't sign on with the reactionary Arab movements that yearn for the country's destruction.

"Let me tell you something that's not very nice," Yehuda said. "There were almost 100,000 Syrians here on the Golan Heights before 1967. And they're not here now. Israel won't let them come back. They live in refugee camps near Damascus."

"Where did they live?" I said. "Is there an empty city up here somewhere? I know about Quneitra, but it was given back to the Syrians."

"They refuse to rebuild it," he said. "Twenty-thousand people used to live there. The rest lived in small settlements. So while the West Bank is like South Africa in some ways, the Golan Heights is like America. America and South Africa have bad histories, but today there is complete equality. It's the same on the Golan Heights. No one under the age of 40 even remembers the Syrians being here. You didn't know there were 100 small Syrian settlements here until I told you about them."

"So what's the future of this place?" I said.

"I don't know anything about the future," he said. "Nobody does. Not even the CIA knows anything. They didn't know the Soviet Union was going to collapse a week in advance. So how can I know? I can do my best to keep the Golan Heights in Israel and that's it. When people want to know about the future, I send them to a woman named Eva in Jaffa. You can take coffee with her and then she'll tell you your future." He laughed. "She's much cheaper than the CIA and no worse. She costs 50 shekels."

"Okay," I said, "so let me ask you this. What if there was an offer on the table from the Syrian government—not this government, a different, moderate, and less hostile government, run by a guy like Anwar Sadat who says, 'Okay, we're going to have real peace and normal relations. No more support for Hamas or Hezbollah. You give us back the Golan, and we'll be as good a neighbor for you as Jordan.' Would you take the deal?"

"Let me tell you," Yehuda said. "What a Syrian leader says doesn't mean anything. It means nothing to me. I would tell him that if Syria is to be governed as a normal country, like Sweden or Canada, then the Syrian government shouldn't mind if I stay on the Golan. Right? I could stay in Canada if I wanted. If they don't want me to stay, then they aren't offering a real peace."

"But what about Jordan?" I said. "You can't live in Jordan. Jews can't even own property there. But the Jordanian government isn't causing any problems for Israel. The Jordanians aren't shooting at you anymore, and they cooperate in a serious way on security."

"At the moment, yes," he said. "I don't know what will happen later.

No one knew Yugoslavia would destroy itself. It was one state. It was quiet. People were friends. Then it exploded. Here we are surrounded by Sunnis and the Muslim Brotherhood. Not in Lebanon but everywhere else. And they are very dangerous. In the Middle Ages, Islam had the most advanced culture in the entire world. Then something happened. We aren't confident the peace treaties with Egypt and Jordan will last. We all saw what happened in Iran in 1979. And look what's happening now in Turkey. What will Turkey look like next year? Maybe it will look like Ataturk's country again, and maybe it will look like Iran. Nobody knows."

"What will happen in Egypt when Mubarak dies?" Hadar said.

"This is why I don't know what will happen in the future," Yehuda said. "And I don't trust people who say that they do. It's a bad idea to deal with an uncertainty by creating a certainty. If we give back the Golan, we will have no idea what might happen next."

Hardly anyone ever hears about the tens of thousands of people who live under Israeli occupation on the Golan. Few outside the Middle East even know they exist. Their plight is not taught in schools. No activists rally on their behalf. Hardly anyone in the world demands with passion that they be liberated.

"We have an undefined nationality," said Faiz Safd, one of the Druze of the Golan, while sipping from a cup of thick Turkish coffee.

He agreed to meet me and Hadar and explain what he and the people in his community think of Israel's occupation. He's is in his mid-30s and, like me, wasn't yet born when Syria lost the territory. Israel has been in charge of it during his entire life, but if the 1967 war had never happened—or if Israel had returned the Golan to Syria for peace in the meantime—his nationality would not be ambiguous. He would be Syrian.

"How do you travel out of the country if you have an undefined nationality?" Hadar said.

"It isn't easy," Faiz said. "We can't get Syrian or Israeli passports, and Syria won't let us visit or move there. They want us to stay here on the Golan so we can help them get it back." They can get Israeli passports, actually, if they accept Israeli citizenship, but most haven't done so. That would be dangerous.

The largest Druze community is in Majdal Shams, high on the slopes of Mount Hermon, where about 9,000 people live. Majdal Shams is the Arabic adaptation of the village's Aramaic name, which in English means Tower of the Sun.

It's an apt name. It's at the top of the Golan, nearest the sun, and it towers above the entire Middle Eastern Mediterranean where Israel, Lebanon and Syria converge.

Its residents are an unusual bunch. The Druze are monotheists who emerged from Islam a thousand years ago, but their religion changed so drastically it became something else. They don't proselytize or wage wars of conversion or conquest. No one is even allowed to convert if they want to. That door closed in the year 1043. You're either born a Druze or you aren't a Druze. And if you die a Druze, they say you'll be reincarnated as one.

Their religious texts are kept secret not only from non-Druze but also from most Druze. The "uninitiated" majority aren't required to observe any rituals. They aren't even allowed to know much about the religion.

There are only about 800,000 of them in the entire Middle East, and they live exclusively in the Levant. The Middle East beyond Israel's borders is often thought of as a monolithic bloc of Arabs and Muslims, but it isn't, especially not here. This part of the region is defined by diversity and disunity. Druze live chockablock next to Arab Christians who live alongside Armenians. Shias live near Jews and Maronite Catholics who often don't even think of themselves as Arabs. Alawites live among Sunnis, Shias, Christians and Jews. Sectarian-ethnic maps look similar to those in the volatile Caucasus and the former Yugoslavia before it unraveled.

The Druze, like the Maronites, are too few to build their own state. They don't even appear to want their own state, opting instead for caution to ensure themselves against persecution. Kamal Jumblatt, the father of Lebanese Druze leader Walid Jumblatt, once explained his people this way: "Ever alert, [Druze] gauge their surroundings and choose their words carefully, assessing what must be said and what can be said."

If the Golan Druze were to accept Israeli citizenship, and if the Israelis were to then hand the Golan back to Assad, they'd almost certainly be denounced as traitors for signing up with the "Zionist Entity." Any number of bad things might happen. They could be imprisoned. They might be killed. They could be thrown off the Golan and permanently exiled to Israel. As far as I know, the Syrian government never once threatened anything of the sort, but it doesn't have to. The Druze are more finely attuned to their political environment than anyone else in the Middle East, and they understand precisely the nature of the government in Damascus.

What distinguishes totalitarian regimes like Syria's from garden-variety authoritarians like Egypt's Hosni Mubarak is their ability to prevent citizens from even thinking like free individuals. When I visited the Balkans a couple of years earlier, I heard about a particularly chilling example from the communist era. "Under the regime of Enver Hoxha," an Albanian human rights official told me, "people were afraid to look at churches and mosques. A friend told me she was too scared to even think about God because Hoxha would know and would throw her in prison."

Assad still has a powerful effect on the minds of the people who live under his rule. He can even affect the minds of Druze on the Golan who were born after 1967 and haven't experienced his rule directly for even a day. They effectively live in Israel and have never known anything else. They've never met a single Syrian policeman or intelligence officer. All they need to know is that someday they might.

"Why," I said to Faiz, "don't you just take Israeli citizenship?"

"We can't think about these things," he said. "We can't take risks. There are only 20,000 of us."

I asked him what he thought might happen to him if he did take out citizenship and was later handed over to Syria. He didn't know. All he knew was that the notion was dangerous.

Israeli journalist and political analyst Jonathan Spyer noticed a similar phenomenon when he traveled from Israel to Lebanon after the war against Hezbollah in 2006. "People have an acute sense of this unseen power, which is both nowhere and everywhere," he told me.

Beirut is a decadent, freewheeling Riviera on the Mediterranean. It has more in common with Tel Aviv than with any Arab capital, but much of South Lebanon is ruled by Iran's proxy Hezbollah. Whenever Spyer mentioned to Beirutis that he had a mind to drive to the south, they strongly advised him against it.

"I'd be hanging out in these lovely bars and restaurants," he said, "with lively people enjoying these nice airy evenings, and as soon as I'd mention that I was going down there, they'd suddenly become serious and say, 'Don't do it.' And I'd say, 'Why not? Tell me why I shouldn't go down there.' They'd just say, 'You shouldn't do that.' To me, that's power. It's real unseen power. Any force that can put that kind of fear into people is something we need to look at."

That's the kind of power Assad has over the Golan even though his soldiers and his police cannot set foot there.

"What do you think of Assad and his government?" I asked Faiz.

I could tell by the look on his face that he wished I hadn't said that.

"I'm not allowed to tell you if the Syrian government is good or bad," he said. "I can say, though, that we want democracy."

Look closely at those words. He's actually telling me what he can say and what he cannot say. Rarely will people who are subject to totalitarian censorship speak with such candor. Usually, if they're not defiant, they'll just recite the party line and that's it.

The feeling of powerlessness coming off him was palpable. His community is tiny and weak. They have no control over what happens to the Golan. No one in the "international community" asks them if they'd rather live in Israel or in Syria. Some individuals have taken out Israeli citizenship and moved to Tel Aviv or Jerusalem, where Damascus can't reach them, but those who want to remain in their home village live in the Assad family's shadow.

"I feel Syrian," he said. "The Israeli government is not our government. I don't hate Israel or Jewish people, but my family comes from Syria. My land-ownership document is Syrian."

Yet he has never visited Syria, at least not the part of Syria controlled by the Syrians. The only country he has ever traveled around and lived in is Israel. And he's at odds enough with the government in Damascus that he says he wants democracy even if he won't say anything bad about the Assads.

He studied economics at Hebrew University in Jerusalem. "It's a great city," he said. "Most of our professionals work in Tel Aviv and Haifa because there's not enough of an economy on the Golan. We have to rely on ourselves. No one will help us, so we work hard—more than eight hours a day, believe me."

His Druze community, he told me, produces more professionals per capita than Israel's Jewish society does. I don't know if that's really true or if it isn't, but he seems to think so.

I'm reasonably sure that an independent Druze state would differ markedly from most other Arab states if one existed. It would be prosperous. It would not start aggressive wars with its neighbors. It would not be a theocracy like Iran or Gaza—not when even most Druze aren't allowed to know the details of their religion. The "uninitiated" majority live entirely secular lives.

"Any impulse for a Druze state?" my Israeli companion Hadar asked Faiz.

"No," he said. "We are not a nationality. We are a religion."

"And you're Arabs," I said.

"Of course," he said. "We speak Arabic. And we feel Arab."

Yet I can't help but wonder if they would still feel like Arabs if they had their own state. Maybe they would and maybe they wouldn't. No matter. The question is entirely theoretical. They'll never have their own state.

The border between the Golan Heights and Syria proper is strange. People and goods can cross, but only once and only one way. The Druze can export agricultural products to Syria, but Israelis can't export or import anything. The Druze also can't import goods from the Syrian side because there's a chance the items would end up in Israel.

If a Golani Druze woman marries a Syrian Druze—and it happens sometimes—she can cross the border to join him, but it's a one-way trip. She will never be allowed to return. She'll get a Syrian identity card on arrival, and that will be that. Israeli filmmaker Eran Riklis brought all this to life in his 2006 film *The Syrian Bride.*

I asked Faiz to explain his religion to me, though I knew the Druze aren't allowed to say much about their religion to outsiders. Faiz laughed when I asked him, probably because he suspected I knew that already.

"You don't need to know," he said. "But if you want to know, you can find out a few things on Google."

If I understand the Druze correctly—and I'm pretty sure that I do—the Druze of the Golan would become completely loyal to Israel if Syria were to relinquish its claim and if the rest of the world recognized the Golan Heights as Israeli.

They'd do it for the same reason the Druze of the Galilee are loyal to Israel and the Zionists. I wanted Faiz to admit this to me, but I knew he couldn't. I was curious, though, what he would say if I put the question to him directly.

"What if Syria says Israel can keep the Golan?" I said. "Would you take Israeli citizenship then?"

"It's not going to happen," he said and laughed.

We both laughed. He knew what I was trying to get him to say, and he knew that I knew that he knew. In a way he was being evasive, but his answer was also on point. My question was so hypothetical there was no sense in his even considering it, as if I'd asked a man who lives in

Nebraska what he'd think if Omaha were annexed to Canada.

I thought he handled my questions well, but he got increasingly fidgety and uncomfortable as I kept at it. He wasn't frightened, as was a Syrian I once met in Beirut who was terrified that the Mukhabarat— the secret police—would overhear our conversation and send him to prison, but Faiz seemed a little unsure of himself. My questions were more direct than he was used to. Druze politics are subtle. Meaning is often found in the things left unsaid.

After a while he called a friend on his cell phone and asked for some backup.

Faiz's English is pretty good, but his friend, Dr. Taiseer Maray from the Golan for Development organization, speaks it perfectly. He was all handshakes and smiles when he showed up. "What is it you'd like to know?" he said.

"Well," I said, "I've spent the last two days talking to Israeli Jews about the Golan Heights, but you live here too."

"And you don't want only one side of the story," he said.

"Exactly," I said. "You know how this works. So tell me about the Golan Heights from your point of view."

"I'm not sure what our Israeli neighbors really think," Faiz interjected, "so if they tell you, please let us know."

Hadar was stunned when she heard that, but she didn't say anything in front of Faiz or Taiseer. She waited until we were back in the car.

"Like it or not," Taiseer said, "the Golan is Syrian land. That's just a fact. It has nothing to do with politics. There were Syrian farms and villages here. I'm not talking about whether Syria is a free country."

I didn't ask him about the dearth of Syrian freedom. He suggested right up front that he did not want to talk about it, but saying even that much was significant. We both know Syria isn't free, and his bringing it up even in the neutral way that he did told me he was thinking about it, he wanted me to think about it, and he wanted me to know that he was thinking about it. He obviously wouldn't have said that if Israel had a land dispute with, say, Denmark.

Like Faiz, he perfectly and precisely split his politics down the middle.

"I care about Israel," he said, "much more than I care about, for example, Egypt. Israel is my neighbor. And I'm not just saying this to be nice. I want the best for my neighbors. If Israel needs to occupy the Golan Heights for security reasons, okay, but Israelis shouldn't build settlements here."

He and Faiz knew my companion Hadar lives on a Golan Heights settlement. She didn't take offense at what Taiseer said, though. The spare room they let me sleep in was built entirely by Druze construction workers from Majdal Shams. She used to jokingly tell the contractor he was doing such a good job because he hoped to move in after Israel withdraws from the territory, but he once told her seriously that if that ever happens, he'll take citizenship and relocate to Israel.

"The settlements are against international law, actually," Taiseer said, "and should be evacuated during a handover. But I also think Jews should be able to live here, along with Christians and Muslims."

Few Palestinians in the West Bank and Gaza say Jews should be able to live in their future state. And no Syrian citizen who lives under the control of Bashar al-Assad would dare even suggest to an American journalist that Israel has the right to hold on to the Golan for security reasons. Yet Taiseer lives as a Syrian Druze under Israeli law and takes the "centrist" position.

He gets along perfectly well with Israeli Jews, but unlike Israeli Druze, he hasn't signed on to Zionism. One reason is perfectly obvious: he must remain loyal to Syria, even if not to Assad, per se. Perhaps another reason, though, is because Druze everywhere eschew religion-based nationalism. They don't yearn to have their own state, and they may have a hard time relating to others who do.

Taiseer thinks—or at least he says—that the safety of Middle Eastern Jews doesn't require Jewish sovereignty.

"We tried that already," Hadar said. "It didn't work."

"But Jews were treated far worse in Europe than they ever have been in the Middle East," Taiseer said. "I'm not making excuses for anti-Semitism in the Middle East. I'm just saying it's not forever impossible for Jews to live here with others. We Druze—like the Shias and Christians and Alawites—also have problems with the Sunni majority because we left Islam. But most of the time we are okay. We should be able to live together in the same state—whether it's in Israel or in Syria—on the basis of civil rights and equality."

Of course it's impossible for Jews to live in Syria on the basis of civil rights and equality under the current regime. Nobody can, and Jews perhaps least of all. And it might not be much easier under the next government, either, especially if radical Islamists take over.

"If I were a good Zionist," he said, "I'd say trade peace for the Golan and the security situation would be resolved."

"But Assad won't exchange peace for the Golan," I said.

"Of course he will," he said.

"I don't think so," I said. "Last year when I visited Lebanon, Walid Jumblatt said something very interesting when I met him for lunch at his house."

Taiseer's eyes widened. Faiz's eyes widened even more. They had no idea I know Walid Jumblatt, the famous leader of Lebanon's Druze. I wasn't trying to drop names or impress him. I just wanted to know how he'd react when I held up his quintessentially Druze-like analysis next to somebody else's different but equally Druze-like analysis.

"Assad doesn't care about the Golan," Jumblatt had told me. "Suppose we go ultimately to the so-called peace. Then later on, what is the purpose of the Syrian regime? What is he going to tell his people? Especially, mind you, he is a member of the Alawite minority. This minority could be accused of treason. It's not like Egypt or Jordan, whereby the government has some legitimacy. Here you get accused of treason by the masses, by the Sunnis. So using classic slogans like 'Palestine will liberate the Golan with Hezbollah' is a must for him to stay in power.

"I had a friend at the time—he is still my friend—when I was in

Syria," Jumblatt continued. "He was the chief of staff of the Syrian army and is now living in Los Angeles. He was quite an important guy and honest with the media. He was a Sunni from a big family in Aleppo. And when Hafez al-Assad was about to fix up the so-called settlement through Bill Clinton, and before they met him in Geneva, a prominent Alawite officer in the Syrian army came to Assad and said, 'What are you doing? We will be lost if you make peace. We will be accused of treason.'"

Taiseer and Faiz didn't know what to say when I brought that up. Perhaps they knew it was true but couldn't say so in public. Maybe they didn't want to contradict Walid Jumblatt even if they thought he was wrong. Whatever the explanation, they neither agreed nor disagreed with Jumblatt's analysis.

Assad and his Alawite community have some things in common with the Druze. They, too, are religious minorities who emerged long ago from Islam and became something else. They, too, have to be sensitive to the majority where they live. If Syria's Alawite rulers made peace with Israel, they may well face a Sunni insurgency as Jumblatt suggested— and it would not be the first time.

Years ago I visited an Alawite village in Lebanon with a Shia woman from the south named Leena. She took me down to her home region from Beirut to show me around. One place we both wanted to visit was a village called Ghajar, a pinpoint on the map where three nations converge and form the strangest of knots. The northern half of the village is in Lebanon. The southern half is controlled by Israel. All of it once belonged to Syria.

After Israel captured the Golan in 1967, Ghajar was stranded in a no-man's-land between Lebanon and Israeli-occupied Syria. The residents couldn't live suspended in limbo between the two countries forever, so they petitioned the state of Israel and asked to be annexed. They were Syrians—Arabs—not Jews or Israelis, but they would rather live in "Syria" under Israeli occupation than in Lebanon.

The Lebanese-Syrian border, though, wasn't marked. Over time, Ghajar expanded northward, without anyone even knowing it, into

Lebanon. And in the year 2000, when Israel withdrew its soldiers from the "security zone" in South Lebanon, the village was thrown into turmoil. The United Nations wouldn't certify the Israeli withdrawal unless the northern half of the village was ceded to Lebanon—which, in the real world, meant to Hezbollah.

Ghajar's residents had been living under Israeli jurisdiction since 1967, and—unlike the Druze of the Golan—most of them took Israeli citizenship in 1981. So when Leena and I arrived in 2005, the northern half of Ghajar was populated with Syrians in Lebanon with Israeli ID cards.

The complexity still makes my head hurt, but that's the Levant for you.

Leena intended to take me there, but in hindsight I believe she mistakenly took me to a different village right next to Ghajar called Arab al-Luweiza.

Ghajar had been under Israeli control for decades, but the place Leena showed me was utterly destitute, in worse shape by far than anything else in the area, whether Jewish, Druze, Christian or Shia. Some houses were crumbling boxes made out of cinder blocks. Others were shanties with tin roofs and walls. Barren ground was strewn with rubble and rocks.

A handful of barefoot children dressed in dirty clothes and playing in filthy streets ran up to us when we stepped out of the car. Somehow they managed to smile.

"What is wrong with this place?" I said to Leena. The conditions were worse than in the Hezbollah areas. "Who lives here? Are these people Shias?"

Leena wasn't sure, so she asked one of the boys.

"Alawi!" he said.

The Alawi—Alawite—sect makes up about 10 percent of Syria's population and a tiny percentage of Lebanon's. Most Alawites live along the Mediterranean coast in Syria and Northern Lebanon, but a few live as far south as the Golan Heights area. They are descendants of the followers of Muhammad ibn Nusayr, who took them out of mainstream Twelver Shia Islam in the 10th century. Their religion has as much in common with Christianity and Gnosticism as it does with Islam, and both Sunnis and Shias have long considered them infidels.

The strangest thing about the Alawites is that they have made themselves rulers of Syria. It's as unlikely as the Druze lording over Lebanon, the Kurds seizing control of Iraq or Coptic Christians mounting a successful coup in Egypt, but it happened. Since the Assad clan is Alawite, most of the elites in the Baath Party, the bureaucracy and the military are Alawites too.

Imam Musa Sadr, founder of the Shia movement Amal in Lebanon, struck a deal with Hafez al-Assad in 1974 and issued a fatwa, or religious ruling, implausibly declaring Alawites part of the Shia community.

Yet the Alawites are not Shias. They're Alawites. The two communities need religious cover for their political alliance, however, and Sadr's fatwa gives it to them. The relationship between Hezbollah and Damascus' Alawite regime is strictly one of convenience. The two feel little or no warmth for each other.

While Hezbollah and Amal are politically aligned with the Alawite government, the Sunnis are not, and Sunnis make up about 70 percent of Syria's population. The fundamentalists among them have long detested Assad's Baath Party regime, not only because it is secular and oppressive but also because its leaders are "heretics."

So the Assad family ended up supporting terrorist groups in Syria's war against Israel for some of the same reasons the Khomeinists do in Iran. As minorities in the region, neither can be rulers of or hegemons over Sunnis without street cred.

In 1982, the same year Israel invaded Lebanon and the Iranian Revolutionary Guard Corps founded the prototype of Hezbollah, Syria's Muslim Brotherhood took up arms against Hafez al-Assad's government in the Syrian city of Hama. Assad dispatched the Alawite-dominated military and destroyed most of the old city with air strikes, tanks and artillery. Rifaat al-Assad, the former president's younger brother, boasted that the regime killed 38,000 people in a single day.

In his book *From Beirut to Jerusalem*, Thomas Friedman dubbed the senior Assad's rules of engagement "Hama Rules." They are the Syrian stick. The carrot is Assad's steadfast "resistance" against Israel. No Arab government in the world is as stridently anti-Israel, in both action and rhetoric, as his. There is no better way for a detested minority regime to curry favor with Sunnis in Syria and the larger Arab world than by adopting the anti-Zionist cause as its own.

As "infidels," Syria's Alawites don't feel they have the legitimacy to force Sunnis to make peace with Israel. That's a risky business even for Sunni leaders, as the assassination of Egypt's Anwar Sadat showed after he signed a treaty with Israel's Menachem Begin.

Because most of Syria's Alawites live along the Mediterranean coast and away from the Sunni heartland, they could, at least theoretically, be separated from Syria into their own Alawite nation. The Middle East would probably be a safer place if they had their own state. Unlike the Druze, they once aspired to one. They did have their own semiautonomous government under the French Mandate from 1930 to 1937 and again from 1939 to 1944.

"The Alawites refuse to be annexed to Muslim Syria," Suleiman al-Assad, grandfather of President Bashar al-Assad, wrote in a petition to France during the second period in 1943. "In Syria, the official religion of the state is Islam, and according to Islam, the Alawites are considered infidels … The spirit of hatred and fanaticism imbedded in the hearts of the Arab Muslims against everything that is non-Muslim has been perpetually nurtured by the Islamic religion. There is no hope that the situation will ever change. Therefore, the abolition of the mandate will expose the minorities in Syria to the dangers of death and annihilation."

The Alawites' semiautonomous government was dissolved back into French Mandate Syria in 1944, and their Latakia region has been an integral part of the country ever since. Had they declared and received independence, they might even have been natural allies of Israel for the same reasons the Middle East's Christians and Kurds are. After all, when the Alawites of Ghajar were given a choice to live under a Lebanese or Israeli government, they chose Israel's. And they made that choice when Lebanon was considered the Switzerland of the Middle East, years before it descended into chaos and horror and war. Israel's occupation of the Golan Heights freed them from tyrannical Syrian rule, and it freed them from the Sunni demand to resist the Zionists.

After Hadar and I said goodbye to Faiz and Taiseer and thanked them for talking with us, I dropped her off at her house before returning to Tel Aviv. We took the long way round, though, so she could show me a couple of things.

"There's a destroyed Alawite village ahead," she said before directing me to turn off the highway. The road to the ruins clearly had not been maintained since the '60s. It is, like the village, in a state of advanced deterioration.

"It must have been lovely here once," Hadar said. "They had this amazing view in a moderate climate and with all these trees above northern Israel. It's a shame, really. We would have gotten along fine with them had they stayed."

She was most likely right about that. The Israelis get along fine with the Golani Druze. And they get along even better with the Alawites living in Ghajar.

"I should have asked our Druze friends why they stayed when the Alawites fled," she said.

"That's a good question," I said. Why did the Druze stay when the Alawites fled? "I don't know why, but I can guess."

"Why?" she said.

"Perhaps," I said, "because they knew already that the Druze in Israel were treated well by the Israeli people and government. They knew they weren't in any danger, but the Alawites had no idea what to expect. There was no precedent for Israelis and Alawites getting along. They would have been fine had they stayed, but they didn't know that. So they left. But that's just a guess."

"I found something Faiz said very disturbing," she said.

"What's that?" I said.

"When he told you he wasn't sure what his Israeli neighbors really think," she said. "We've been telling them exactly what we think now for decades. We want them to join us and take citizenship. It's not a trick. That's exactly what we want and hope for, and we've never told them anything else."

Faiz, like all the other Druze on the Golan, surely hears this message from the Israelis, but it seems he isn't prepared to accept it at face value. Perhaps he suffers from cognitive egocentrism, what Professor Richard Landes describes as the tendency to project one's own mentality on others.

"My guess is that he was projecting," I said. "He doesn't necessarily tell you what he really believes, for political reasons beyond his control, so maybe he thinks Israelis do the same thing. It's completely normal behavior from his point of view. In his experience, everyone does it."

"We've perfectly integrated Israeli Druze into our society," she said, "and he knows that, so why doesn't he think we could do the same with the Druze of the Golan?"

Israel has done a good job integrating even non–Middle Eastern minorities. "We accepted Vietnamese boat people as refugees in the 1970s," she said. "They're Israeli citizens, and their children are Israeli citizens. They aren't Jewish, but they fit in very well. They speak Hebrew and they serve in the army."

She was a little bit bothered by our entire conversation with Faiz and Taiseer. They told me more or less what I thought they would say, but she was uncomfortable with the differences between their point of view and that of her Israeli Druze friends.

"I just wish they would meet us halfway," she said.

"They are," I said, "compared with the Syrian Druze. If they lived under the authority of Assad and took their opinions from him, they wouldn't say they're more concerned with your welfare than the welfare of Egyptians. They wouldn't say Israel has the right to occupy the Golan for security reasons as long as Israel doesn't build settlements. They'd champion the 'resistance' and say you have no right to exist in this region at all."

"That's true," she said. "I once saw them in Majdal Shams carrying placards demanding Israel leave the Golan. Only a tiny number of people showed up at the rally, and they looked terribly bored. It doesn't cost them anything to protest against Israel, but they don't dare protest the Syrian government even though they live here."

She later sent me an email after she thought about our conversation some more.

"It's no good from their point of view," she said, "our being nice neighbors and offering them full citizenship if we don't come out once and for all and make it very clear that we have no intention of ever giving up the Golan. As long as Israel does this silly peace dance with the Assads of any generation once every few years, Faiz and the rest of the Druze will still be in that impossible position. I can see entirely where he's coming from and how unfair it is to them—all we're offering them is something they can't take. They need us to operate on the 'strong horse' principle, but it's against our nature."

Much of the world supports the Palestinian cause, partly because they've been stateless for decades but also because Palestinian leaders, both religious and secular, have waged relentless campaigns of terrorism. The squeaky wheel gets the grease, as they say. Few would take an interest in the Palestinians if they acted like Druze.

Hardly anyone yearns to return the Druze of the Golan to Syria. Even they come across as only half interested. If they were passionate, though, and if they mass-murdered Israelis, their cause may well get traction on university campuses, in activist circles and perhaps even in the White House. Terrorism works, at least up to a point. If the Druze adhered more closely to the regional mainstream instead of to their own local mainstream, they might resort to terrorism themselves, but they don't.

The Alawites are a little bit different. Most who live in Ghajar enthusiastically took Israeli citizenship as soon as it was offered. They seem to think it makes them safer. Those who live in Syria enthusiastically embrace the Sunni cause of "resistance," and they do it for the same reason. It's safer that way.

The war between Syria and Israel will last a long time, for the rest of Assad's life, more likely than not.

Six

On the Hunt in Baghdad

Baghdad, 2008

"If your men conduct any raids," I said to Captain Todd Looney at Combat Outpost Ford on the outskirts of Sadr City, Baghdad, "I want to go."

"We might have something come up," he said. "If so, I'll get you out there."

Less than an hour later Haji Jawad, one of the most dangerous terrorist leaders in all of Iraq was spotted holding a meeting at a house in the area. An arrest warrant had already been issued by the government of Iraq, and Captain Looney's company was the closest to his location. They would be the ones to go get him.

"Do you still have room for me?" I said.

"Get your gear," Captain Looney said.

Last time I was in Baghdad, in the summer of 2007, I was told that most suspects surrender the instant they realize their house is surrounded. Fighting would be suicidal, and most terror cell leaders do not seek martyrdom. But the guy we were after was far more vicious and crazy than average.

"Is he the kind of guy who might shoot at us during a raid?" I said to Captain Clint Rusch in the Tactical Operations Center.

"Oh yeah," he said. "He's definitely the kind of guy who will shoot at us. He's a really bad dude. A few weeks ago he and his men lobbed huge bombs at a JSS in the area and almost destroyed it, then called up the commander and asked how was his morning. And he said if we didn't stop chasing him, he'd start wearing a suicide vest wherever he goes.

The tip-off came in over the phone late at night when the terrorist leader's meeting was almost scheduled to be finished. By the time everyone had their gear and was ready to go, we had seventeen minutes or less to drive across a portion of Sadr City and break down the door before the meeting was over.

We ran to the Humvees.

"Go with Sergeant Gonzales," Captain Looney said to me. "When we dismount, catch up to me and stay on me." He looked angry all of a sudden, but mostly he was just being serious. Any of us might be killed in less than an hour.

Our convoy of Humvees roared down Baghdad's streets in the dark without headlights. I checked my watch. No time to waste. We had eleven minutes to catch the bastard before his meeting was scheduled to end. Hopefully he and his pals were on "Arab time" and would hang out and drink tea for a while before heading out.

Almost every house we drove past was dark. Few streetlights worked. It was hard to believe I was in the middle of a city of millions. Iraq's electrical grid is still in terrible shape. Baghdad is only marginally better lit than the countryside. It produces perhaps only one or two percent as much ambient light after dark as cities in normal countries. Baghdad at night from the air looks more like a constellation of Christmas lights than, say, the brightly lit circuit board of Los Angeles.

The Humvee in front of mine suddenly stopped. Our driver slammed on his brakes.

"Dismount!" Sergeant Gonzales said from the passenger seat in the front.

Here we go.

I got out of the Humvee. Even hopped up on adrenaline it's impossible to throw those doors open quickly. They weigh hundreds of pounds because they're up-armored with several inches of steel.

Every soldier could see better than I could. They all had night-vision goggles. I had to rely on my eyes in a near-pitch black corner of a dark city. It takes thirty minutes for a man's eyes to adjust to darkness, and we had left the brightly lit interior of the base less than ten minutes before.

Sergeant Gonzales motioned for me to follow him alongside a wall toward an opening that led into the neighborhood. I stepped in a deep puddle of mud. At least I hoped it was mud. Sewage still runs in the streets in much of Baghdad, and we were in one of the most decrepit parts of the city. But I hardly cared *what* had just splashed up onto my pant legs. Any second now I might be shot at or worse.

One at a time we poured through the hole in the wall. Every single house on the other side of that wall was cloaked in darkness. I had no idea which house we were about to storm into, but the soldiers knew and I followed them up to the gate.

The gate was locked. One of the soldiers--I couldn't tell anyone apart in the dark--kicked the gate with everything he had. Twice. And it did not open.

"Goddamn it!" Captain Todd Looney said.

He pulled out an enormous hammer and swung it hard against the front of the gate.

BANG.

The gate merely shook.

BANG.

The metal gate shuddered, but it did not break.

BANG.

Everyone in the neighborhood must have heard us by then.

If a meeting were still going on in that house, they knew we were coming. I kept as close to the wall as I could in case we fot shot at. No one inside the house would be able to hit me as long as I didn't back up into the street.

Taking the house would be much more dangerous now, but the soldiers brought flashbang grenades. Flashbangs stun and blind everyone in a room for up to ten seconds. All the soldiers had to do was toss one of those babies into a room ahead of them. Ten seconds is an eternity in room-to-room combat. American soldiers can do whatever they want in a room full of terrorists in less than two seconds.

BANG.

The hammer came down on the gate once again, but it still didn't break. We would have to climb over the wall.

"Keep busting it open while we're climbing the wall!" Captain Looney said.

BANG.

The wall was about seven feet high and made of cement. Most of us couldn't get over it without some kind of boost. I'm not used to throwing myself over walls taller than I am, and the soldiers were weighed down with 80 pounds of armor and gear. Someone crouched on all four and let everyone else use his back as a step ladder. That effectively knocked two feet off the height of the wall. It's easy to climb five feet.

"Keep going over!" the captain said. "Keep going over!"

The gate was locked from the inside. Those on the other side desperately tried to unlock it, to no avail.

"Bolt cutters coming over!" somebody yelled and tossed a pair of cutters over the gate. They came prepared.

And yet still the gate did not open. We had wasted almost a minute while making one hell of a racket.

I felt useless just standing there and trying mostly in vain to take photographs in the dark. What was I supposed to be doing? I'm not trained for kinetic raids. I didn't know the procedure.

So I selected a soldier at random and asked. "Is everyone going over the wall? Do I need to go over, too?"

At that point I was ready to take orders from even a private.

"Yes, sir," he said, whoever he was. "You need to go over."

Can't say I was thrilled about that. Unless they got that gate opened, I'd be pinned in the tight enclosed courtyard in front of a suspected terrorist's nest. There would be no running away if something happened. But that was preferable to being left all alone on the street in front of that house while the soldiers--my *de facto* bodyguards--were inside and over the wall.

One of the soldiers who had gone over the wall ahead of me kicked in the front door of the house with his boot. The sounds of smashing glass and twisting metal surely alerted anyone in the house who somehow might not have heard the banging on the gate with the hammer.

If the target inside were indeed wearing a suicide vest, this was most likely when he would martyr himself and take some of us with him. I waited a moment before climbing onto the wall. I had cover from an explosion as long as I stayed where I was. But I didn't hear anything

The soldier crouching in the mud was waiting for me to use his back as a step ladder onto the wall. So I planted my muddy boot in the small of his back. Not that it mattered. He was plenty filthy already. I had five more feet of wall to clear, and for an absurd moment I worried that I might humiliate myself by not being able to make it over the top. That was ridiculous. It was only five feet, and besides--I had so much adrenaline in my body I could have thrown a car.

As soon as I pulled myself onto the wall I realized that every single one of us climbed up in the wrong place. Climbing straight over would have put us in the neighbor's yard. I had to shimmy along the top of the wall several feet so I could drop down in the courtyard of the house we were raiding. I could barely see, and I was terribly exposed.

Yes, he's the kind of guy who will shoot at us.

I was more exposed at that moment than anyone while crawling along the top of that wall.

Get down, get down!

I dropped into the courtyard of the target house.

"Top floor's clear!" I heard someone yell from inside.

No one had fired a shot yet. No one had exploded a suicide vest.

Then the gate broke open and five more soldiers poured through.

Lights were on in the house when I ran inside. The front door had been violently kicked off its hinges. It leaned up against the couch in the living room.

Shards of glass crunched under my feet. Mud and nasty muck from outside was tracked all over the carpets inside--and this is a culture where almost everyone takes off their shoes before stepping inside. We might very well be in a terrorist leader's house, but a small part of me still felt bad about the mud and the door.

My digital voice recorder was turned on and inside my pocket. It recorded everything, but I have no idea who said what.

"Where's the terp at?"

Terp is short for *interpreter*. Our interpreter, Eddie, was an Iraqi from Baghdad who had spent the last several decades in San Diego, California.

"They've over there at the next house."

"Go! Go! Next house! Let's go!"

"Out! Out the gate!"

Every soldier in the house ran out the gate. I followed. The house we had just hit was empty. No one was sure exactly which house in a row of three Haji Jawad was supposed to be in. So we went house to house.

Some poor bastards would soon return home from wherever they were to find their door broken down, mud all over their carpets, and no explanation.

We ran to the next house and had no trouble unlatching the gate. Each soldier took up position. I stood near the front door and away from the windows. My eyes were beginning to adjust to the darkness and I could sort of see.

"Hit it," someone said. "Go right fucking in there."

A soldier kicked the door in with all his might. It crumpled like an empty 7-Up can. Glass shattered. A woman inside screamed. Soldiers streamed into the house.

Someone flicked on the lights.

The woman in the front room screamed again and put her hands on her head. Small children ran behind her for protection.

"Get down! Get down!"

She looked at me in wide-eyed animal terror as if she had just seen Godzilla, and she said something to me in Arabic that I did not understand.

"La etkellem Arabie," I said. *I don't speak Arabic.*

I wanted to say "it's okay," but it was not okay. I had no more an idea what was about to happen than she did.

"Go upstairs," said one of the soldiers.

"Hey, you, in there," said another to the woman who had just spoken to me. "Get in there."

They were rounding up all the women and children into one room and all the men into another.

"Get in there now!"

Two soldiers led three Iraqi men down the stairs. The men looked frightened and disoriented, but much less so than the women and children. Two were turned around and flex-cuffed.

The Americans were *not* fucking around. Odds were high that we were in a terrorist's nest and still might be shot at any moment from any direction.

The one Iraqi man who had not yet been flex-cuffed spoke to me calmly in Arabic.

"I am a police officer," he said. "I have a badge."

I understood him perfectly well, but I nevertheless told him I didn't speak Arabic. He needed to explain himself to somebody else.

Men were taken into the front room of the house. Women and children were herded into the back.

Then the power went out and the house plunged into absolute darkness.

Eddie, our interpreter, screamed at these Iraqis in a rage that I had never heard from him. He sounded like he was prepared to beat any and all of them any second. His voice demanded instant obedience. While it was possible he spoke to them this way for effect, I suspect his anger at the mass-murderers who had car-bombed his home town for years was totally genuine.

Flashlights came on and I could see again.

Captain Looney stood before the Iraqi man who had told me he was a police officer and asked whether he knew anything about Haji Jawad.

"I've never heard of him," the supposed police officer said.

"Hey!" Captain Looney said. "Everybody knows who he is. Saying you've never heard of him is like saying you've never heard of Moqtada al Sadr."

I stepped outside the front door and into the courtyard for some air. Glass crunched under my feet again. The door hung at a crazy angle from the only hinge that didn't twist off when it was kicked in.

Two men from inside the house had been taken outside and planted face down in the mud with their cuffed hands behind their backs. They trembled in fear.

I went back inside. Captain Looney was speaking to another Iraqi man in a wife-beater t-shirt whom I hadn't seen before. What did *he* know about Haji Jawad?

"I've never heard this kind of name," he said. His hands shook and he looked at his feet.

Two soldiers in the kitchen briskly opened every cabinet and drawer and searched for anything that was not supposed to be there--weapons, intelligence, anything incriminating or out of the ordinary.

They didn't mess the place up, but they rifled through everything with a practiced thoroughness.

I heard Captain Looney's voice in the back room where the women and children had been corralled. The woman who had screamed when her door was broken down was crying hysterically.

"I've been in Iraq too long for your crying to affect me," Captain Looney said in a hard, even, and no-bullshit voice.

She stopped crying instantly. She didn't even continue to sob. She just stopped as if the captain had flipped off a switch.

"I've lost too many of my own soldiers in this country," he said.

In COP Ford's Tactical Operations Center hang three photographs of American soldiers in his company who were killed in Sadr City by

Shia militias. All were personal friends and comrades of every American soldier I was with that night on the raid. "We fight for the men next to us," the captain had said to me earlier that evening in his office before we set out.

The woman who was somehow able to stop crying instantly also said she had never heard the name Haji Jawad. Everyone in the room knew she was lying.

"Do you know what this guy *does*?" said one of the soldiers. "He *rapes* women like you. He *cuts* off the heads of men like your husband. And he *murders* children like yours."

He also kills American soldiers, but that went unsaid.

Every person in that house did one of two things that night: they either covered up for Jawad, or they revealed they were deathly afraid of him. There is no chance whatsoever that none of them had never heard of the guy. He is a notorious mass murderer on the loose in their own city. Imagine meeting an adult American who says he or she has never heard of Timothy McVeigh or Osama bin Laden. It just doesn't happen.

"I have a daughter," the woman said. She did, indeed, have a daughter. The little girl held onto her mother's leg for dear life.

"Lots of insurgents have daughters," Captain Looney said. "Having a daughter does not make you innocent."

The two soldiers who were searching the kitchen moved into the living room and started opening closets and cabinets.

"I had better not find anything other than one Glock in this house," Captain Looney said.

One of the soldiers found the Glock pistol that apparently had been declared. The man who told me he was an Iraqi police officer said it was his. But everyone knew that police officers in Iraq sometimes moonlight as terrorists or insurgents. It meant something that he was a police officer, but it didn't clear him.

I stepped out of the house and into the courtyard again, not quite sure what to do with myself. So I paced. And I needed some air. There was a tremendous amount of emotional violence in that house. I could feel it. All of us felt it. All of us knew we might be shot or even blown up at any moment. But I noticed, only in hindsight, that no one had been struck or even shoved by a single American soldier. The raid was intense, but it was also restrained.

Nobody was arrested. Haji Jawad wasn't in there. We would have known. He lost a foot in a fight once and now limps around on a prosthetic. Captain Looney said it was time to go back to the base. The residents of each house that had been raided could file some paperwork and get a cash reimbursement for the damage caused on the way in.

Then a call came in over the radio.

A suspect with a bad foot had just been spotted limping away from the house a few streets over. So instead of going back to the base we circled around to where the suspect had been spotted.

After rounding a corner I was back in near-total darkness. My eyes had adjusted to the dim light in the house, so I could hardly see again in the darkness that is Baghdad after midnight. This neighborhood was dark even compared with most of the others. Only the faint outlines of homes against the cold backdrop of stars were visible. Still, I could see that the housing conditions dramatically deteriorated as we walked. The homes we had just broken into appeared to be more or less middle class, but behind them was slum housing. What little I could see resembled the hillside *favelas* in Latin America.

My boots squished and sucked in the mud and the muck. The street obviously was not paved. All of Baghdad is strewn with trash, but this area choked on it.

I followed Captain Looney.

Slum dogs barked and charged from every direction. Captain Looney pointed his rifle at one. I saw a red laser dot on its side.

Please don't shoot the dog.

I didn't want to see a dog shot right in front of me, and I didn't want to hear any gunfire. We were possibly homing in on one of the most dangerous terrorists in the world, and I could hardly see a damn thing. Whoever it was we were chasing probably couldn't see any better than I could. That was a good thing. Gunfire would reveal our location.

If I hear gunfire too close that isn't ours, I thought, *I'm throwing myself onto the ground and planting my face in that muck.*

"The target's pushing southeast," someone said. "That's back behind us."

But then we heard a gun shot just a few blocks ahead of us on the other side of some houses.

"Shot fired," someone quietly said into the radio.

It sounded like a rifle shot, not like a pistol. But it wasn't close enough that I needed to face-plant in the mud just yet.

There was no return fire, but I knew this whole thing could turn kinetic and violent at any second.

The mud got deeper, and I had to navigate around giant holes in the road. It wasn't even really a road. It was more like an alley. Most cars were too wide to drive down it.

"Look at that big-ass rat," somebody said.

I couldn't see the rat without night vision. I wondered whether I would accidentally kick it.

I kept near the walls more than the soldiers did. They had night vision goggles and rifles. I didn't have either, and I felt more vulnerable.

Stars shimmered above us. They were the same stars that shine above my house back in Oregon. That surprised me on some irrational level. Sometimes Iraq feels like a different planet. Somewhere overhead I heard the distant roar of a jetliner, probably on its way to Kuwait. That put me back in the world. Kuwait is clearly on the same planet as Oregon. And though it's right next to Iraq, it seemed terribly distant because it's so civilized and luxurious. Trust me: unless you're Iraqi, if you fly from Iraq to Kuwait you will feel like you're home.

No one was walking around except us--and the person up ahead we were about to detain. The night was as silent as if we were camping out in Alaska.

Just ahead on the left was a dump site where an enormous amount of garbage had been tossed. I gave it a wide berth. Insurgents sometimes bury anti-personnel IEDs in those piles and detonate them as platoons of soldiers walk past. The entire neighborhood might have been laced with traps for all I knew.

More dogs barked. I faintly heard men speaking in English up ahead and saw the black outlines of motionless soldiers a hundred feet or so up ahead. It seemed they had caught the fleeing suspect with the bum foot.

"They got him," Sergeant Gonzales said. His job was to monitor the radio with an ear piece and listen to chatter.

"*Him*?" I said.

"They got the guy who matches the description," he said. "We don't yet know if it's him."

The area got more and more slum-like as I moved toward them. Then I realized I was inside a junk yard. IEDs and other booby traps could be anywhere and everywhere, but probably weren't.

A small Iraqi man sat on the ground. Three American soldiers stood over him.

"Stand up!" Captain Looney said when we reached them.

Eddie translated.

"Why were you running?"

"I did not run away," the man said.

"We were watching you," Captain Looney said. "We watched you run. Only the thief fears the judge. Why were you running from us? Why were you hiding? We saw you hiding. How do you think we found you?"

The man mumbled something in Arabic. I could hardly hear him. I don't think Eddie heard him either because he didn't translate.

"Somebody bring some zip strips," Captain Looney said.

Someone brought the zip strips. The suspect was then flex-cuffed.

I noticed another man had also been captured. He stood in silence a few feet away and trembled in fear.

The identification cards of both suspects were checked and called into the base. Someone in the Tactical Operations Center compared their names with those in the known terrorist database.

"You still haven't answered my question," Captain Looney said. "Why were you running? Are you a Muslim?"

"Yes," the man said.

"Do you read the Koran?"

"No," the man said.

"You know," Captain Looney said, "that it says only the thief fears the judge, right?"

A loud and low military plane roared overhead.

"We were scared," the man said.

"Why were you scared?" Captain Looney said. "Look at me."

The man looked up at Captain Looney. The captain shined a flashlight in the man's face and checked his appearance against a color photograph of Haji Jawad.

He wasn't the guy.

But the other captured man, the man standing just a few feet away and trembling violently, bore a more striking resemblance to the man we were after.

Captain Looney approached him.

"Why were you running?" he said.

"We were scared," the suspect said.

"Well, you know what?" Captain Looney said. "When the police come into my neighborhood, I don't run. You know why? Because I haven't done anything wrong."

"I am afraid of you," the man said.

"Why?" Captain Looney said. "Why do you fear us? We don't just go running around here *killing* people like Saddam Hussein did."

"I am afraid because of the explosion," the man said.

"What explosion?" Captain Looney said.

"It was four months ago," the man said.

"What does that have to do with *now*?" Captain Looney said.

"I am sorry," the man said. "I apologize."

A soldier frisked the suspect firmly and thoroughly in a way you do *not* ever want to be searched. This wasn't your typical airport security line pat-down where the TSA guy knows very well that you almost certainly are not a terrorist.

On the other side of a chain link fence was a van surrounded by enormous piles of junkyard refuse.

"Are you living in that van?" Captain Looney said to the suspect. "Go check out that van," he said to one of his men.

Two soldiers climbed over the chain link fence and poked around inside the van.

"What the fuck are you doing out here, man?" the captain said.

"We are security guards."

"Yeah, but what are you *guarding*," Captain Looney said.

"There are air conditioners out here," said Eddie, our interpreter.

"It's junk," Captain Looney said. "It's just junk."

Almost every encounter I have ever seen between an American soldier--especially an American officer--and an Iraqi has been polite. Terrorist suspects, especially terrorists with American blood on their hands, obviously get treated differently. No one had physically harmed either of these men, though. I didn't even see either of them get shoved, let alone struck.

"He's shaking pretty good," one of the soldiers said, referring to the second suspect.

"I was a prisoner in Iran," the man said. "I have the flu and a bad heart."

I felt bad for the guy. He did match the physical description of Haji Jawad, but he was just a random guy who coincidentally had a bad foot. And he got spooked and ran. The fact that he wasn't missing a foot was all the proof we needed that he wasn't the guy. At this point he was only being interrogated because he ran from American soldiers. In and of itself that's not a big deal, but he ran right after the soldiers raided a house that was thought to be a meeting place for terrorist leaders. He picked a bad time to freak out.

Captain Looney asked him the same questions over and over again and could not get a straight answer. All he got were stock boilerplate answers larded with filler words like "Inshallah."

"Inshallah" means *God willing* in Arabic, and it's often associated, from the American point of view, with the evasion of responsibility. "I'll see you tomorrow at three o'clock, Inshallah," is often correctly interpreted as meaning "There is a good chance I won't be there." Earlier that day I heard an American soldier tell an Iraqi bureaucrat that his wristwatch didn't come with the word *Inshallah* on it anywhere.

It's often difficult to get a straight answer out of Iraqis. Evasion is a habitual survival mechanism that evolved in a society that was ruled for decades by a totalitarian police state. It survived the destruction of Saddam Hussein's regime because so many neighborhoods have been ruled by psychopathic militias. It is still not clear to some Iraqis that American soldiers aren't just another psychopathic militia. Canned phrases and stock responses are all you can get out of some people.

"I'm tired of this Iraqi talk," Captain Looney said to the suspect. "I'm going to hand you over to the interrogators. That's what they get paid to do. I'm tired of hearing *Inshallah*. Listen up. You can have this conversation with me, be honest with me, and stop giving me these bullshit answers like *Inshallah* and *walah adim*, or I'm going to take you to the interrogators and let them talk to you."

The man mumbled something and ended his sentence with "Inshallah."

"You're saying it," Captain Looney said. "You're saying *Inshallah*. I don't want to hear that word."

A pair of blackhawk helicopters flew overhead. Military air traffic over Baghdad is constant, partly so insurgents and terrorists will always feel like they're being watched from the air as well as the ground. And they *are* being watched from the air and the sky as well as the ground.

My Kevlar helmet was beginning to make my head hurt. I wanted to take it off, but I didn't dare in the slums of Baghdad. The air smelled of garbage and piss. Home felt not only thousands of miles away, but years away.

Captain Looney asked the suspect what he knew about Haji Jawad. The man said he had never heard of him, which was a lie.

"That's like saying you don't know who Ali or Mohammad is," Captain Looney said. "What *do* you know?"

The suspect kept talking in platitudes and had nothing of substance to say whatsoever.

"I'm tired of these motherfuckers," one soldier said.

Captain Looney spoke into his radio. "These two individuals are living in squalor," he said. "They're pretty uneducated. I don't think either one of them would be smart enough to even hit the switch on an IED. But we can still bring them in for interrogation, over."

No one, including me, seemed to think either of them should be brought in and interrogated.

"Ugh," said one of the soldiers and stepped back. "This guy breathed on me and I just about dry heaved."

"Don't get so close to him," said Sergeant Gonzales.

"I was worried I was going to have to shoot a dog back there," Captain Looney said to me.

"I thought you might," I said, "when I saw one painted with the red laser dot."

"I was just trying to scare them away," he said. "They're only doing what comes naturally. Dogs don't make a choice. People make a choice to be good or bad."

The radio squawked and he answered. "I think it was bad intel," he said. "I don't think these guys have anything to do with who we're looking for."

One of the soldiers who was searching the van stepped out with something in his hand. "Sir," he said. "We found three M4 magazines and a military map of Fallujah."

A military map of Fallujah?

"Let me see that," Captain Looney said.

The soldier produced the map and unfolded it. Sure enough, it was exactly like the maps I had seen on the walls inside U.S. Marine bases in

Fallujah last year. An American Marine sergeant's name was written on top of the map with a red pen. How did these guys get that map?

"It's not wise to have U.S. military stuff in your house, bro," Captain Looney said to the suspects.

"Okay," said the first.

One of the soldiers scrolled through the names in each suspect's cell phone.

"What's your boss's name?" Captain Looney said to the second.

The man mumbled Abu something-or-other. I could not quite make it out.

"Abu" means *father of*. Arab men often adopt a second name for themselves after they have a son. Palestinian Prime Minister Mahmoud Abbas is also known as Abu Mazen, for instance, which means his son is named Mazen.

"Abu…" Captain Looney said. "What's your boss's *real* name?"

"I think it's Mohammad."

"You *think* it's Mohammad?" Captain Looney said. "Seriously? You don't even know who you work for? Listen. If you keep acting this goddamn stupid, I'm going to detain you for the simple fact that no one can be this stupid unless they're hiding something."

It is not at all apparent from this exchange, but Captain Todd Looney has a lot of respect for Iraqis in general. I have spoken to him at length, and I've seen him interact with Iraqis who aren't being detained on suspicion of terrorism. It's only fair that I point that out.

It's also only fair to point out that these Iraqis may not be as dumb as they come across. It's common knowledge that Iraqi police officers frequently abuse those they arrest. Not everyone in Baghdad knows or believes that American soldiers rarely do so and will get in serious trouble if they are caught. And you'd be scared, too, if you were flex-cuffed and aggressively questioned. No one wanted to say anything about Haji Jawad because they were rightly afraid of violent retaliation.

And don't be shocked by the profanity. Military men don't talk like accountants, and they never have. "I don't trust an officer who doesn't cuss," I heard Captain Looney say to another officer earlier that same day. "We have a nasty job. Our job is killing people."

He really does not like to kill people. "I'm a pacifist, man," he had told me in his office. "At least I'd like to be. Of course I know *how* to fight any time that's what the enemy wants. I'm ready whenever they are. But it's not what I'd rather be doing."

Some soldiers and Marines I've spoken to feel slightly uneasy in Iraq now that they rarely get into firefights. Many don't feel comfortable with nation-building and peacekeeping, partly because it is not what they trained for, and also because it is not the kind of thing warriors generally do. Nation-building is political work. Most soldiers don't join the army to become politicians.

One night I asked Captain Looney which he prefers: kinetic fighting or nation-building?

"I vastly prefer this," he said. He meant nation-building. Killing people does not make the would-be pacifist happy.

"Some soldiers tell me they prefer fighting," I said.

"They're immature," he said.

"That's a good answer," I said. And it was. Killing people really is a nasty business, no matter how necessary it sometimes may be. So is raiding the wrong house in the middle of the night and scaring old women and children. It had to be done--don't get me wrong--but I felt horrible watching it happen.

"Get up," Captain Looney said to each of the suspects who knelt in the mud in the slum junkyard.

"I am at your service," said the second suspect, the man who had been shaking in fear the entire time. "If I'm guilty, take me."

"Get out of here," Captain Looney said. Then he cut the man's flex-cuffs.

The other man's flex-cuffs likewise were cut. Both were free to go.

They were afraid of American soldiers that night, so they ran. God only knows what they think of Americans now. Did they feel humiliated? Or were they more surprised that they weren't arrested and beaten up?

The Iraqi police might not have been nearly so lenient. And the Iraqi police today are extraordinarily lenient compared with Saddam's Iraq police that these men had grown up with. The two suspects might have an even lower opinion of American soldiers than they once did, or they might think better of them today. I have no idea.

All of us--Captain Looney, Sergeant Gonzales, the rest of the soldiers, and I--walked back toward the waiting and idling Humvees that would return us to base. We had come up empty. We did not have the most-wanted terrorist flex-cuffed and blindfolded in the back of one of the trucks. All we had was more mud and muck on our boots to show for the effort.

"Why the *fuck* are you here voluntarily?" Captain Looney said to me.

I didn't know what to say.

Seven

The Woman Who Blew Up the Arab World

"Does the flap of a butterfly's wings in Brazil set off a tornado in Texas?"
– Edward Lorenz, mathematician and chaos theorist

Tunisia, 2012

On June 28, 1914, Gavrilo Princip shot and killed Austria's Archduke Franz Ferdinand in the streets of Sarajevo—a fateful act that triggered a series of events culminating in the First World War.

Ninety-six years later, on December 17, 2010, an impoverished Tunisian fruit vendor named Mohamed Bouazizi set himself on fire in front of city hall in the small town of Sidi Bouzid—another fateful act that changed the history of an entire region forever.

Protests supporting Bouazizi first turned to riots and then revolution. The crooked authoritarian ruler Zine el-Abidine Ben Ali was overthrown in Tunis less than a month later. A copycat uprising in Egypt led to a bloodless military coup against strongman Hosni Mubarak. Libya's Muammar Qaddafi was next on the list, though this time it took civil war and aerial bombardment from NATO to be rid of him. Protests against Syria's Bashar al-Assad mushroomed into a multi-sided civil war featuring the Free Syrian Army, Lebanon's Hezbollah, the Al Qaeda-linked Jabhat al Nusra, and the even more terrifying Islamic State in Syria and Iraq, which eventually--and perhaps inevitably--sucked int he United States.

Princip died in prison four years after killing Austria's archduke. He knew what his actions unleashed on the world. He couldn't participate any further than he already had, but he knew.

Bouazizi only survived his self-immolation for a couple of weeks. He languished, comatose, in a hospital in Sfax the entire time. He had no idea he inspired even a protest, let alone a revolution, a coup and a number of wars.

He killed himself because he could not make a living. And he did it before city hall because he blamed the government.

According to rumors and initial reports, a female police officer spent months picking on him for selling fruit from his cart without a license. Things came to a head when she confiscated his goods and allegedly slapped him. When city officials refused to give his stuff back, he poured gasoline over his head, lit a match and set the world ablaze.

The woman who allegedly slapped him is named Faida Hamdi. I met her at a quiet park just off the main street in town, where she said almost everything published in the media about her is wrong.

We sat in plastic chairs on the grass behind a swing set for children. She ordered—and insisted she pay for—glasses of sweet tea from a concessionaire. A man who looked like an ultraconservative Salafist brought the tea over. I wondered what he thought about a local woman hanging out with an obvious foreign infidel, but if he was perturbed, he didn't let on.

"First of all," she said. "I'm not a cop." She worked for the municipality as a civilian. "My job was to chase away illegal fruit vendors. I don't carry a gun. I don't have a truncheon. I don't carry a weapon at all."

She said she hadn't been picking on Bouazizi, that she had never even spoken to him before that day.

"I had been tolerating his illegal work for a long time," she said, "but that week I had an order from the ministry to confiscate any merchandise sold from any illegal vendor from that particular place. So I was doing my job. When I confronted him, he said, 'Why are you targeting me? If I paid you bribes, you wouldn't target me.'"

She said she didn't take bribes, but the city was known to be crooked. Maybe she was clean. I don't know. Either way, her bosses were not.

Though she said she confiscated the electronic scale Bouazizi used to weigh fruit, she emphatically denied that she ever slapped him.

"He pushed me," she said, "and actually wounded me. So I screamed."

Some local men told me he may have grabbed or hit her breasts. No one seemed to be sure. I didn't ask her about it. Why embarrass a modestly dressed Muslim woman with such a question? She suffered enough humiliation during the revolution. The entire country and much of the rest of the world thought her a tool of a repressive police state.

The flip side of everyone believing Bouazizi grabbed or hit her breasts is that such a story—even if it isn't true—improved her image in the minds of others. She was no longer perceived, at least not by everyone and at least not exclusively, as the aggressor.

I didn't ask her to talk about her breasts, but she did tell me Bouazizi hit and pushed her.

"I called the police," she said. "They weren't armed either when they showed up, nor did they attack him. They just pushed him away so he couldn't hit me. They confiscated his things and took him down to the station."

An eyewitness told a reporter from the London-based Arabic newspaper *Asharq al-Awsat* that she didn't slap Bouazizi but that the police really did beat him. Maybe they did and maybe they didn't. We'll never know.

"In a small town like this," she said, "a woman hitting a man is a headline. But the rest of the day was normal for me. I went home as if nothing had happened. Then I got a call that Bouazizi had burned himself."

According to the international news media, Bouazizi was a university graduate struggling to eke out a meager existence, the Tunisian equivalent of an American with a master's degree in literature or philosophy working the barista counter at Starbucks. It made for a great story, but it wasn't true. His family said he did not even graduate from high school. Lots of kids in towns like Sidi Bouzid don't finish high school. Their families sometimes struggle so mightily that it makes at least short-term sense for the kids to drop out and work.

Don't get the wrong idea, though. Tunisia isn't Third World. Sidi Bouzid is about as bad as it gets, but it's clean, orderly and not too hard on the eyes. It isn't horrifying like the slums of Bangladesh or Cairo's City of the Dead. Sidi Bouzid is just depressed and a little bit hopeless for most who don't leave.

Everyone I spoke to in town, and in the also impoverished nearby city of Kasserine, said Tunisia's poor are yearning for jobs. No one said they wanted handouts or subsidies from the state. They wanted to work. They'd work their fingers bloody for scandalously small amounts of money. Hamdi herself made only $50 a month. The cost of living in Sidi Bouzid was low, but still. Fifty dollars a month is practically nothing. My lunch that day cost less than $2, but it was 4 percent of her monthly salary. An average house rents for $200 a month. A big one rents for $300 a month.

Government spokespeople said Bouazizi sold fruit without a vendor's license. His family said he didn't need a license, that the real reason the law brought down the hammer was that he didn't pay bribes. Whichever version of the story is true, the government tried to wring money from him that he didn't have.

I don't know what his politics were, but the complaint that drove him over the edge was hardly based in radical Islam. His complaint was libertarian, frankly, though he likely hadn't heard such an American word.

Activists erected a statue of his fruit-vendor's cart just down the street from city hall, two blocks from where he set himself on fire. Beneath it someone spray-painted the words "For Those Who Yearn to Be Free."

The city government, in his view, was a corrupt and obnoxious regulatory state that made it hard—well nigh impossible, actually—

for him to work and support his family. Thirty percent of the town's population was unemployed. Enterprising people like Bouazizi who took the initiative to work for themselves were held down by the state. And for what? For not having a license to sell a banana?

Hamdi understood. She was part of the state, but she understood.

"I believe in the law," she said, "but it's unfortunate that my job is the suppression of somebody else's job. I believe the law should rule, though, so I have to do it. It's like when a police officer pulls you over for running a red light. You might think, 'Ack, why is he doing this to me,' but it has to be done because it's the law. You obey the laws in your country, right? Why shouldn't it be the same here?"

Much of the country saw her as a villain when the revolution broke out, but she insisted she had nothing to apologize for.

"It's my job to serve citizens," she said. "When they go into a café and it's dirty and unhealthy for customers, it's my job to confiscate the filthy equipment and order the café to be closed."

Her self-image was an honorable one. She wanted to be a part of order, law and good government. And she was willing to accept an exploitatively low salary in return. How long can a decent and idealistic person serve an arbitrarily repressive regime? She managed for 10 years, but the roof still caved in.

"I spent three months and 20 days in jail," she said, "from December 31 to April 19. I was jailed on the orders of Ben Ali. I was accused of taking bribes, but I did not break the law. He used every tool he had to make me look like a scapegoat so that people would shut up and stop protesting."

She strained mightily to keep herself from crying and paused to collect herself. I would have handed her a Kleenex if I had any.

"I was sentenced to five years in prison for extreme violence against citizens," she said, choking up. "Before Ben Ali left the country, no lawyer would represent me. But after the revolution a lawyer helped free me. So the revolution is a good thing even though I was the first one oppressed by it."

Post-traumatic stress disorder came next. She couldn't work all the following summer when she got out of jail, but she recovered. "I have my old job back," she said, "though I no longer do field work."

She didn't hate Mohamed Bouazizi, nor did she blame him much for what happened.

"I didn't know him," she said. "I never spoke to him before that day. I knew who he was, though, because he always worked in that spot and I'd been tolerating him for a while. It's unfortunate that he killed himself and that he was poor. He was also an orphan."

She felt wronged by the powerful, not only by the former regime but even by the president of the United States.

"I have a grudge against your president," she said, though I didn't ask her about him. "Barack Obama mentioned me in a speech. He said I was a cop. He said I slapped Mohamed Bouazizi. He's a stupid fool for not checking. Americans are great people, but you need to do a better job checking your information."

"Well," I said, "that's why I'm here. That's why I wanted to meet you."

She smiled and nodded. The media got her wrong, but perhaps the history books will treat her more fairly.

Bashar al-Assad, the Butcher of Damascus, was in the fight of his life as an indirect result of something routine she did a year and a half earlier. Violent clashes between Sunnis and Alawites were breaking out in Lebanon as a (very) indirect result of something routine she did a year and a half earlier. The suppurating catastrophe in the Levant eventually sucked in the United States just as Libya had. History was exploding in dangerous and unpredictable ways. All these events could be traced back in a straight line to her encounter with Bouazizi on December 17, a date she's sure not to forget.

We all change the course of events by existing in this world, but most presidents can hardly leave marks that are this big. Her own act was a small one, but it lit the fuse.

How must it feel for an ordinary person in a random little town to ignite a revolution, to be made a scapegoat by a dictatorship, to be mentioned in a speech by the president of the United States, to be arrested and jailed for what was at worst a minor infraction, to see her cynical jailer toppled in a revolt, to watch the warden of Egypt toppled in another revolt, to see the Libyan regime bombed by America, to see open war break out in Syria and spill into Lebanon and to see Mali—an African country that is not even Arab—broken in half as an aftershock of the Libyan war? All because she confiscated a fruit vendor's scale. At least Gavrilo Princip expected something to happen when he shot Ferdinand in Bosnia on the eve of the war.

"A revolution cannot be solely the cause of one person," she said. "Even though I didn't really participate in it, I'm proud of the revolution and proud of my country."

She may not have participated in it, but she sure did precipitate it. Her name is Faida Hamdi and she is Tunisian. She is also Lorenz's butterfly, a small soul who by flapping her wings set off storms of tornadoes for thousands of miles in every direction.

Eight

Egypt's Botched Revolution

Cairo, 2011

Egypt's revolution against Hosni Mubarak captivated the world. It inspired an armed rebellion against Muammar Qaddafi's hellish dungeon in Libya and, at least initially, peaceful protests against Bashar al-Assad's Baath Party regime in Syria despite his government's ruthless repression. But the Egyptian revolution wasn't a real revolution. It was a coup d'état against the president by the army.

The coup had the support of the people, of course. It might not have happened had mass demonstrations not broken out, and it certainly wouldn't have otherwise happened on the day that it did.

I returned to Cairo during the country's chaotic transition. The Supreme Council of the Armed Forces (SCAF) ruled the country as a military junta, though you'd hardly know it as a casual visitor. The men with guns who were everywhere on the streets of Cairo when I visited years earlier were elsewhere, perhaps in their barracks. Egypt was bereft of any portraits of a strongman in charge. I wasn't sure who the head of state even *was*—highly unusual for an Arab country. If you pressed me, I'd say the head of state was SCAF chairman Mohamed Hussein Tantawi, but many Egyptians thought he was just a front man, that someone else in the junta was the real man in charge. No one I asked was sure one way or the other, not even official American sources who spoke to me off the record.

156

Tens of thousands of citizens who were snatched up during the uprising in January and February still languished in jail under snap collective sentences. The millions who took to the streets and pressured the army to oust Mubarak felt their work was incomplete, and on the second Friday of July they staged another mass demonstration downtown.

The police and the army had retreated from the capital's center. Tahrir Square, so often a scene of anarchy and mayhem, was relatively civilized that day. Activists from every group in the country—from the liberals and the socialists on the left to the Muslim Brotherhood—teamed up and provided their own security in case anyone from the plainclothes police or the Baltageya—fellah-class thugs who beat people up for a few bucks or even some smokes—stirred up trouble.

I went down there with my American colleague Armin Rosen and our Egyptian colleague Yasmin el-Rifae. She knew her way around better than Armin and me and could translate when necessary. She said the men from internal security could be identified as such on their ID cards, so everyone who entered the square had to show identification. When I flashed my American passport and said I was journalist, I got a very warm welcome, including high-fives and handshakes.

I couldn't accurately count the number of people in the crowd, but tens of thousands of people were down there. And I couldn't help but compare Egypt's revolutionaries with Lebanon's. The massive demonstrations in Beirut in 2005 against Syria's occupying military dictatorship that I'd covered earlier in my career looked and felt strikingly different. Far more women joined Lebanon's Cedar Revolution and fewer wore Islamic headscarves, partly because almost half of Beirut's demonstrators were Christians, but also because Lebanon is more secular by an order of magnitude.

Lebanon's revolution looked and felt cosmopolitan and middle class. Egypt's was significantly more masculine and Islamic. The crowd at Tahrir was also much poorer. No one would describe this movement as a Gucci Revolution, as a handful of Occidentalist Westerners rudely dubbed Lebanon's.

Most of the women at the square wore the headscarf. Yasmin dressed like a Westerner, and I saw other uncovered women there, too, but most dressed conservatively, even those affiliated with the liberal and socialist parties. One of the iconic images of Egypt's revolution showed a victorious young woman wearing the hijab flashing the V-for-victory sign. The headscarves, though, did not necessarily indicate membership in the Muslim Brotherhood or adherence to any Islamist principles. Headscarves were just the standard dress code for women in Egypt regardless of politics.

Almost all the slogans I heard and saw painted on signs and walls emphasized freedom from state oppression, but there was a darker current there too. Many in that crowd were vengeance-seeking reactionaries. I saw a number of nooses on banners and even found one bearded man—who was probably with the Brotherhood or the Salafists—carrying an actual noose.

A scruffy man in an orange hat saw my camera, deduced that I was a journalist and decided that was the time to yell about Israel. "We will go to Israel next!" he said. "Israel is next!"

Yasmin grimaced, embarrassed, as the man raged incoherently. She's Egyptian and not exactly a fan of Israel either, but she could discuss it in a rational manner without getting hysterical or wallowing in paranoia and hatred. This guy, though, was one of the crazies.

"Okay, okay," she said and shooed him away. "That's enough."

An Egyptian man standing next to me also cringed.

"That's just his opinion," he said. "There are many opinions in Egypt. Why must Israel always be our enemy? Why? Why must the U.S. be our enemy?"

Yasmin called a famous socialist activist she knew named Hossam el-Hamalawi, and he agreed to meet us for a few minutes in front of the local KFC franchise. I saw a banner beneath the KFC showing a Muslim crescent and a Christian cross fused together, a symbol of tolerant anti-sectarianism that I first saw at liberal rallies in Lebanon.

"This won't just be a one-day event," Hamalawi said when we found him. "It will turn into a sit-in." He was right about that, and it dragged on for weeks. "I have no idea how long it will last, but at the end of the day the battle is not necessarily going to be settled here in Tahrir. What brought down Mubarak wasn't Tahrir, and it wasn't the army. It was the mass strikes that broke out all over the country that forced the military junta to ask Mubarak to step down or else the system would collapse. The main battle for us, the people on the left, is to take the battle to the factories, to take Tahrir to the universities, to take Tahrir to the workplaces. In every single institution in Egypt we have a mini Mubarak waiting to be overthrown."

The working-class labor strikes, he said, had been ongoing ever since the army arrested Mubarak. "The middle-class activists were happy to suspend protests here in Tahrir," he said, "and go back to their well-paying jobs. They were happy to establish a dialogue with the military junta. But the working class has been continuing its mass strikes."

There were strikes all over the country, it's true, but at the same time most Egyptians tired of all this revolutionary activity. They yearned for normality and an end to the upheaval that brought the economy—an emergency-room case to begin with—to its knees.

"I used to work as an editor before the revolution," Hamalawi said. "I could go back to my job at any time and still get paid thousands of Egyptian pounds, but the public-transport worker whose strike brought this country to a halt cannot go back to his starving family and say it's okay for him to get 189 Egyptian pounds after 20 years of service and wait for the military to solve his problems. So the strikes are ongoing."

Activists are by their nature optimists, especially in police states. Few will risk a beating or worse if they know they're going to lose. So Hamalawi, like every other activist I spoke to, thought his side would win.

"People said we were crazy when we were chanting against Mubarak in 1998," he said. "As student activists, people thought we were crazy when we started advocating general strikes before the outbreak of the strike wave. People thought toppling Mubarak, an American-backed dictatorship, could never happen." Yet it happened.

"We've had 7,000 years of civilization," he said, "and 7,000 years of oppression. And I'm optimistic that for the first time in our lives, for the first time in 7,000 years, we will be able to achieve a real democracy."

Fat chance, I thought.

Sorry to be a downer—and I kept my thoughts to myself—but I knew better. Most revolutions end in tears, and revolutions in the Middle East are especially perilous. The region is a great teacher of pessimism. I'd already seen one revolution in the Arab world hit the rocks, and that was in Lebanon, a country that's far more liberal and culturally democratic than Egypt. Tahrir Square was an intoxicating place in July, but it was a bubble. It wasn't the country.

Egypt's liberals were out in large numbers, but they were a sideshow. The army and the Islamists had far more supporters and power. Events the following Friday proved it.

Hundreds of thousands of Islamist activists from the Muslim Brotherhood and the totalitarian Salafist movement seized control of the square. They didn't go down there just to yell at the army. They aimed to intimidate liberals, and it worked. The Islamists "told their supporters to join in the demonstrations to fight against the liberal infidels," a caller on a state TV show said. Thirty-four revolutionary groups—and that would be almost all of them—packed up and left.

Then the army went in and cleared out the rest. The soldiers tore down the tents and stepped aside as thugs from the Baltageya beat the shit out of people while nearby shop owners cheered and applauded.

The liberals, the leftists, the Islamists and even the army were unified, sort of, when Mubarak was everyone's hated target, but the interim phase pitted them against one another. Competing revolutions and competing demonstrations wracked Cairo as citizens egged on a popular government crackdown.

The real battle for the heart and soul of Egypt was on. The victor would determine the Arab world's direction for a long time.

Tarek Heggy made himself slightly famous through books, newspaper articles and television appearances in Egypt and abroad. He stood out not only for lacking any feelings of hostility toward Israel but also for advocating rapprochement. In 2008, along with Professor Naim Mahlab, he established the Tarek Heggy scholarship at the University of Toronto for postgraduate studies in comparative Jewish/Muslim relations.

I met him in a hotel lobby outside the Mediterranean city of Alexandria, where he and his wife were escaping the heat, smog, noise and congestion of Cairo.

"I personally think there is nothing worse than Mubarak's era," he said as we sipped from tall glasses of Egyptian-brewed beer. "All the problems we have now come from Mubarak's era. Even if we end up in the hands of the Muslim Brothers, it is because of Mubarak. He didn't handle them properly."

"How would you have dealt with the Muslim Brotherhood?" I said.

"He handled them only with a stick," he said, "and you can't handle Islamism with only a stick in your hand. I would have exposed them to open debate. I would have let all Egyptians know that their ultimate objective is power, the caliph system and the implementation of Islamic law. I would have made sure that more women, more liberals and more Christians knew exactly what would happen to them under the Muslim Brotherhood. I would have used the media appropriately. I would have shown people what happened in Iran."

He meant the 1979 revolution, of course, when Islamists seized power in the wake of the Shah's downfall and built a regime even more oppressive than the previous one.

"Mubarak's Egypt was a very strong police state," he said. "It shouldn't have fallen easily, but it did, partly because of the popular movement but also because of the army. You can't look at one and exclude the other. There was a coup d'état. That's why less than a thousand people were killed."

Heggy knew a bit more about what happened behind the scenes and off-camera than most journalists and foreign observers, partly because he knew some of the actors personally. Former intelligence chief Omar Suleiman, for instance, was his neighbor. Sometimes they talked.

"Here's the dramatic story," he said. "On the 10th of February, Mubarak signed a decree sacking [Defense Minister Mohamad Hussein] Tantawi and appointing the head of the republican guard. The decree was sent to TV stations to be read on the air. The head of the TV station took it in his hand and went to Tantawi. So Tantawi was warned 24 hours before Mubarak stepped down. A half-hour later, the first announcement was made, and it was vague: the Supreme Council of the Armed Forces will continue meeting until the problem is sorted out, and the army will always side with the people. That was the first announcement, which, for somebody like me, was a sign of the coup d'état.

"The following day," he continued, "Omar Suleiman was asked to read a statement that Mubarak was supposed to have written, but instead he read something crafted by the army. Mubarak heard it for the first time on TV just like the rest of us, and he was removed to [the resort city of] Sharm el-Sheikh. The head of the republican guard has been in jail since that minute. The main function of the republican guard is to prevent a coup d'état."

"That's what it's for," I said.

"It's not for anything else," he said. "It's there to protect the president from his own army."

Yet Mubarak's republican guard failed to protect him. That's how transitions of power often take place in the Middle East and North Africa. Mubarak was an army man, as were Nasser and Sadat, but his son Gamal, whom he had groomed to succeed him, was not. Maybe that's why the army removed him and maybe it isn't. I don't know. I'm not sure anyone does. All that matters is that the army did remove him and has the power to remove anyone else it doesn't like, for whatever reason, in the future.

"Egyptian-Israeli relations will be decided by the army," Heggy said, "and the army is totally against confrontation with Israel. In the streets people say they want to renegotiate the Camp David agreement, but the army will never go for anything like this."

"Is that because the army knows it lost the 1973 war even though the government pretends Egypt won?" I said.

"I like the way you phrased that," Heggy said. "Everyone here thinks we won in 1973 and only lost in 1967. We did very well during the first week in 1973, but wars are judged by how they end, not how they begin. Sadat didn't want to fight in 1973 to win. He wanted to fight for some pride when he sat at the negotiating table. That's what his wife, who is a very good friend of mine, said to me at her house in Maryland. Sadat told her many times that the best he could do in a war against Israel is put in a good performance at the beginning. The Israelis have a better army, better training, and they have America behind them. He said he needed to be able to sit down and talk to Israelis with his head held high, and he could only do this by first giving them a good punch. They will give him two good punches, but at least he will have given them one."

Sadat didn't only need to "punch" Israel so he could hold his head high. The entire country felt, and still feels, humiliated by its repeated losses to Israel. It isn't easy for even a military dictator to keep his finger off the trigger when a whole country is crying for war.

Egypt's army was certainly more rational in its behavior toward Israel than it would be if it heeded public opinion, but the army was partly responsible for shaping public opinion. The brass hardly liked Israel or the United States any more than the Muslim Brotherhood did.

Few Egyptians I spoke to other than Heggy seem to have paid even the slightest attention to what happened in Iran after the 1979 revolution, when Ayatollah Khomeini's Islamists took over. There are at least two excellent reasons for that. First, Egypt's Free Officers regime, unlike the Shah's, didn't go down with Mubarak. And second, the Muslim Brotherhood stood virtually no chance of creating its own army inside the country as Khomeini had done when he built the Revolutionary

Guard Corps in Iran and Hezbollah in Lebanon. There's only room for one army in Egypt. An attempt to create a second would be suicidal.

So Egypt's revolution was very different indeed from Iran's, but history doesn't need to start repeating exactly before its lessons ought to be heeded.

"Do people here take Iran seriously?" I said.

"I don't think so," he said. "It's not on the screen."

"Why?" I said.

"It's far away," he said. "Egyptians are among the most localized people in the world. They look inward and greatly exaggerate their value in the world. I'm sure you must know that."

I did know that. I saw it in Egypt's military museum at the Citadel on a hill overlooking Old Cairo. Everyone who set foot inside learned how the Egyptian army—and therefore the government—saw itself.

The Citadel's museum was the kind of place a superpower would build. Architecturally it looked like it was built by Victorian-era imperialists from Great Britain but with a bombastic Russian, even Soviet, style. Not even in an alternate dimension would such a grandiose place be built by the bumbling Iraqi or Lebanese armies. I couldn't imagine anything like it being built by any Arab army other than Egypt's, with the possible exception, I suppose, of Algeria's.

The Citadel is a medieval fortification overlooking Old Cairo and was built in the 12th century by Salahaddin (a.k.a. Saladin), the Kurdish warrior who reconquered Jerusalem from the Crusaders and made himself sultan of Egypt and Syria. It's fitting that the Egyptian army built its museum there. Its officers saw themselves as modern-day descendants of Egypt's ancient and medieval warriors.

Egypt's military adventures abroad against Israel, Yemen and Iraq under Saddam Hussein in the first Persian Gulf War were celebrated. North Korea's government donated the services of one of its painters to illustrate an Egyptian-Israeli air war over the Sinai in 1973. The painting was commissioned during Mubarak's tenure in 1993, many years after Sadat signed the peace treaty with Israel.

Egypt's geopolitical clout fell after it signed that treaty. It no longer resembled a mini regional superpower. The elite in the armed forces, however, yearned to see Egypt rise again if it could unshackle itself from American requests that it be a status quo power for regional peace and stability. They saw themselves as bigger and more important. Serious moves in that direction would play very well indeed on the street.

H ala Mustafa was distraught. She was one of Egypt's most promi-nent liberal intellectuals and the founder and editor-in-chief of *Democracy* magazine. The authorities had been hounding her for years by smearing her name in the press, wiretapping her phones and sending anonymous death threats. Her name appeared in newspapers all over the world when the government launched an official investigation into her private life after she met the Israeli ambassador in her office at the al-Ahram Center for Political and Strategic Studies.

My colleague Armin Rosen and I met with her in that same office.

"I hope this doesn't come across as a paranoid question," Armin said, "but do you think your office is bugged?"

"Of course!" she said. "Yes. It's very bugged."

"So I guess if I have a message for Egyptian intelligence," I said and chuckled, "this would be the time to deliver it."

Perhaps I should have been alarmed at the possibility that the Mukhabarat might be spying on me as well as on her, but the news wasn't as disturbing as it would have been if I were interviewing dissident intellectuals in a place like North Korea or Syria. Cairo's regime was an Arab Nationalist military dictatorship, but it was built on the standard-issue authoritarian model rather than a totalitarian one. The odds that anyone in her office would be arrested were small, and the odds that any of us would be kidnapped or assassinated by the state were infinitesimal. Even so, Egypt was not the free country some mistook it for at the time.

"The moment of liberal change hasn't come yet," she said. "The regime today is the same one that was founded in 1952. This is still the

Nasserist regime. I was hoping this revolution would bring something different, that we could return to the liberal tradition that existed before Nasser destroyed it. Egypt had a historic opportunity to revive its liberal past, but the moment has passed. The military didn't encourage that path, the Muslim Brotherhood jumped over everybody to manipulate the process, and the liberal secular forces retreated."

Egypt did go through a relatively liberal period before the Free Officers launched their coup against King Farouk in 1952. Egypt was hardly a democracy at the time, but it was much more open, tolerant and Western-oriented. Nasser changed everything when he imposed socialism (in the Russian rather than Scandinavian style), pan-Arab nationalism and a virulent strain of violent anti-Zionism. Yet with Soviet backing he transformed Egypt into something that looked like a regional superpower.

Many Sunni Arabs throughout the region swooned to his pan-Arabism and wished to be annexed by Cairo. Syria actually did get annexed to Egypt for a couple of years when the two merged into the doomed United Arab Republic. Nasser even started military adventures abroad when he sent soldiers to Yemen and sparked the Six-Day War against Israel. Both conflicts led to disaster, especially when the 1967 war ended with the Israeli occupation of Egypt's Sinai Peninsula.

The regime was a secular Arab-nationalist one, but radical Islam gained strength with Nasser's squelching of Egyptian liberalism. The overwhelming majority of women throughout the country wore headscarves during and after the Mubarak era, whereas few did in the first half of the 20th century. A startlingly large number of men sported bruises on their foreheads—acquired by hitting their heads on the floor during prayer—to show off their piety. I saw more men with bruised foreheads in a single day in Cairo than in all other Muslim-majority countries I've visited, combined, in more than a decade.

The revolution, coup d'état or whatever we ought to call it did not return Egypt to 1951, the year before Nasser. History has no rewind button. Egypt couldn't regain what it lost when King Farouk was overthrown any more than the United States could suddenly return to the Truman era.

"All we can do," Mustafa said, "is preserve the minimal amount of our liberal tradition that still remains. But the military rule and the growing Islamization of the society make it very difficult. The conservative forces are trying to prevent any sort of progress in the country. The military rulers are different from the Muslim Brotherhood, but they don't contradict each other."

Most Western analysts described Mubarak's government as an American ally that was at least moderately cooperative with Israel, which was accurate to an extent, but his state-controlled media cranked out vicious anti-American and anti-Israeli propaganda every day for three decades. No one should have expected liberalism (and I'm using that word in its general sense, not in the parochial American sense) to emerge anytime soon after all that.

"I've read many American analyses of the Arab Spring," she said, "but most neglect the presence of the regime. Americans seem to think the regime went down with the dictator, but it's not true. So they're basing their analysis on what the people in the street do and say, but they don't realize the regime is directing the process. The Salafists right now are completely controlled by the state security apparatus, and so they've suddenly become a major power. They weren't in the past."

"What does all this mean for the United States?" I said.

"That the moment of change hasn't come yet," she said. "It was a premature revolution. Mubarak's regime wasn't Mubarak's. It was the regime that was founded in 1952, and it's still here. The regime's attitude against Israel is the same. Americans thought Mubarak was with Israel, but it's not true. Mubarak did nothing to change the propaganda or advance peace. You have to rethink what was happening."

I saw for myself what kind of message the military regime put out when I visited the October War Panorama commemorating Egypt's supposed victory against Israel in the Yom Kippur War of 1973—a war Egypt actually lost.

The North Koreans built that museum, the largest and most outrageous of its kind that I have ever seen. Unlike the Citadel, this place was a cartoon.

Outside, across the street from a Soviet-style apartment complex, fighter jets, missiles and tanks were on display for everybody to gawk at. You could easily see them from the sidewalk without paying admission. You couldn't even miss them while driving past in a car. That's how I first found out that the panorama existed. My taxi driver took me past the gate on my way to the airport in 2005.

"What's that?" I said as I gestured toward old air-force jets propped up on stands and pointing to the skies.

"It's a museum celebrating our victory against Israel in 1973," he said as if he actually believed Egypt won. Hezbollah's empty boast of a "divine victory" at the end of the disastrous 2006 war was part of a preposterous tradition that goes back a long time.

Inside the main entrance I saw a series of murals in the ancient style that showed Semitic slaves captured and tormented by the Pharaonic regime alongside modern Israeli soldiers trampled on and humiliated by 20th century Egyptians.

The set piece, and the museum's namesake, was an enormous panoramic painting depicting the Yom Kippur War, when Egypt mounted its temporarily successful surprise attack against the Israeli forces in the Sinai before Israel counterattacked and finished the war on its terms.

Visitors sat in theater-style chairs on a raised platform that slowly spun around so they could leisurely take it in.

Bogus history punctuated with bombastic martial music and cries of *"Allahu akbar"* (God is great) played over a single-channel audio track. All the women in the audience wore headscarves, and everyone in the audience, men and women alike, stared at me as though I had purple paint on my face. They must have wondered what on earth I was doing there and what I thought of it all.

The elite in the government and the army knew they lost the war in 1973. How could they not? They lied to puff themselves up. And they never stopped broadcasting the message that Israel and the United States were their enemies even as Israel and the United States described them as friendly moderates. The army blamed all Egypt's problems during the post-Mubarak chaos on foreign (i.e., Israeli and American) saboteurs and subversives and tightened entry requirements on Western visitors, even tourists. This is not the way a peaceable ally behaves, but aside from the new visa requirements, it was nothing new, really. Mubarak's government did the same thing.

It was next to impossible to get an interview with anyone in the junta. I was laughed at when I tried. "They won't give interviews to the Egyptian media, let alone the American media," my Egyptian colleague Yasmin said.

No one from the army gave speeches. No one from the army went on television to talk about what it was doing or what it wanted. SCAF had little contact with the society it ruled. Its soldiers were not ubiquitous on the streets like those of so many Arab armies. Once in a while the junta sent out a press release, and it did so at least once via Facebook, but the officers were so distant and removed from their subjects, they may as well have been holed up in a bunker in the sky over the horizon.

I asked Hala Mustafa what she thought about the game Mubarak played with the United States, how he claimed the Muslim Brotherhood would only get stronger if he opened up Egypt's political system as Washington asked.

"The army is trying to prove he was right," she said and laughed. "His men, his establishment want to prove he was right. He's gone, but they are still here, and that's why they're co-opting the Muslim Brotherhood."

She insisted the regime had been far more consistently anti-liberal than anti-Islamist. "The army recently released Anwar Sadat's assassin," she added. "It's bullshit."

The street activists I met were optimistic, but Mustafa was not. "The regime and the Islamists hate liberalism and Westernization," she said. "This has been the problem since King Farouk was toppled by the Nasserists. Egypt's liberal bourgeoisie and the liberal thinkers are associated with the imperial power of the moment, so they are rejected. Leftists and Marxists, however, overlap ideologically with the regime because they are anti-liberal and anti-American." This was also, in her view, part of the reason Israel had to be demonized: "not because it's Jewish but because it's Western and liberal."

That right there is why I couldn't shake my feeling that no matter what happened, no matter who might win Egypt's upcoming election, the country's near- and medium-term future would be grim. Aside from the fractious activists in the square, Egypt was for all intents and purposes a two-party state pitting the army and its supporters against the Islamists. Political liberalism can't grow in a place where the two main factions are both anti-liberal.

That was the problem from which most others sprang. Egypt need not copy the West down to the last detail in order to flourish, but there's no getting around the fact that people who reject everything the West stands for are guaranteed to live in poverty with boots on their necks. The only question is which brand of boot.

Nine

Hanging With the Muslim Brotherhood

Cairo, 2011

My second interview with Muslim Brotherhood spokeman Essam el-Erian in Cairo is one of the strangest of my career. I'm reproducing it here in its entirety so you can experience the Brotherhood raw and unplugged.

First, some context. This interview took place after the overthrow of Hosni Mubarak and before the election of the Brotherhood's Mohamed Morsi to the presidency. Morsi was later overthrown in a military coup by General Abdel Fattah el-Sisi, and Erian was arrested along with the rest of the Brotherhood's leadership.

In early 2014, more than 600 Brotherhood members, presumably Erian among them, were sentenced to death at the end of a single show trial, making General Sisi Egypt's most vicious ruler in decades.

My friend, colleague and traveling companion Armin Rosen joined me in Erian's office.

Armin Rosen: Can you tell us about the Muslim Brotherhood's vision for Egypt at this point?

Essam el-Erian: Egypt has changed, and change is ongoing. It has been changing not only in the last 10 years but for 100 years. We have been struggling for freedom and independence for a long time, ever since we were occupied by the British in 1882. During this period we had two big attempts to build a democratic state. Both failed. One was a good attempt after the big revolution in 1919. We had a liberal life, a parliament and a constitution, but the monarchy stopped everything. Then we had a military coup in 1952. We hoped to have a good democratic system, but when the military rules, you can forget about having a democracy.

This is our third attempt, and it's different this time because the people themselves went to the streets to revolt. No one dares to say he's a leader of the revolution or behind the revolution. The people are making this happen through their own efforts. We Muslim Brothers were among the people because we represent a sector of the population, but we'd never dare to say this revolution is an Islamic revolution. It's a national revolution.

MJT: You guys were completely taken by surprise by this, weren't you?

Essam el-Erian: We all need a free and independent democratic state. We have struggled for a strong and independent Egypt not only for 100 years but for 200 years, since Muhammad Ali. He was also supported by foreigners. There was no USA at that time, but the French, British and Germans put him under siege, and this was an insult to Egyptians. We were under the authority of the Ottoman Empire, and we respected Muhammad Ali and the Ottoman authorities, but he wanted reform within the empire and to have a good modern country as a symbol. He never achieved this. In 30 years, he was broken. And ever since we've wanted an independent and strong modern state.

MJT: What do you think of the liberal era before Nasser came to power in 1952? When you look back on that, does it look better than the current era or worse?

Essam el-Erian: The Bush administration invaded Afghanistan, and it failed. You're facing disaster there now and don't know how to escape. [*Laughs.*] A safe escape from Afghanistan will just add another disaster added to the disaster of the occupation. And the Bush administration tried to create a democratic model in Iraq. It also brought a disaster not only to the Iraqi people but to the nation of America and the values of America. And to the economy of America. [*Laughs.*]

This was, of course, not in the American interest, but in the interest of some people who are governing the think tanks and the media. Now that Obama is facing this disaster, the Republicans are putting this burden on his shoulders. This is a big lie. He inherited this.

It is time for you to respect others, to respect your values and to be a real democracy. Respect multiplicity in the world. We are different. This county is different from Saudi Arabia. It is different from America and the U.K. This is the most important lesson of the Egyptian and Arab revolutions. You need to respect their choice. Don't intervene in their domestic affairs. Treat them as equals, as human beings, not as an oil field. [*Laughs.*] People are not going to drink oil.

I hope after the success of the revolution, if the revolution has an impact in Saudi Arabia, that the Saudis will only produce the oil they need, not what you need. If they keep their own oil for their own future generations, that will teach the Americans to respect others and not to insult the Saudis and the Arabs.

Armin Rosen: How are Americans insulting the Saudis?

Essam el-Erian: Yes. Yes. Yes. I'll give you some examples. Your administrations—while your people are silent—have been supporting tyrants and dictators all over the Islamic world for more than 60 years.

MJT: The government has, yes.

Essam el-Erian: You supported the Shah of Iran. You supported Suharto, the generals in Pakistan, all Arab leaders.

MJT: You do understand that was government policy.

Essam el-Erian: Yes, but the American government is an elected one. You don't only vote on your taxes. You also vote for foreign affairs.

MJT: During our election campaigns, we don't get the choice between supporting or not supporting Mubarak.

Essam el-Erian: You insult Arab people.

MJT: You insult Americans.

Essam el-Erian: No.

MJT: There is a lot of anti-American sentiment in Egypt, especially from you.

Essam el-Erian: Please respect my intelligence. When you vote for Republicans who create wars in the Arab world, and when a million people take to the streets while having no effect on the administration, what can you call this?

The second thing, of course, and you know this from media reports and human-rights organizations, is that people are tortured and killed on American orders. The third is that you never respect the rights of Palestinians. You never give equal opportunities to Palestinians and Zionists. All the time you are biased. You're biased now and will be in the future. You're biased.

Hillary Clinton just said Bashar al-Assad is not important to Americans anymore. Before this declaration, he was important! You supported him! People here are intelligent. They consider every word.

How can people here explain or understand the last decision in Congress which prevents Mr. Obama from training the revolutionaries in Libya?

MJT: What do you think about what's going on over there?

Essam el-Erian: Look, sir. It's a big game. You cannot convince me that the American administration is sticking to American values. Qaddafi is your man.

MJT: He's our man?

Essam el-Erian: Yes.

MJT: Now, wait a minute.

Essam el-Erian: Yes.

Armin Rosen: He bombed a disco full of Americans.

MJT: He has been an anti-American dictator since the day he took power.

Essam el-Erian: French people are now having secret talks with Qaddafi and his son. [*Laughs.*]

MJT: We are not French.

Essam el-Erian: You neglected everything about Qaddafi when he declared that he'd get rid of so-called nuclear weapons. You neglected to think about him killing people and destroying his country. Your administration neglected everything. So how can I understand that Qaddafi was behind the attack over Lockerbie, Scotland? Megrahi [the supposed mastermind of the attack] is still living in Libya and is a very big symbol of the hypocrisy of the West. All the West.

MJT: I want to back up for a second. You said that Qaddafi is our man because we restored relations with Libya. Is that all it takes for a dictator to be "our man"? That we have diplomatic relations?

Essam el-Erian: Sir. Who protected Qaddafi's military coup d'état? Who protected him? You had all this military power. You could have stopped him.

Who protects all the dictators of the Arab world? Your men are there everywhere, from the king of Morocco to the king of Bahrain. They are your men.

MJT: The king of Bahrain is an American ally, but Qaddafi was never an ally.

Essam el-Erian: These men represent foreign interests. I study history. You might not be convinced by what I say, but this will all be clear after secrets become available in documents. Some people here in this country believe Nasser was protected by the Americans. You advised Mubarak during this revolution to stay in power by making reforms.

Armin Rosen: What sort of relations would you like to see Egypt have with the United States?

Essam el-Erian: Ordinary relations. I think Americans are on the same track. And the world is not America. The world is very wide. We have Africa, we have Asia, we have the Arab world, we have Moscow, we have India. All those are ready to have ordinary relations with the Arab world. China is now the big purchaser of oil in the Sudan.

Armin Rosen: The government in Sudan is far more oppressive than the government in Libya.

Essam el-Erian: No. No. No. Look, sir. China, Iran and France are the three players in Africa. America is now out. And the Arab world may be lost to America if it doesn't revise its strategy. It may be lost. All the Arab world. This American attempt to stop the revolution in Syria and Libya and Yemen is going to fail.

MJT: Now, wait just a minute.

Armin Rosen: You think it's okay for China to buy oil from Sudan, but it's not okay for the U.S. to re-establish ties with Qaddafi after he gave up his nuclear-weapons program? Isn't that a double standard?

Essam el-Erian: China's interests are economic only. It doesn't link economics and politics. All your candidates say they will transfer your embassy from Tel Aviv to al-Quds [Jerusalem].

MJT: They always say that, but they never do it.

Essam el-Erian: But what's the message to the Arab world? This is very dangerous for the image of Americans. You are biased!

MJT: Yeah, but you're biased too. You guys are completely biased toward the Palestinians.

Essam el-Erian: When congressmen stood up 30 times to salute Netanyahu when he gave his speech in the Congress, it destroyed any dream for peace.

MJT: Why should Americans be unbiased, but it's okay for you to be biased?

Essam el-Erian: We are fighting for and defending our interests.

MJT: So are we. That's how the world works.

Essam el-Erian: This is our right.

Can you imagine a democratic Syria or a democratic Jordan assimilating Palestinians in their lands? They cannot. It is a matter of time. Those people must go back [to Israel]. You prevent Mexicans by force from secret immigration.

MJT: Only illegal immigrants, not legal immigrants.

Essam el-Erian: This is illegal. We cannot have noncitizens in our lands. They take our jobs.

MJT: Palestinian refugees have been living in Lebanon, Syria and Jordan for more than 60 years.

Essam el-Erian: No! Even if they've been there for 200 years, they must go back [to Israel].

MJT: What about all the Jews in Israel that got thrown out of places like Baghdad?

Essam el-Erian: Let them live together.

MJT: Should they go back to Baghdad?

Essam el-Erian: Let them live together. Why not? Live together.

MJT: They can't live together, because they don't like each other.

Essam el-Erian: What about the Jews who came from Russia? Why do you put pressure on Syrian people, or Lebanese people, to compensate and tolerate Palestinians? You never put any pressure on Israel to compensate or tolerate Palestinians. Is this biased or not biased?

MJT: It's biased, but why should we not be biased and not stick by our allies, while you are biased and stick by your allies? That's just how the world works. Look, I don't expect Egyptians to suddenly like Israel, so why ...

Essam el-Erian: Our only war is the war for democracy. Those guys in Tahrir Square and Syria and Yemen are struggling for democracy. When democracy flourishes, it will solve everything, including the conflict with Israel. Democracy will solve it, peacefully, without bloodshed. We need democracy and freedom. These are human values. Are we an exception? We are not an exception!

You spend $40 million here to promote democracy. This was declared in the Congress. This is good. But you can keep this for yourselves, and we can build our democracy without any aid.

MJT: You would rather that Americans who support Egyptian democracy not help you?

Essam el-Erian: Keep your money for poor Americans. It's better for you.

MJT: Well, a lot of Americans would agree with you about that.

Essam el-Erian: You have trouble with your health care system. Sick people in America need this money. It would be good for them. And good for us.

Hosni Mubarak is Egyptian. If we dislike him, we will put him on trial. I was tortured in prison by Hosni Mubarak, but I am for giving him a fair trial and the opportunity to defend himself. I faced a military trial but never called for a military trial for Hosni Mubarak. You know why he won't face international charges? Because he will be asked about everything. And when he says everything, it will destroy the images of many leaders around the world. Your leaders are against a trial for Hosni Mubarak. There will be big surprises when we try Hosni Mubarak. Israel will send a spy to kill him before the trial! [*Laughs.*] We want to know why a former Israeli minister described Mubarak as a "treasure."

Please, if you want to describe what is going on in Egypt and the Arab world, it is a big change. No power can stop this change because it's the will of the people, the power of the people. People want to live in peace, not in war, in independent democratic states, preserving their human dignity, keeping their wealth for themselves and future demonstrations.

MJT: Do you think they'll win in Syria? Assad is killing lots of people.

Essam el-Erian: Others killed even more. His father killed 20,000 people in one day in Hama. Change can reach everyplace. The kings of Morocco and Jordan are making reforms.

MJT: What do you think of the Saudi government?

Essam el-Erian: They are intelligent. Kings are more intelligent than tyrants. They have the wealth and the power. If they give some power to the people, they keep the wealth. And this is good.

I hope you transmit the truth to the American people and also advise politicians that they must revise their strategy.

MJT: What would you like American foreign policy to look like?

Essam el-Erian: Of course, that is up to Americans. You should advise them. I cannot advise them. You in the media play a very important role.

MJT: A little role.

Essam el-Erian: The media and think tanks play a very important role. You created a ghost, a monster, this terrorism. You magnify terrorism, and we face its vengeance. You in the media link every Arab, every Muslim, to terrorists. We were pushed to take off our shoes in your airports.

MJT: I have to take off my shoes too.

Essam el-Erian: Why?

MJT: I don't like it either.

Essam el-Erian: You make people live in terror.

MJT: Who does?

Essam el-Erian: You do. The media.

MJT: Who is living in terror?

Essam el-Erian: Your politicians. Your media. Your media.

MJT: We don't live in terror. I don't know a single person in the media who lives in terror.

Essam el-Erian: Can you answer one question? Why don't we hear about trials for September 11?

MJT: Because the people who did it are dead. They killed themselves in the towers.

Armin Rosen: There was a civilian trial.

Essam el-Erian: Four thousand innocent people were killed, and there has been no trial.

MJT: That's because the people who did it are dead.

Essam el-Erian: Nobody was put in a cage to face a trial.

MJT: They were on the planes. They blew themselves up in the towers.

Essam el-Erian: No. Who was behind it?

MJT: Osama bin Laden. And we just killed him too.

Essam el-Erian: We know you have about 600 people in Guantánamo Bay. None of them have faced trials. Why? This is a very big mystery.

MJT: Well, what do you think happened? What's your theory?

Essam el-Erian: And another 4,000 Americans were killed in Iraq and Afghanistan. You have almost 10,000 innocent Americans killed.

Never mind the millions killed in Iraq and Afghanistan. You never put anyone on trial. Who is behind all this? Who made the conspiracy? Is Osama bin Laden alone? Who is behind Osama bin Laden?

Armin Rosen: Who do you think is behind Osama bin Laden?

Essam el-Erian: I want to know!

MJT: What's your theory?

Essam el-Erian: You have the documents now that Osama bin Laden is dead.

MJT: What's your theory?

Essam el-Erian: I don't know.

MJT: You have a theory.

Essam el-Erian: I want to know. That is the question.

MJT: Everybody has a theory. What's yours?

Essam el-Erian: Why 10,000 Americans killed? Why? Without any investigation.

MJT: Why does it have to be a conspiracy? It really isn't that complicated.

Essam el-Erian: Is Osama bin Laden alone, or is somebody with him?

MJT: Why does anyone have to be behind Osama bin Laden?

Essam el-Erian: This must be investigated in America! There is this case in the U.K. about hacked telephones—160 news people were fired.

MJT: [*Laughs.*] That has nothing to do with Osama bin Laden.

Essam el-Erian: A very old newspaper was closed. There was no drop of blood. If 10,000 Americans don't expect to have a full investigation about the killings in New York, Iraq and Afghanistan, we want to know.

MJT: Look, it really isn't that complicated. Osama bin Laden had some support in Saudi Arabia and from Pakistan's ISI.

Essam el-Erian: Look, sir. It is not enough that Osama bin Laden admitted in public that he did it. Osama bin Laden can't do it alone.

MJT: He had some support in Pakistan and Saudi Arabia.

Essam el-Erian: If you're saying Saddam Hussein supported him, it's a lie. Colin Powell said Saddam Hussein had biological weapons, but this was a lie. Colin Powell now regrets this.

We want to know.

MJT: What is it that you don't know?

Essam el-Erian: You tell me.

MJT: This isn't complicated.

Essam el-Erian: Yes, it's complicated. I agree!

MJT: No. It's not complicated.

Essam el-Erian: I am a physician. If a lady comes to me and suffers from any complaint, I will investigate. A complicated case must be fully investigated.

It has been 10 years. When will Americans will know the truth about who killed 10,000 people?

MJT: The American people are satisfied that we know who did it.

Essam el-Erian: No.

MJT: Yes, we are.

Essam el-Erian: No.

MJT: You aren't, but we are.

Essam el-Erian: The people cannot forget. The victims and their families will face everyone who keeps silent and protects the real people who were behind this and have drawn a curtain over the truth.

MJT: Who do you think did it? You think the United States government did it?

Essam el-Erian: The American people faced Joe McCarthy. And there were the Chinese people after the Cultural Revolution.

MJT: Are you suggesting the United States government was behind 9/11?

Essam el-Erian: Nobody knows! I don't know.

Armin Rosen: Let me suggest …

Essam el-Erian: You are very naive people.

MJT: I'm not naive. I do this for a living.

Essam el-Erian: So Osama bin Laden admits he's the murderer. You gave him $25 million, then you killed him, so fine, now the file is closed. For me, it is not closed.

Armin Rosen: Let me be even more blunt than Michael. There is a clear line between the founders of the Muslim Brotherhood and the ideology that inspires al-Qaeda.

MJT: That's absolutely true.

Armin Rosen: Is there some queasiness on your part in blaming 9/11 solely on him as opposed to the dictators that you believe the U.S. supports?

Essam el-Erian: Of course. We are victims of 9/11.

MJT: Ayman al-Zawahiri was a member of your organization.

Essam el-Erian: This region [*pounds table*] is a victim of 9/11. This region was put under dictatorship because we were accused as a nation of being behind 9/11.

MJT: Nobody thinks Egypt committed 9/11.

Essam el-Erian: Mohammed Atta is from Egypt.

MJT: Yes, he's from Egypt, but he himself is not Egypt.

Essam el-Erian: We were all called criminals. The entire nation.

MJT: Nobody thinks that.

Essam el-Erian: Yes. For 10 years. Why do you support those dictatorships that torture us in our prisons?

Armin Rosen: Do you see any relation between the ideology of the Muslim Brotherhood and al-Qaeda? There is a history there.

Essam el-Erian: Al-Qaeda has been against the Muslim Brotherhood all its life.

MJT: That's true, but Ayman al-Zawahiri was once a member of the Muslim Brotherhood.

Essam el-Erian: I was surprised when a congressman visited me last week and said it is well known in America that the Muslim Brotherhood is linked to al-Qaeda.

MJT: I'm not saying you are al-Qaeda.

Essam el-Erian: You know, but he is a decisionmaker. He says the Muslim Brotherhood and al-Qaeda are the same.

MJT: If you were al-Qaeda, I wouldn't be sitting in your office.

Essam el-Erian: Look, sir. If you don't dare to learn the truth about 9/11, we will. We were victims of this dirty and bloody crime.

MJT: You think you're victims because Egypt was blamed?

Essam el-Erian: All the nation. The whole Arab and Muslim nation was called terrorists. And you put these nations under dictatorship to face this ghost.

MJT: We didn't put Egypt under dictatorship.

Essam el-Erian: Your administration did.

MJT: Mubarak was already in power.

Essam el-Erian: And you put Hamas in the same cage as al-Qaeda. They are fighting for their liberty, but you describe them as terrorists.

MJT: What do you think of Hamas' martyrdom operations [suicide bombings]?

Essam el-Erian: Hamas was elected in a democratic process that your former President Jimmy Carter witnessed, but you neglect everything and call them terrorists.

MJT: So you think they aren't terrorists.

Essam el-Erian: Of course. They are fighters for liberty. Their land is occupied by the real terrorists. Real terrorists who kill innocent farmers in Qana and children in Egypt. They killed children in school here in 1968. They are the real terrorists.

MJT: Hamas kills children in schools.

Essam el-Erian: Why do you describe one as terrorist but not the other? Say both are terrorists. If you make an excuse for someone, you must have this excuse for others.

MJT: Not all violence is terrorism.

Essam el-Erian: Israelis kill children. They killed 300 children in Gaza. Those 300 children were fighters?

MJT: Children get killed in every war, but that doesn't mean everyone who fights in a war is a terrorist. Egypt sent troops to Yemen to fight there and help the revolutionaries. Is Egypt a terrorist state? Do you seriously believe that no Egyptian soldier ever killed a child in Yemen?

Essam el-Erian: Look, sir.

MJT: I asked you a serious question.

Essam el-Erian: For three centuries your grandfathers killed the Indians.

MJT: We can do this all day.

Essam el-Erian: If you want to go to history, we can walk through history together. But we are speaking about the present. [*Bangs table.*] In the present, you are biased.

MJT: Of course we're biased. So are you.

Essam el-Erian: Your media and administration are biased.

MJT: Everyone is biased.

Essam el-Erian: The politicians are no longer making the rules here. The people are. And the people are very intelligent in Egypt, even farmers in Upper Egypt. They know who is our enemy. Don't link yourself and your nation to the enemy of the Egyptian people.

MJT: Who is the enemy of the Egyptians?

Essam el-Erian: Israelis.

MJT: You guys have a peace treaty with Israel.

Essam el-Erian: If they respect it, the Egyptian people will respect it, but the Israelis do not respect it.

MJT: Israel is not attacking Egypt.

Essam el-Erian: Israel attacks everybody.

MJT: Israel is not attacking Egypt.

Essam el-Erian: Why are you neglecting the attack on Gaza?

MJT: Gaza is not Egypt.

Essam el-Erian: Bombs came over our borders. Why do you neglect the treaty? We have no comprehensive peace and no Palestinian state.

The whole world is changing. This is a time to revise the whole world order, as George Bush the father said. We need a new world order. Human beings should have equal lives and equal opportunities with the West. We must share in this new order and not be neglected all the time.

Armin Rosen: There are a lot of people in the U.S. who think the Muslim Brotherhood wants a moderate Islamist state supported by the military like they have in Sudan.

Essam el-Erian: Sudan is not an Islamist state. [*Laughs.*]

Armin Rosen: It's a constitutionally Islamist state backed by the military.

Essam el-Erian: All the Arab states are constitutionally described as Islamic states. All of them.

Armin Rosen: Well, what sort of ideal state structure do you want?

Essam el-Erian: An Egyptian state.

Armin Rosen: What does that mean?

Essam el-Erian: All of your colleagues ask me that question. The British made a democracy, and the French made another one, and the Americans made a third one, and the Germans made a sixth one. All are democratic. We have diversity and different interpretations, so we can have different models of democracy.

MJT: Lebanon has its own model of democracy, and Iraq has a slightly different one. What would Egypt's look like structurally?

Essam el-Erian: Lebanon is a special circumstance.

[*His cell phone rings. He has been ignoring most incoming calls, but he has to take this one, and he talks for 10 minutes in Arabic. He eventually hangs up and switches back to English.*]

Thank you, sirs. It was a nice hot meeting. [*Laughs.*]

MJT: Before we go, can I at least ask why you aren't down in Tahrir Square with everyone else? Every party in the country is demonstrating against the regime except the Muslim Brotherhood.

Essam el-Erian: We were in Tahrir Square.

MJT: But you aren't there now.

Essam el-Erian: Because now is very confusing. I went down there yesterday. I looked at the faces of the people, and they are not the people I know.

MJT: The people down there are liberals and socialists.

Essam el-Erian: It's chaos.

Armin Rosen: We've talked to a lot of activists there, and almost all of them say the Muslim Brotherhood is not on their side, that you're opportunists.

Essam el-Erian: We were there on Friday, but we are not backing the sit-in.

Armin Rosen: I mean in general. They don't feel like you're on their side.

Essam el-Erian: Look, sir. When the history of this revolution is written, everything will be clear. We are not going to say anything about our role in the revolution. Let the others say what they want.

Ten

The Children of Hannibal

Tunisia, 2012

The Arab Spring didn't go well. Egypt managed to rid itself of Hosni Mubarak, only to foolishly elect the Muslim Brotherhood's Mohammad Morsi to replace him as its new pharaoh. General Abdel Fattah el-Sisi then removed Morsi in a popularly-backed military coup, but imposed a military regime far more vicious and cruel than Mubarak's.

Libya degenerated into a failed militia state. Earlier it suffered from far too much government—Qaddafi's system was thoroughly totalitarian and modeled on Nicolae Ceausescu's in Romania—but the new state was so weak it hardly existed.

Civil war erupted in Syria, one in which the revolt against the tyrannical house of Assad was just the opening chapter. The fighting eventually blew across the borders into Lebanon and Iraq. The Islamic State of Syria and Iraq, an outfit so extreme that even Al Qaeda disowned it, finally committed one atrocity too many and brought down the wrath of a US-backed military coalition.

But things look different in Tunisia. The Islamist party Ennahda won more votes in the first election than any other, but it still won less than half and was forced into a coalition government with secular liberal parties. The Islamists outright lost the second election to the aggressively secular party Nidaa Tounes--or Call of Tunisia in English. No one person or party could get its mitts on all the levers of power, and in early 2014 Tunisia adopted the most liberal constitution in the entire

Arab world.

Why did the Arab Spring turn out so much better in the country in which it began? The answer lies back in time more than 3,000 years.

The northernmost point on the African continent is just outside the Tunisian city of Bizerte at the tip of Ras Angela cape. Here is where the Mediterranean bottlenecks. The Italian island of Sardinia is barely 100 miles away. Sicily is but 100 miles across the water from Tunis in another direction. The Italian town of Pantelleria, on the island of the same name, is only 37 miles off the east coast. Palermo, Sicily's largest city, is closer to Tunis than it is to Rome.

It should come as no surprise, then, that this area became the overseas core of the Roman Empire.

What is now the greater Tunis urban area, though, was an advanced civilization even before Rome was founded. Roughly 900 years before Christ, Elissa (whose Greek name, Dido, was immortalized by the Roman poet Virgil in his epic *The Aeneid*) was exiled from the Phoenician city of Tyre in southern Lebanon. She founded a new city on the southern shores of the Mediterranean and became its first queen.

That city, which at its height became known as the "shining city," was Carthage.

It grew into an innovative and technologically advanced, cosmopolitan sea-based power with one of the most formidable navies in the ancient world. At its peak it controlled most of the southern Mediterranean, from Morocco to Libya.

Three hundred thousand people lived in the capital alone, making it a megacity by antiquity's standards. The city was so dense that the Carthaginians had to build six-story apartment buildings in order to house everyone, something never before accomplished anywhere in the world. The apartments even had indoor plumbing.

"To some extent you could compare it to Manhattan," Stefan G. Chrissanthos, the author of *Warfare in the Ancient World,* told the

History Channel. "It was a huge population living in a relatively small area. This was an important commercial and cultural hub not only for North Africa but for the entire western Mediterranean world."

They built baths, a complex sewer system and enormous cisterns that you can still see today. Some of the more backward and impoverished parts of the Arab world still don't have all the things the Carthaginians had, but the city now known as Tunis had them even before ancient Rome did.

Carthage was truly a superpower. For hundreds of years it rivaled Rome in prestige, strength and wealth. No other nation at the time could challenge and threaten Rome as it did. When the two finally clashed, Carthage produced one of the greatest military generals in history—Hannibal—who fought a hard and bloody 15-year campaign against his chief rival. His army swung through Spain and Gaul and invaded Italy from the north on the backs of elephants. Europe was very nearly conquered from Africa. And while Hannibal failed, he put cold fear into the hearts and minds of Rome's citizens.

The Roman statesman Cato the Elder was later reported to have uttered the words *"Carthago delenda est"*—Carthage must be destroyed—after every single one of his speeches.

At the end of the Third Punic War (Punic is the Latin word for Phoenician), Rome did destroy Carthage, and it did so utterly. Barely a stone remained on top of another. The conquerors killed or enslaved all the inhabitants. Julius Caesar rebuilt the city in the Roman style, settled it with Roman citizens and made the new Carthage the principal European city in Africa.

Three wars with Carthage—two of them existential—convinced the Romans that they needed a serious empire lest they be conquered by somebody else. "It was in Tunisia," Robert D. Kaplan writes in his book *Mediterranean Winter*, "where Rome began to build its empire in earnest ... Tunisia became to Rome what India would be to Great Britain, its 'jewel in the imperial crown.'"

The Romans first annexed it and then renamed it Africa. Tunisia is hardly a typical country in Africa—it is at least messily democratic, and 60 percent of its citizens are middle class—but the entire rest of the continent was later named what Rome used to call it. The Romans eventually conquered the whole of North Africa, but they developed none of it as much as the area that now surrounds Tunis.

You can see that even today if you visit. Roman ruins are scattered all over the place and can be found as far south as the sand seas of the Sahara. The largest coliseum outside Rome was built just a few hours' drive south of Tunis in a place called el-Djem.

"The closer to Carthage," Kaplan writes, "the greater the development." Of course that development wasn't started by Rome. Rather, it was continued and accelerated by Rome.

Little remains of Hannibal's Carthage. The archeological site just to the north of downtown Tunis is mostly Roman, though there is a Phoenician portion just outside the museum. Ahmed Medien, a local journalist I toured the area with, didn't think of the ruins there as something left behind by somebody else, the way many Americans might view Native American sites in Arizona and Colorado. He saw a straight historical line between himself and ancient Carthage and described the Roman and Phoenician ruins as parts of his own cultural heritage.

Modern-day Tunisians admire and identify with Hannibal. There's even a statue of him with two elephants all the way down in Tozeur at the edge of the Sahara. Stores and hotels are named after him. The last light-rail stop before the lovely seaside suburb of Sidi Bou Said is called Carthage-Hannibal. The international airport is named Tunis-Carthage. Tunisians love the idea of ancient Carthage as a sophisticated, prosperous, cosmopolitan, sea-based superpower. Today's Tunis-Carthage is in some ways just like the old Carthage, although—unlike Egypt—it has been blessedly shorn of its militarism.

Fragments of Phoenician culture persist in small ways, as well. During the spring and summer, for instance, Tunisian men walking the streets will place jasmine flowers behind their ears, a fashion that was popular even in Hannibal's time.

The Roman Empire, however, left an even more lasting imprint, one that goes well beyond names and flowers and statues of ancient war heroes. Its legacy is one of urbanism and legitimate government, two things that are still extremely weak—at times dangerously so—in some Arab countries, even in ones like Jordan, which are relatively trouble-free.

Roman Carthage was an extremely important city in early Christianity. The biblical canon was confirmed there. Early Christian theologians Tertullian and Cyprian hailed from the area. The famed Christian philosopher and writer Saint Augustine, a Berber, was also from this part of Roman Africa. His hometown of Hippo is now called Annaba and lies on Algeria's Mediterranean coast, but it's barely inside Algeria just on the other side of the Tunisian border. That border is a modern invention. During Rome's time, Hippo was very much a part of greater Carthage.

Rome's culture and political system were firmly implanted not only into the cities and soil but also into the cultural DNA of the people who lived there. Tunisia belonged to Western civilization for nearly 1,000 years, more than four times longer than the United States has so far existed. Rome eventually fell, of course, but Tunisia remained part of the West for several more centuries.

In *The Decline and Fall of the Roman Empire, Volume 3*, Edward Gibbon describes Tunisia as seen by the conquering Vandals from Germany: "The long and narrow tract of the African coast was filled with frequent monuments of Roman art and magnificence." Of the Vandal King Genseric he writes, "[he] acquired a rich and fertile territory which stretched along the coast ... from Tangier to Tripoli ... He cast his eyes toward the sea; he resolved to create a naval power, and his bold enterprise was executed with steady and active perseverance. The woods of Mount Atlas afforded an inexhaustible nursery of timber; his new subjects were skilled in the art of navigation and ship-building."

So the Vandals ruled Tunisia for a while but lost it again to the Eastern Roman Empire, which had become the Byzantine Empire, in

534 A.D. Not until the 7th century A.D. did Arab armies finally take it for themselves.

The newcomers didn't impose the culture of the Arabian Peninsula wholesale on the inhabitants. They couldn't. The people of Carthage were too strong for that. The newcomers met them halfway and adjusted themselves to the advanced civilization that was already there. Conquering Arabs did this everywhere to an extent, as have imperialist peoples everywhere. The same happened when ancient Mongolia conquered China: the Mongols became Chinese. In few places, though, was the indigenous culture as resilient as it was in Tunisia. In few places—the most notable exception being Andalusia in Spain—was the pre-existing culture part of the West.

The Hafsid dynasty ruled from Tunis from the 13th century to the 15th and, at their peak, controlled the parts of Libya and Algeria that even today orient themselves somewhat toward Tunis-Carthage. The Hafsids ramped up trade with Europe dramatically during the time of their rule. Tunis was a culturally and artistically advanced place during this time and produced one of the Arab world's greatest historians, Ibn Khaldun, whose masterwork, the *Muqaddimah*, is still read today by Western students of the region. One of his arguments in the book is that desert nomads must be brought under the control of an urbanized state to prevent anarchy from overwhelming the realm. Roman statesmen learned this lesson the hard way. At the time of this writing, the Arab governments of Libya and Yemen still haven't figured out how to do it.

Later, and far more recently, the French ruled Tunisia. They took it from the Turkish Ottomans in 1881 and didn't entirely leave until 1963, seven years after the country achieved independence.

After all that history, Tunisia has emerged as unique. It doesn't have tribes as do most Arab countries. Its citizens make up an entirely modern and coherent nation-state. Its culture is cosmopolitan and tolerant, its enthusiasm for religion relatively mild. The whole population even beyond the urban core—including those who live deep in the southern desert—is both fluent and educated in the language of Paris.

It is at an angle to the rest of the Arab world. A serious angle.

"Our future," said Tunisian diplomat Ahmed Ounaies, who was briefly the foreign minister after Ben Ali was overthown, "is with Europe."

The coastal region of Northern Tunisia—directly across and just a short hop from Italy—is where most people live. The middle is sparsely populated, and the south is Saharan and empty. Whole swaths of the urban architecture are strictly Western—French—and nearly all the ruins are Roman. The Frenchification of the greater Tunis area is startling when seen for the first time. It is much more extensive than in Beirut. Parts of the country almost look and feel as though they're *in* Europe.

The north has things in common with southern Europe that it does not have with next-door Libya and Algeria. It even has things in common with southern Europe that it does not have with its own hinterlands. The divide between city and countryside forms one of the most controversial sociopolitical issues in the country. The coastal elite feel they have a hybrid identity. They are not entirely Arab or European but a mixture of both. People in the conservative rural areas are more comfortable defining themselves simply as Arabs.

"There is a fine line between the two sections in Tunisia," said Karim Dassy, a history professor at the University of Manouba. "There is the elite who have this double European-Arab identity and who are proud to be the descendents of Hannibal. For the more poor factions of the society, there is no connection with Hannibal whatsoever."

The non-elite do have a connection with Hannibal, though—at least their country does—whether they realize it or not and whether they like to think about it or not.

"They are aware of the fact that they're made of tidbits," said Hedi Ben Abbes, the secretary of state to the minister of foreign affairs. "But some of them cannot cope with the contradictions, though these contradictions are absolutely important. This is what French philosopher

Edouard Glissant calls the poetics of relations, that tension inside the body made by contradictory influences. It is a positive tension. We are not unicolored. We are made of different flows that make our bodies alive."

Even the least-educated citizens know their country is at a cultural crossroads smack in the middle of the Mediterranean where East and West, Europe and Africa, and Islam and Christendom have blended for millennia. The elite are just more aware of it. And the coastal inhabitants are more profoundly affected by it.

"For Tunisia," professor Dassy said, "imperialism means Roman imperialism and Greek imperialism. French imperialism here was similar to both in some ways. It was Roman in the sense that there was a military force here and Greek in that it was partly philosophical. This is why the elite has this dual culture."

"We've had some 20 civilizations pass through," said Zouheir Touiti, a professor of international relations, "from the Roman and Byzantine empires to the Vandals and Christians. So the output of this long process of history is giving us what you are seeing now."

Geography is important. Not only has Tunisia's location made it possible for the likes of the French and Romans to show up in force, but it has also brought certain kinds of non-imperialist immigrants to its shores.

"The Muslims were expelled during the reconquest of Spain," said Abdelhamid Largueche, a history professor at the University of Tunis, "and the Jews who came to Tunisia to develop commerce and trade are two additional factors in how Tunisia became more cosmopolitan. We deal here with exports and trade. Our proximity to the sea is crucial to the openness of the society."

There is a third component, too, neither European nor Arab, that should not be discounted. The indigenous population is Berber, or Amazigh. Most Berbers assimilated over the centuries to the culture imposed by Europeans and Arabs, but fragments of their language and culture are part of the mosaic even today.

"There was not a very strong Arabization of the Tunisian society," said Khadija Ben Saidane, a Berber activist from the south who learned Arabic and French as second and third languages. "Tunisia has not 3,000 years of civilization, but 15,000 years of civilization. Tunisia is the way it is now because of all the civilizations that came here, not only because of the Arabs."

Tunisia set itself on a different course from the other 20th century Arab states the instant it achieved independence from France. The country's first president, Habib Bourguiba, was a dictator in the mold of Mustafa Kemal Ataturk, the founder of the modern Turkish republic. Like Ataturk, he wanted his country to orient itself toward Europe rather than the East or the south.

"Bourguiba tried to make Tunisia a somewhat Westernized state," said professor Touiti, "closer to the West than to the African states. Don't lump us together with the Arab Spring countries. Each state has its own reality. You cannot compare us to Egypt." He described the country's liberal tradition as "Tunisianity." "We have our own Islam," he said. "We were the first Arab state to abolish slavery. We were the first Arab state to join the Human Rights League. We have a historical progression that's unlike the other states."

Bourguiba decreed that education should be in French rather than in Arabic. He admitted, at least privately, that his brief experiment with socialist economics failed, so he shifted to a market economy. Today, as a result, the majority of Tunisia's citizens are middle class—unlike any other Arab state without oil. Bourguiba implemented the Arab world's first progressive personal status code that granted equal rights to women and men. He referred to the veil as "that odious rag" and banished it from schools and government offices. I saw vastly fewer women than in other Arab countries wearing headscarves and veils even on the streets, where they're free to wear what they want.

"No other Arab country has tried the same policy we tried," said former Foreign Minister Ahmed Ounaies, "to free ourselves from the religious legacy and make religion merely a cultural reference rather than a way of ruling the country."

Ben Ali replaced Bourguiba in a bloodless coup in 1987. He didn't alter the state's ideology, but nor did he govern with vision as had Bourguiba. He just crookedly ran the place as if it were his own private property and smashed anyone who got in his way. Whatever enlightened ideals the state had under Bourguiba were lost to torpor and time.

Ben Ali's Tunisia was an authoritarian police state, but a relatively mild one by regional standards. He was no mass murderer like Syria's Bashar al-Assad or Iraq's Saddam Hussein, nor was his system totalitarian like Muammar Qaddafi's. It was more like the authoritarian regimes that Portugal and Spain suffered under in the 1970s before they joined the Western European democratic mainstream.

When I visited for the first time in 2004, I sensed that the country was predemocratic, that if the autocracy could be cleared out of the way, Tunisia might have a real shot at advancing to the next level. Most citizens seemed to share at least some of Bourguiba's views of the modern progressive society. They were relatively liberal and tolerant on their own initiative, not because the president ordered them to be. Ben Ali could hardly be bothered with ideological Bourguibism anyway. By the time Mohamed Bouazizi set himself ablaze in Sidi Bouzid, Tunisian political life had been stagnant, oppressive, vision-free and corrupt for a whole generation. The relative liberalism of Tunisia's street-level culture was hardly being forced on the citizenry by the palace.

Christopher Hitchens visited in 2007 and came away with the same impression. "I could not shake the feeling," he wrote in *Vanity Fair*, "that its system of government is fractionally less intelligent and risktaking than the majority of its citizens." His local friend Hamid compared Tunisians with their neighbors in Libya. "We are the same people as them," he said, "but they are so much *en retard.*"

So neither Hitchens nor I were surprised to see a mostly nonviolent democratic revolution break out. (There was never any chance of that happening in Libya or Syria.) It makes perfect sense that the Arab Spring began here, that it did not lead to civil war, that an orderly election was held on time, that the majority of Tunisians voted against the Islamist party and that even the Islamists were compelled to say that they don't want an Islamic state.

My optimism doesn't come naturally, not in this part of the world. I witnessed firsthand how the Cedar Revolution in Lebanon in 2005 was smashed by the Syrian-Iranian-Hezbollah axis and wrote a book about it, *The Road to Fatima Gate*. I never thought Egypt had much of a chance. The country is too poor, too Islamist and too authoritarian for political liberalism to take hold anytime soon. Qaddafi turned Libya into a vast prison. His total-surveillance state is still the most terrifying system of government I've ever seen up close and in person.

Tunisia is exceptional. It is not yet, however, the Italy or France of North Africa. There are still grounds for pessimism. The biggest hitch is Ennahda, the party of the Islamists. They're described in the Western press far too often as moderate. They're moderate compared with the totalitarian Salafists, sure, and they're moderate compared with Egypt's Muslim Brotherhood, but they're extreme by the standards of Tunis.

Party leader Rached Ghannouchi has praised suicide bombers who murder Israeli civilians. "Gaza," he said of the Palestinian territory ruled by totalitarian Hamas, "like Hanoi in the '60s and Cuba and Algeria, is the model of freedom today." He declared war on the United States during the run-up to the first Persian Gulf War. "There must be no doubt that we will strike anywhere against whoever strikes Iraq," he said. "We must wage unceasing war against the Americans until they leave the land of Islam, or we will burn and destroy all their interests across the entire Islamic world."

Americans are hardly the only ones disturbed by him and his party. Secular Tunisians across the political spectrum find Ennahda alarming.

"It is a fascist party," said Rami Sghayier, a local activist with Amnesty International. "They tried to convince people they're just defending religion and they won the election that way, but they have a fascist program. They're protecting the Salafists and other extremists. We don't only have the Salafists here—we also have Hizb ut-Tahrir. The interior minister did not even move his finger when the Tunisian national flag was attacked at Manouba University by Salafists. They took down our country's flag and replaced it with their black flag."

It's important to note, though, that Ennahda *campaigned* on a moderate platform. Ghannouchi didn't pimp his creepy ideology during the election season, nor did he serve in the government. (He was an influential party head, but he had no more actual power than Bill Clinton or Sarah Palin in the United States.) Hardly anyone in Tunisia wanted to vote for someone who thinks suicide bombers are healthy role models for their sons and daughters. Hardly anyone in Tunisia wanted to transform their country into the Gaza of Africa. Ennahda was forced by the society and its coalition partners in government to surrender to Tunisianity.

"There is a potential for extremism in Ennahda's philosophy," said Ounaies, the former foreign minister. "But they will try to adapt and become pragmatic so they can stay in power and be admitted by the Tunisians and by the world. Any ideology based on religion is extremist, but that is not the Tunisian way."

Indeed, it is not the Tunisian way. Tunisia, perhaps more than any other country in the Arab world, save Morocco, values moderation and centrism.

"Tunisia has always favored the center and rejected extremism," says professor Largueche, "and Ennahda has started to grasp that. So they're changing. Salafism has always been rejected in Tunisia. In the 19th century, Wahabbism was also rejected. Mohammad Abdul Wahhab in Saudi Arabia asked the bey of Tunisia to adopt it, but religious leaders here asked the bey to reject this school of thought. They didn't want it."

One of the most important developments after the revolution was Ennahda's formal announcement that it supports a secular state and not an Islamic one. "That was the one big impediment in the way of a secular constitutional framework," said professor Dassy. "Fifty percent of the problem is now resolved. But even though Ennahda dropped the Sharia provision, there is no guarantee it will protect individual liberties, political freedoms or women's rights—that's the other half."

The country could still go either way then. Plenty of things can and usually do go wrong after revolutions, especially in countries like Tunisia that, while politically liberal in some ways, have only a little experience with working democracy.

"My feeling is that Tunisia will cross five years of uncertainty," said Ounaies. "But the trend is toward a strong Arab democratic society. Within five years I think we will stabilize with a new legislative assembly and create a new tradition of democratic rule in the country. We are the ones who are creating this pattern of Arab politics. We are the first."

Tunisia's relations with the West after the revolution were better than one might expect, considering the fact that Islamists won almost half the votes in the first election and that the U.S. and Europe tacitly supported the former dictatorship.

Secretary of State Hedi Ben Abbes—who was from a secular liberal party, by the way, not Ennahda—described American-Tunisian relations as "state of the art."

"The relationship has never been so good," he said. "It hasn't always been good, but it's excellent now because the United States pays great attention to human rights and universal values. We also subscribe to those principles since we are involved in a democratic process. We believe in transparency, good governance, the separation of powers, freedom of speech, freedom of the press and so on and so forth. These values make Tunisia a model country in the Arab world. I'm crossing my fingers because it's a very delicate process. What we are sure of, though, is that we will never go back to dictatorship."

Tunisia's relations with Israel remained terrible, though. The two countries don't even *have* diplomatic relations. A loud minority even clamored to forever ban normalization of ties in the new constitution. But even Ennahda went on the record and said that's not going to happen, that the constitution is no place to regulate relationships between states.

I suspect that Tunisia, once things settle down, may have more in common politically with Turkey than with any Arab system of government. Turkey has plenty of problems, but it's in much better shape than most Arab states. Islamists and secularists are more or less evenly matched in both places. They scrap with each other ideologically rather than with bullets and car bombs. Neither is able to fully dominate the other.

Tunisia has advantages over Turkey, however, insofar as it's less culturally self-referential and more open to the world beyond its frontiers.

"Turkey is closed," said Touiti, the international-relations professor. "They have not a second language. They only speak Turkish. Ataturk taught them that Turkey is the only civilization they should believe in. Habib Bourguiba kept the French language and forged international relations with the European Union. Turkey is more nationalist. We are more open."

So while the Arab Spring soured in Egypt, Libya and Syria, the place where it was born looked better every year. If Tunisia succeeds—and if it becomes a model for others—for that we can partly thank Carthage and Rome.

Eleven

Lebanon's Israel Syndrome

Beirut, 2013

Lebanon has a serious problem with Israel. The country has technically been at war with its southern neighbor since the Jewish state declared independence in 1948. Israeli citizens are banned. Even foreigners are banned if they have Israeli stamps in their passports. Lebanese citizens aren't allowed to have any communication of any kind with Israelis anywhere in the world. If citizens of the two countries meet, say, on a beach in Cyprus or in a bar in New York, the Lebanese risks prison just for saying hello. Israel doesn't even exist on Lebanese maps.

At the same time, with the possible exception of Morocco, Lebanon is in important ways the least anti-Israel country in the Arab world. Indeed, decades ago many Israelis assumed it would be among the first Arab countries to sign a peace treaty. It made sense at the time. With its enormous one-third-Christian minority (it used to have an outright Christian majority), it's the least Muslim and most religiously diverse of all the Arab countries. And since a huge number of its Christians insist they aren't even Arabs, Lebanon might be the least Arab of the Arabic-speaking countries. Its capital, Beirut, has more in common with Tel Aviv than with any Arab city, including others in Lebanon. Put simply, Lebanon is just about the only Arab country where Israel can find natural allies.

Decades ago, many Israelis believed Lebanon would be the first Arab country to make peace, yet today it's widely assumed that Lebanon

201

will be the *last* Arab country to make peace with Israel.

It's a paradox, but that's Lebanon for you. To say it's a nation of contradictions is a cliché, but it's a cliché because it is true. It is simultaneously Western and Eastern, Christian and Muslim, modern and feudal, democratic and illiberal, secular and sectarian, cosmopolitan and parochial, progressive and reactionary, tolerant and aggressively hateful. That's because there is more than one Lebanon.

The country is divided roughly into Christian, Sunni and Shia thirds, with a 10 percent Druze population to make things even more complicated. The Christians have had ties with the West for centuries. Most of the Shias look to Iran for leadership and support. The Sunnis are generally aligned with the more liberal and moderate forces in the Arab world, as well as with the Saudis. Thanks to all of this, as well as Lebanon's location between Israel and Syria, Lebanon gets sucked into regional conflicts.

And because Lebanon was a vassal state of Syria, and because it's where Hezbollah lives, even discussing peace and normal relations with Israel can get you imprisoned or killed. That's been the case since the middle of Lebanon's civil war, when international peacekeepers withdrew from Beirut and Syria's ruling Assad family came to dominate Lebanese politics.

Lebanon is more or less a free country that protects freedom of speech, but on the Israeli question it is effectively a police state. Lebanese are afraid to talk to each other about it. They'll talk to me, though, because I'm an outsider. They're extremely careful, of course, and much of what they say is strictly in confidence, but once in a while someone will talk to me on the record, knowing perfectly well that I'm going to publish what they have to say.

I've been working in Lebanon on and off since 2005, and things changed after the Syrian civil war broke out in 2011.

The red line on Israel isn't as bright as it used to be. Except for the usual warmongering rhetoric from Hezbollah, I sense more moderation and sanity than I used to. It doesn't surprise me. Peace between Israel and Lebanon is still a long way off, but the possibility is now at least conceivable, mainly because the end of Syrian tyrant Bashar al-Assad will be the beginning of the end for Hezbollah. And they're the ones who enforce the red line on Israel.

This became clear to me when I had lunch with Mosbah Ahdab, a Sunni politician and former member of parliament from Tripoli, Lebanon's second largest city.

"Lebanon's post-Assad transition is going to be tough," he said as we shared a bottle of wine in his living room, "because we have Hezbollah still around. But Hezbollah will be cut down to a more realistic size. They will still have their weapons, but they can't continue provoking the tens of millions of people who live around here that they've been aggressive to all these years."

Indeed, Hezbollah will be surrounded by enemies. With the Assad family out of power in Syria, Hezbollah will be left exposed as a Shia minority in a Sunni-majority region. Their immediate neighbors are Jews, Christians and Druze, none of whom have the time, patience or tolerance for an Iranian proxy militia in the eastern Mediterranean.

"There will be the real possibility of development," Ahdab said. "We could have train service all the way down to Cairo. It could be fantastic."

Michael Young, the opinion-page editor of Beirut's *Daily Star* newspaper, once said that Lebanon is a place where what isn't said matters just as much as what is. This was one of those times.

Look at a map. The only way a train can travel from Beirut to Cairo is by passing through Israel. Lebanon and Israel will need an open border and normal relations before something like that could even get started. Yet a former member of parliament—not a Christian, but a Sunni Muslim—is openly, if a little obliquely, discussing it.

But he can't discuss it with the Israelis. He can't talk about anything with Israelis or he'll go to jail. And he isn't happy about that at all.

"I was once invited to a European Union conference," he told me.

"There was an Israeli guy from the website BitterLemons.net sitting near me and trying to talk to me. There was a camera around and I couldn't respond. When the session started, he said to the president that he didn't know why he was invited to a place where people from Arab countries are present and refuse to speak with him. When it was my turn to speak, I addressed the president. I said, 'The previous gentleman is totally right. It's ridiculous to be unable to communicate, but the laws in my country forbid me from speaking to him. I'll go to jail.'"

I've heard lots of stories like this over the years from Lebanese and Israelis. Israelis are offended when they run into Lebanese people who refuse to acknowledge them, but Ahdab isn't kidding when he says he'll go to prison. He used to be part of the government, but he's afraid of that government's laws. And if he had tried to change the law when he was in parliament, he almost certainly would have been killed by Hezbollah or another of Syria's allies.

I told Ahdab I think that law is insane.

"Absolutely," he said.

But what if there's a new regime in Damascus? What if, as he said, Hezbollah gets cut down to size?

Samy Gemayel, in a long-standing family tradition, serves as a member of the Lebanese parliament. He's the son of former President Amine Gemayel and the nephew of Bashir Gemayel, who was Lebanon's president-elect in 1982 before he was assassinated. Samy's brother Pierre was an MP in 2006, when men wielding automatic pistols shot him to death through the windshield of his car.

The Gemayels founded the Kataeb Party, which had a militia best known as the Phalangists during the civil war of the 1970s and 1980s. It was a hard-right party back then, but like most parties in Lebanon (except Hezbollah) it has mellowed with age. Today, the Kataeb has more in common with European social democratic parties than with its militant and ruthless old self.

I met Samy Gemayel in his office in the mountains above Beirut and asked what he thinks might change in Lebanon without the Assad regime next door, especially if it also means a chastened and weakened Hezbollah. And, I added, "will there be any possibility that people might at least start discussing a Lebanese-Israeli peace track with a new government in Syria? Nobody even talks about it now, even though Israel and Syria have negotiated repeatedly."

"It's a syndrome of the Lebanese people," he said. "For 20 years anyone who even opened his mouth and said we should think about having a peace treaty with Israel went to prison or was killed."

That was because of the Syrians and Hezbollah.

"People are afraid," he said. "It's like someone who has been in prison for 30 years. When he gets out of prison, he's afraid to walk on the street and talk to people. It's the same for the Lebanese people. They haven't gotten over this syndrome. Especially since Hezbollah is here to remind them."

A peace treaty is a long way off, of course, and will certainly require the destruction or transformation of Hezbollah before it can happen. But the first step will be getting over this syndrome and dissolving the red line. And there may be a relatively simple way to accomplish it.

"What if," I said to Gemayel, "people from Washington came here and said, 'Hey, you need to talk to your neighbors.' Would things change?"

"Yes, it can change," he said.

And why shouldn't it? The syndrome is simple. It's based on fear, silence and punishment. If the United States pressures Lebanon to negotiate with Israel, the Lebanese will at least be able to discuss the fact that they're being pressured by the United States to negotiate with Israel. And those who think it's a fine idea will be given international cover. Just as the red line was imposed from the outside, it can be erased from the outside.

Indeed, powerful Lebanese people are walking right up to the red line right now without pressure from the outside.

"Remember," Gemayel said, "when Hezbollah had indirect talks with Israel through the Germans? I went on TV. It was the first time someone talked about this. I said, 'How come Hezbollah is allowed to talk to the Israelis indirectly through the Germans to get their prisoners back, while the Lebanese state is not allowed to do indirect talks?'"

Hezbollah didn't respond to that challenge. What could they possibly say?

The Gemayels and their party were allied with Israel during Lebanon's civil war. Samy Gemayel's uncle Bashir swore to vanquish Yasser Arafat's Palestinian state within a state in southern Lebanon, to throw out the Syrian army and to sign a peace treaty with Jerusalem. Naturally, the Israelis backed him to the hilt in 1982, when they invaded and he was elected president.

According to Thomas Friedman's account in his book *From Beirut to Jerusalem,* one of the last things Bashir Gemayel ever said was, "To all those who don't like the idea of me as president, I say, they will get used to it." A few moments later, he was blown to pieces by terrorists from the Syrian Social Nationalist Party.

Bashir's brother Amine replaced him as president. Lebanon's civil war raged on; it was only halfway through at that point. And the Kataeb's alliance with Israel began to wane. Jerusalem's peace partner was dead and replaced with his more cautious brother. Hezbollah was on the rise in the south—from which Arafat's PLO had been evicted—and in the northern Bekaa Valley. The Assad regime's military forces weren't planning to leave Lebanon anytime soon. The Israeli dream of a friendly and terrorist-free Lebanon was premature and would have to be deferred for a generation at least.

I asked Samy Gemayel about his party's former alliance with Israel, and I did it carefully. "You can answer me twice," I said, "on the record and off the record. I can turn off my voice recorder because I want to know what you really think, but I also want to know what you would say publicly."

"Let me be very clear," he said, "and this is my answer publicly and nonpublicly. We believe we had no choice back then but to have an alliance with Israel. I've said it on TV. And if we find ourselves in the same position today, we would do it again. I also said that on TV. We couldn't do anything else. The Syrians were against us. The Palestinians were against us. The Lebanese Muslims were against us. The entire Arab world was against us. What were we supposed to do? Say, Please kill us? We would take support from anywhere, and the only country that supported us at that time was Israel. We really don't have anything to hide on this matter. And we believe that there should come a day when we negotiate with Israel on all pending and disputed issues in order to have permanent peace on our southern borders. We should end this. We should have stability."

He went on. I thought he might be careful and cautious, that he'd rather discuss something else, but no, he walked right up to the red line and told me I could print all of it.

"There is no excuse," he continued, "why Egypt is allowed to have a peace treaty with Israel while we cannot negotiate for an armistice. Why can Jordan have a peace treaty while we also cannot negotiate for an armistice? Even Syria, without a peace treaty, has had peaceful relations with Israel since 1974. Why can't we? More, why can Hezbollah, a paramilitary group, negotiate with Israel twice through German mediators in 2004 and 2009 to release its prisoners, and the official Lebanese state is not allowed to?"

How many Lebanese people agree with Gemayel? Who knows? They aren't really allowed to discuss it. There certainly aren't any polls on this question, and they wouldn't be reliable if there were.

When I asked how many people he sensed agreed with him, he put it this way: "We have to take into consideration that a lot of people were killed here by Israel. We have to be very careful when we talk about it because people died. But it's the same for Syria. Syria also killed a significant number of Lebanese from 1976 onward—more than what Israel killed, it may be argued. So if you want to have this attitude toward Israel, why not have the same toward Syria? Syria has done more harm to Lebanon than Israel."

There are two reasons it's considered acceptable to be a Lebanese ally of Syria but not of Israel. First of all, Syria is a "brother" Arab country. And second, Syria conquered Lebanon, transformed its political system and still has agents and proxies inside.

"We just want peace in this country," Gemayel said. "We want to build this country that has been destroyed for the last 40 years. And we can't build this country as long as it is at war. We don't want to be at war anymore. It's as simple as that. The future should be a future of peace."

The Future Movement party, founded by the late Rafik Hariri—who was assassinated in 2005 by the Syrians and Hezbollah, kicking off the Cedar Revolution—is the primary political vehicle for Lebanon's Sunni population. It gets roughly 90 percent of the Sunni vote in elections. (The local Muslim Brotherhood is an irrelevant fringe party.) Hariri essentially agreed with Gemayel, and so does his son and successor, former Prime Minister Saad Hariri. The Future Movement, as its name implies, looks to the future and not the past. Its ideology is one of liberalism and capitalism, which cannot flourish in war zones. Neither Hariri campaigned for peace with Israel, but neither waged war on Israel either. Instead, both struggled against Israel's regional enemies. And they paid the price, the elder Hariri with his life and the younger with self-imposed exile in France.

I had dinner with Saad Hariri shortly before he became prime minister in 2009, and though I can't quote him directly because our conversation was off the record, I can say that this man, who is the leader of Lebanon's Sunnis, isn't an obstacle to peace.

What about Lebanon's Shias? They make up roughly a third of the population, and roughly two-thirds of them are at least nominal supporters of Hezbollah. But another third or so are staunchly opposed to the party.

Lokman Slim is the Shia community's most prominent anti-Hezbollah activist. He lives right under the Party of God's nose in the *dahiyeh,* Hezbollah's stronghold in Beirut's southern suburbs. He has dedicated his life to building a liberal alternative to the self-proclaimed Party of God. His opinions are his own. Politically, he's a minority figure. But he's not at war with his community. He is at war with its dominant political party, which is not the same thing at all.

"The Shia want to be a respected partner in the globalization of the world," he told me. "I can't accept that the shitty island of Cyprus is part of the European Union and we, just a few miles away, are ostracized. We want to enjoy prosperity and suffer recessions, to be a part of the world with all its problems and all its benefits. We want to be part of the world like Israel and Syria."

How many people in the Shia community agree with what he is saying?

"Much more than you think," he said.

Lebanon is one of the few Middle Eastern countries not ruled by a monarch that never went through a socialist phase. Even Israel went through a socialist phase, though fortunately not on the Arab or Soviet model. Capitalism and trade come naturally to the people of Lebanon. They don't have much choice. It's a small country without any resources. Even after decades of military occupation and war, Lebanon is more prosperous than the other resource-poor Arab countries. Wouldn't its economy heat up if Beirut had a peace treaty and free trade with Israel?

"Obviously," Slim said. "We should take advantage of the fact that people want peace. Don't only listen to [Hezbollah leader] Hassan Nasrallah. Talk to people in the street. The people in the south will tell you they want peace, while Nasrallah always says he wants war. Of course the old woman in her shop selling cigarettes and sandwiches to UNIFIL soldiers wants to expand her small business."

He wasn't referring to any old woman in particular, but there are plenty of merchants in the south who have done business with the Israelis, and not all of them are in their 70s. When Israeli soldiers invaded southern Lebanon in 1982 to demolish Yasser Arafat's PLO statelet, the indigenous Shia population hailed them as liberators. Hezbollah doesn't talk about this, and the party is extremely unhappy when anyone else brings it up, but everyone in Lebanon knows it's true.

At the time, it did not even occur to Lebanon's Shias that Israel was their enemy. Their foe was an ancient one, which had been kicking them around since just after Islam was created: the Sunnis. Palestinians are overwhelmingly Sunni, and in the 1970s their construction of a belligerent mini-state in the Shia heartland of south Lebanon was a most unwelcome development.

"The Shia of the southern hinterland," wrote Johns Hopkins professor Fouad Ajami, who hails from that part of Lebanon, "had endured Palestinian power, the rise in their midst of a Palestinian state within a state. The Palestinian gunmen and pamphleteers had had the run of that part of the country. Arab nationalists in distant lands had hailed that Palestinian sanctuary; Arab oil wealth had paid for it. The Shia relief in 1982, when Israel swept into Lebanon and shattered that dominion, was to the Arab nationalists proof that the Shia stepchildren were treasonous. Then a Shia militant movement, Hezbollah, rose to challenge Israel. Its homicide bombers, its policies of 'virtue and terror,' acquitted the Lebanese Shia in Arab eyes."

But it took years for Hezbollah to convince the average Lebanese Shia civilian that they were the good guys. If the Israelis had not stayed too long in southern Lebanon—the occupation lasted almost two decades—Hezbollah would have had a much harder time getting started.

"The Shia peasants denounced Hezbollah to the Israelis," Slim said. "They would go to the Israeli soldiers and report strange things that were happening. Hezbollah spent a long time changing the mentality of these people."

If Hezbollah is weakened or collapses entirely, this mentality should eventually revert to the norm, because Jews have never been the principal enemy of the Shias. That dubious honor has always gone to the Sunnis. And as Ajami points out, the Shia "resistance" against the "Zionist entity" was from the start as much about acquiring status and respect, and thus acceptance, from the Sunnis as it was about Israel.

"Go to the south," Slim said, "and ask people if they want a new war, another divine victory."

I have, and they say no. Lebanon's Shias are simply not interested in war anymore. The Second Lebanon War in 2006 was the high-water mark in support for Hezbollah aggression. Nasrallah himself was forced to admit it. He all but apologized to his community in the smoldering aftermath, saying, "If I knew the process of capturing [Israeli soldiers], even with a 1 percent probability, would lead to a war like this, and then if you asked me would you go and capture them, my answer would be, of course, no—for humanitarian, moral, social and security reasons."

Obviously, he wouldn't have said that if his constituents had enjoyed his destructive adventure. But that doesn't mean they want a peace treaty and normalization. They don't.

"They want a cold peace," Slim said. "Right now they are ideologically conditioned. Don't forget all the anti-Jewish propaganda. Because we're not just talking about Israel. Anti-Semitism has been rooted in our culture from the 19th century up through Hezbollah. So people in the south just want a cold peace. They will not mind taking advantage of a warmer peace, but don't involve them in its creation."

Hanin Ghaddar, the managing editor of the online magazine *NOW Lebanon,* is another liberal Shia from the south who dissents from the mainstream opinion in her community, and she's free to say things Hezbollah and its supporters will not.

"People had different opinions," she told me, "but the general impression was that the 1982 Israeli invasion was great. The Israelis overstayed their welcome, but they were *really* welcome at the beginning. Everybody was very happy. I remember it. A lot of my relatives were happy, including my father. We had no problems with the Israelis."

But they expected the Israelis to leave. The strangers from the south were welcome as liberators, but not as occupiers. If they had left, Hezbollah would have had a much harder time establishing itself. She concurs with Lokman Slim. Hezbollah, she said, "used the occupation to rally the people around them."

The Israelis should have left sooner, but the error is perhaps understandable. They were welcomed at first, so they thought they'd be welcome to stay. And they wanted to stay to prevent another hostile group like the PLO from establishing itself on the border. Obviously, it didn't work out.

But anti-Zionism was not an indigenous belief in this part of Lebanon. The Israelis didn't foresee that Iran's revolutionary new government would export its ideology to its distant coreligionists, partly because Iran's ambitions in the Levant had not yet taken shape and also because the Shia history of dispossession and neglect was not—and still is not—widely understood in Israel. The Iranians understood it, however, because it is their story as well. The rise of Hezbollah was welcome among the Shias for the same reason the Israeli invasion was welcome: both promised relief from Sunni oppression, ancient and modern, real and imagined.

Ghaddar lives in Beirut, but she grew up in the south and often visits family there. Like Slim, she's convinced that her community will be more relaxed on the question of Israel in the future.

"They're very flexible, she said. "The war with Israel ended in 2006. Everybody knows that. It's not going to happen again, not if Israel doesn't start it. Hezbollah cannot strike first again. They don't have enough support. For the people, the war is over. They're convinced Israel isn't going to strike unless Hezbollah starts something."

None of this means that peace and normal relations are around the next corner, but what about relative peace and quiet?

"There is a way," said Eli Khoury, CEO of the M&C Saatchi advertising company in the Middle East and co-founder of the Lebanon Renaissance Foundation. "Hezbollah has already agreed in principle to return to a nonaggression treaty, the original armistice that has been in place for more than 60 years. [Druze leader] Walid Jumblatt campaigns for it. [Former Prime Minister] Fouad Siniora also campaigned for it."

He's referring to the armistice the Lebanese government and the new state of Israel signed at the end of the first Arab-Israeli war in 1949. Lebanon was hardly even involved in that war and hasn't actively waged war against Israel since. The Israelis have fought wars *in* Lebanon, but not against the Lebanese army or government. Their enemies were Palestinian- and Iranian-backed terrorist organizations. In the middle of the 2006 war, Lebanese and Israeli military officers sat down over tea and worked out a plan to ensure that neither side accidentally shot at the other.

"Everyone is at least paying lip service to neutrality now," Khoury said. "It used to be only the Christians who said they wanted neutrality. So today at least lip service is paid by every party, even the harshest, to neutrality, decentralization, border control, cleaning up agreements with Syria and a return to the armistice with Israel."

The Christians have always wanted Lebanon to be neutral in the Arab-Israeli conflict. The Shias wanted it, too, until 1982. Back then it was only the Sunnis who wanted Lebanon to be involved. It was they who embraced Egyptian tyrant Gamal Abdel Nasser's pan-Arabism and invited the PLO into the country.

Since then, however, the Sunnis in Lebanon have quietly moved on from the conflict with Israel, just as Sunni Arabs have moved on pretty much everywhere else. For them, the war ended with the PLO's last stand in 1982. As for the rest of the region, not a single Sunni Arab government has actively participated in a full-blown war against Israel since the 1973 Yom Kippur War. Lebanon's Sunnis, in moving on, are hardly unique. Indeed, they have even more reason to move on than do Sunnis in places like Tunisia and Morocco because Tunisia and Morocco don't get torn to pieces when the rocket launchers are fired up. Contrary to popular belief in some quarters, most Lebanese people do not enjoy getting blown up and shot at.

"The most recent study we commissioned," Khoury said, "and it was thorough—we surveyed 4,000 people—showed that 95 percent of the Sunnis don't care about Salafism or the Arab-Israeli conflict anymore. They're interested in other things. You have to remember that Saad Hariri's party is by far the most popular movement among the Sunnis."

Only Hezbollah keeps the fight alive, and historically speaking, the default position of their constituents has been radically different from what it is now. Hezbollah's sponsors in Syria and Iran are still standing, and it might take a generation for attitudes to change even after guns, money and ideology stop coming in from Tehran and Damascus. But it should be clear by now there's nothing eternal about the attitudes and behavior of Israel's northern neighbor. And if it's still too soon for optimism, it is not too soon to say a faint hope flickers on the horizon.

Twelve

Can Beirut Be Paris Again?

Beirut, 2013

Before the city became the poster child for urban disaster areas in the mid-1970s, Beirut was widely known as the Paris of the Middle East. With its French Mandate architecture, its world-class cuisine, its fashionable and liberated women, its bevy of churches in the Christian half of the city, its thousand-year-old ties to France and with French as a second language, it fit the part.

Then civil war broke out in 1975 and a gravitational black hole seemed to appear beneath the city, sucking in interventionist powers from the Middle East and even the more remote parts of the world. The Palestine Liberation Organization, the Israelis, the Syrians, the Iranians, the Soviets, the French and the Americans descended on Lebanon when its orgy of violence—the worst in the region since the collapse of the Ottoman Empire—tore city and country to pieces. More than 100,000 people were killed at a time when the population was less than 4 million. Beirut still hasn't fully recovered.

No country inflicted more damage than Syria under the rule of the Assad family's Arab Socialist Baath Party. The Syrian army was one of the most destructive belligerents when it invaded during the Lebanon war and sponsored one militia after another to keep the country off balance. After the war ended, the Syrians smothered Lebanon with a stultifying military occupation for 15 years until the Cedar Revolution forced a withdrawal in 2005. Even after Syria left, Damascus and its violent local proxies—Hezbollah, Amal and the Syrian Social Nationalist Party—laid

215

waste to Lebanon from the inside, first by provoking a disastrous war with Israel in 2006 and again by invading Beirut in 2008 and toppling the government.

Now with Syria's Bashar al-Assad possibly on his way out, or at least too busy to export mayhem to his neighbors as he faces the likes of Jabhat al Nusra and ISIS, will Beirut have the chance to be Paris again?

The truth is that Beirut never really was Paris except in a bastardized sense. The city is what you'd get if you put Paris, Miami and Baghdad into a blender and pressed *puree*. Gleaming glass skyscrapers rise above French-style villas adjacent to bullet-pocked walls and mortar-shattered towers. Hip entrepreneurs set up high-end boutiques next to crumbling modern-day ruins. A downtown Ferrari showroom sits across the street from a parking lot that was recently a bombed-out field of rubble. Beirut's fabulous cuisine never went away, nor did the city's high-end shopping districts, cafés, nightclubs and bars, but English has eclipsed French as the second most spoken language, and none of the reconstruction or new construction looks even the slightest bit French.

Beirut is a city that devours its past. Postwar progress means that some of its most beautiful buildings and even entire streets are being demolished and replaced with high-rises. Some of the new towers, like those along the city's new waterfront, are architecturally outstanding. Others are standard-issue generic blocks that function as little more than vertical placeholders: imagine a 20-story bank building in a place like Dayton, Ohio. Sure, they beat the junky 12-story apartment complexes built during the war-torn 1970s and 1980s, but they're replacing some of the most charming urban vistas in the entire Middle East.

"Construction in Lebanon has reached an alarming stage where much of the architectural memory of a city like Beirut is being erased," says Michael Young of Beirut's *Daily Star* newspaper. "Where once we had a relatively charming Mediterranean city, what we now have increasingly is a city of impersonal high-rises, many of them of questionable architectural value. Everywhere there is concrete and almost no green space."

"The tragic thing," says a graduate of the American University of Beirut who can't stand the mismanagement, "is that they are destroying ruins that are over 2,000 years old to build structures that could very likely be uninhabitable within a year because the political situation could dramatically worsen. They destroyed a Phoenician port. They are destroying Roman and Byzantine ruins. For what? The chic new buildings they are erecting could very easily look like the blown-up Holiday Inn in the near future."

Beirut is a small city. With only a million residents, it's less than half the size of metropolitan Portland, Oregon. A hundred years ago it was hardly bigger than a fishing village. Nevertheless, Beirut has a lot of history to devour, some of it lovely, much of it horrible.

The year 1975 was when it all went to hell, but before 1975, back when Beirut was still "Paris," the Levantine hell was in Syria. Damascus was the unstable place in the region. Syria, in fact, was among the least stable countries on earth. Throughout the 1950s and early 1960s, military coups came as often as Christmas. Not until the Baath Party seized power in 1963 did Syria settle down, and only then because the Baathists erected a total-surveillance Soviet-style police state that terrorized the population into passivity.

Hafez al-Assad, father of the current ruler, Bashar al-Assad, took the helm in 1970, and he cleverly figured out that Syria's inherent instability could be exported and that the easiest place to export it was Lebanon.

Lebanon's religious groups have different cultures, different values and different regional and international sympathies. The Christians have historic ties to the West dating back to the Crusades. Lebanon's Sunnis are backed by much of the Arab world, which, outside Iraq, is overwhelmingly Sunni. The Shias have Iran as their patron, one of only a handful of Shia-majority countries anywhere in the world. Since Lebanon is small, divided by nature and weak by design, it's easy pickings for a totalitarian state looking for hapless prey to divide and conquer.

Syria didn't start the Lebanese war—it was sparked in Beirut by clashes between Palestinian and Christian militias—but it would have ended much sooner without Syrian interference, and it would have ended much better. The Taif Agreement at the conclusion of hostilities required the disarmament of every militia in Lebanon. Assad's army oversaw their disarmament but left Hezbollah in place, partly because it was a useful proxy in Syria's relentless war against Israel and also because it could be used in a pinch to checkmate Beirut if Damascus' new vassal got a little too uppity.

Hezbollah was used for both purposes after the Syrian army's withdrawal. The 2006 war between Hezbollah and Israel—which Hezbollah started when it killed three Israeli soldiers along the border and kidnapped two others—cost more than a thousand Lebanese citizens their lives, created more than a million refugees (almost 25 percent of the country) and shattered infrastructure from the north to the south. Despite the fact that Hezbollah and its local allies lost the most recent election, they're in charge of the government, thanks to their slow-motion takeover of the country that began with the invasion and brief occupation of West Beirut in 2008.

In the end, it hardly mattered that the Lebanese managed to evict the Syrians, since Assad can still partly rule from a distance by proxy. But Assad can't rule Lebanon even by proxy if he's thrown from his palace in Syria. And now that his state is collapsing—the government has already lost control over huge swaths of the country to relatively moderate rebels and to psychopathic jihadists—Syria's inherent instability has nowhere to go but inward.

The gravitational black hole that shattered Beirut and made Lebanon into one of history's epicenters has shifted 52 miles east to the Syrian capital. The Free Syrian Army battles alongside the al-Qaeda-linked terrorists of Jabhat al-Nusra to topple Bashar al-Assad's regime. The formerly al-Qaeda linked Islamic State in Iraq and Syria (ISIS) is at war with everyone in the country. The war isn't only political; it is also

.

sectarian. Syria's Sunni Muslim majority is at war with the heterodox Alawite minority, to which the Assad family belongs, while the Christian minority keeps its collective head down and the Kurdish minority wants out altogether. Wealthy Arabs from the Arabian Peninsula are funneling money and guns to the opposition. The Israelis launched a number of air strikes against Syrian weapons depots to prevent their transfer to Hezbollah in Lebanon. The United States decided to assist the moderate factions and bomb the terrorist factions. The Russians and Iranians are backing Assad to the end, as is Hezbollah. Syria has become Lebanonized.

"Syria before Assad was a playground of foreign intervention," says Martin Kramer at the Washington Institute for Near East Policy. "Hafez al-Assad turned Syria into a regional player in its own right, occupying Lebanon, running his own Palestinian factions and enabling Hezbollah. But now Syria has reverted to what it was before: a jumble of clashing interest groups and resentful sects, pitted against one another, all seeking foreign backers who might tip the balance in their favor. In the long view, fragmented weakness may be Syria's default condition, and the Syria of Assad père, an aberration."

At the time of this writing, no one can say for sure if Assad will survive the revolutionary war waged against him, but most Lebanese people I know think he will fall and that Syria could fall with him.

"Bashar's balloon has burst," says Eli Khoury. "He's lost control. Pandora's box is open. The Kurds, the Christians, the Sunnis, the leftists, the conservatives, they're all asking what they're going to get."

"I don't see Syria as heading toward transition," says Jean-Pierre Katrib, a Beirut-based university lecturer and human-rights activist. "I see Syria as heading toward disintegration."

The truth is that Syria makes no more sense as a state than Iraq does, which is why it took a totalitarian regime to keep it from fracturing. Both Syria and Iraq, each wired together with minority-backed Baath Party governments, have in some ways more in common with the former Yugoslavia than with internally coherent Arabic-speaking nations like

Egypt, Tunisia and Morocco.

"Syria and Iraq have so far only been governed by ruthless, centralized iron," Khoury says. "It's otherwise hard to make sense of these places. They're too big. The Baath propaganda says Lebanon was taken away from Syria. Even some Lebanese people believe this. But historically there was never a state called Syria. The theory that the Sykes-Picot Agreement broke Arab countries into pieces shortly before the end of World War I is wrong. It also glued some countries together, such as Iraq and Syria. Maybe history is going to reverse Sykes-Picot."

Damascus under the current regime has exerted such a toxic influence on Lebanon for so long that regime change there may do wonders for Beirut, even if the aftermath of the Syrian war is disastrous—which it probably will be.

B eirut recovered somewhat from its own Syria-style destruction even during the Syrian occupation, and not all the reconstruction and recovery has taken the form of erasure. Most of downtown has been rebuilt, although the results look and feel a bit odd. Stone buildings that delightfully blend Parisian and Ottoman styles have been lovingly restored, but the area is a bit antiseptic and fake-looking, almost as if it were built yesterday as a faux imitation of a past that no longer exists.

But it wasn't built yesterday. It is authentic. The city center sustained such heavy damage during the civil war that all the buildings had to be completely resurfaced, making them look brand-new even though they are not. They are so clean, unblemished and unmarked by time that they don't quite look real, especially compared with the rest of the city, which is chaotic and wild. Downtown Beirut looks even more pristine than the most pristine parts of Paris, giving the impression that it's trying too hard. After 20 more years of weather and age, it should look properly broken-in and lived-in again, but right now it looks like a Levantine Disneyland.

The company responsible for downtown's renovation, Solidere, was founded by Rafik Hariri, the former Sunni prime minister whose assassination in 2005 sparked the Cedar Revolution against the Syrian military occupation. Not everyone is happy with Solidere, and not only because downtown looks and feels like a theme park. Solidere has a near monopoly on the reconstruction of the city center and uses considerable muscle against property owners and residents who get in the way of its plans. I've seen billboards and graffiti saying "Stop Solidere" around Beirut for years.

The first time I visited the city in 2005, the area immediately northwest of the restored downtown was a wide urban blank space laid waste by war. Today it has been rebuilt from scratch as the new Souks of Beirut, in a style that never existed before. It sort of looks and feels like a traditional Middle Eastern bazaar, but not really. It's more like an open-air mall with a hint of traditional style to give it some flavor. Most of the shops are well above the price range of not only most Lebanese citizens but also of middle-class Americans like me. The new Souks of Beirut cater almost exclusively to wealthy Gulf Arabs on holiday. The area certainly looks better than the rubble field it replaced, but most Beirutis feel a bit alienated by the place, as do I.

There's another problem too. The new Souks of Beirut sucked half the merchants out of downtown, and they have not been replaced. Lebanon's economy can only sustain so many high-end restaurants and stores at a time before they're spread out too thin. Solidere, it appears, rebuilt too much too quickly.

But there is a major advantage to Beirut's unnatural-feeling and now half-empty downtown. Like the Latin Quarter of Paris, cars are banished from most of it. The city desperately needs a little island of breathing space, because streets and sidewalks everywhere else are stressful, loud and even a little bit dangerous.

The rest of the city is a pedestrian nightmare. Streets are so narrow that cars often have to be parked on the sidewalks, forcing everyone on foot into roadways turned to rivers of steel by the worst drivers in the world outside of Albania.

Stop signs merely act as suggestions. Traffic lights scarcely exist and are only really obeyed when traffic is as its peak. Even then, drivers are constantly running red lights. Traffic is so out of control in Beirut that I suspect even the most ardent American opponents of red-light cameras at home would approve of Beirut's after trying to cross the street a handful of times.

The city is currently installing parking meters for the first time in its history. Parking meters. In Beirut! They are as alien and incongruous there as a topless bar in Saudi Arabia or a Lamborghini showroom in Somalia. Nobody takes them seriously. I recently walked down a street where every parked car—one after another for several blocks in a row—had a parking ticket tucked under the windshield wipers. Citizens may eventually catch on and learn to drive and park like everyone else in the world, but until then, the city careens out of control.

Messiness aside, though, Beirut is the most cosmopolitan, liberal and even Western Arab city by far. Foreigners from Europe and the United States will find far more fragments of their own culture in Beirut than will Arab tourists from the Persian Gulf region, though plenty of Gulfies holiday in Lebanon anyway. To an extent, you can chalk up Beirut's partial Westernization to the cultural influence of Lebanese Christians and imperial France, but the Sunni parts of town are no less culturally developed than the Christian side. Fantastic bookstores, art galleries, film and music festivals and even gay bars—unthinkable in cities like Baghdad and Cairo—proliferate in both parts of the city.

One reason is that Beirut isn't very religious. It's hard to say for sure what percentage of people believe in God and take religion seriously, but let's put it this way: bars and clubs are much more crowded than churches and mosques. Beirut's houses of worship aren't as empty as Europe's, where you'll often find more tourists with cameras inside than the devout, but they're close.

When Lebanese self-identify as Christian, Sunni, Shia or Druze, they aren't telling you what they believe theologically. They're telling you which community they belong to. Religious sects in the eastern

Mediterranean function like ethnicities, just as they do in Northern Ireland and the former Yugoslavia. Atheist Sunni Muslims in Lebanon and Syria are just as much Sunni Muslims in sectarian terms as Jews in Israel are Jews whether or not they're religious. Each sect has its own history, its own culture, its own aspirations and fears and its own constellation of allies and enemies.

The people of Lebanon, Syria and Israel can't exempt themselves from all this just because they choose to be secular. Even the most liberal and cosmopolitan secular humanists find themselves trapped by their sectarian identity, sometimes willingly and other times not. It's inescapable because during times of armed conflict, people can be killed for what's printed next to Religion on their identity card—and nobody's card says None next to Religion. Sectarian murderers do not ask, nor do they care, whether or not their victims believe in God or have even set foot in a church or a mosque. During times of armed conflict—and even to an extent during times of sectarian tension, which is near constant— people can only truly find safety amid the confines of their sect.

Lebanon's diverse sects make up the constituent parts of its culture, and the sectarian boundaries define the human geography. The eastern half of the capital is almost entirely Christian. The western half is predominantly Sunni. And the southern suburbs are all but monolithically Shia.

The city split apart during the civil war into mutually hostile cantons. Christian militias squared off against Palestinian and Sunni militias across a burning gash known as the Green Line, which ripped through the center of the city on a northwest-by-southeast axis. Beirut wasn't so neatly divided before the civil war, and today you'll find Christians on the west side and Muslims on the east side, but the city remains mostly divided along the same line today.

Each half of the city looks and feels different. For a host of reasons, the Christian side sustained less damage during the war. Fewer buildings were destroyed, so it's a lot more French-looking today. It's also more culturally "French," since many Lebanese Christians feel a political, cultural and religious kinship with France and the French language that Lebanese Muslims do not.

The west side of the city is more culturally Arab and architecturally bland, because so many of its buildings were flattened during the war. The Sunnis on the west side of town also never bonded as strongly with France. They're more liberal and cosmopolitan than Sunni Arabs in most other parts of the region, but their culture, religion, language and loyalties are for the most part in sync with their more conservative neighbors.

East and West Beirut are nearly identical, however, compared with the southern suburbs. Collectively known as the *dahiyeh*, which means suburb in Arabic, this part of the metro area is the de facto "capital" of Hezbollahland. The central government has no writ there. Hezbollah provides its own security, its own services, its own hospitals and its own schools. Drive down the streets and you'll see the Hezbollah flag and the Iranian flag but rarely if ever the Lebanese flag. It looks, feels and functions like a ramshackle satellite of Iran even though you can walk there from central Beirut in roughly an hour.

Once known as the "belt of misery," it was and remains a slum, even if it's a little less miserable than it used to be. Most of the buildings are shoddily constructed 12-story apartment towers built without permits and with no attention whatsoever to grace, style or aesthetics of any kind, especially not the French kind. There are places in East Beirut where, if you try hard enough and squint at the city just so, you could fool yourself into believing you're somewhere in France, but there's no chance you could ever get away with that in the *dahiyeh*.

The dividing lines between these three parts of Beirut are the flash points when armed conflict breaks out. A half-mile or so south of the city center along the old Green Line near Sodeco Square is what's commonly called the Yellow House, at least what's left of it. This once beautiful row of apartments and shops was the posh home of some of Beirut's finest before it was shattered to the core early on during the war. The bullet-pocked stone skeleton still stands in a state of ruin that is hardly less advanced than that of the great gladiator coliseum in Rome.

It is finally being renovated after decades of sitting there like the blasted-up hulk that it is, but it's not being renovated the way downtown has been renovated. The Yellow House will not look antiseptic and fake when it's finished. The chewed-up facade will be encased in glass with only the inside fixed up and refurbished. It will become a war museum, its torn-to-shreds husk preserved as if in amber as a constant reminder that urban civil war is one of the worst catastrophes the human race can inflict on itself.

If they aren't careful and wise, the Lebanese may end up inflicting it on themselves all over again. For the sectarian monster stalking Syria is again clawing its way to the surface in Lebanon. Sunni Muslims, by and large, support the Syrian opposition, while most of Lebanon's Shia community backs the Assad regime. Hezbollah is now openly involved in the Syrian war—without anything even vaguely resembling an exit strategy—and is taking such heavy casualties that Michael Young, in *NOW Lebanon,* dubbed it "Hezbollah's Vietnam." Meanwhile, Lebanese Sunnis in the Bekaa Valley are giving shelter to their brethren in the Free Syrian Army. Some are even volunteering as soldiers.

Lebanese Sunnis and Lebanese Shias are killing each other right now in Syria. It may be but a matter of time before they stop bothering to first cross the border and just start killing each other at home.

The reason both sides manage to restrain themselves despite it all is that both know neither can win an offensive war inside Lebanon. Amine Gemayel, the former president, summed up the futility of civil wars there when Lebanon was chewing off its own leg in the 1980s. "Everyone is against everyone else," he said, "and it all keeps going around and around in circles without anyone ever winning or anything being accomplished."

Eli Khoury concurs. "The beauty of Lebanon," he says, "is that everyone is a minority and no one can kick anyone's ass. If there's a war, it won't go anywhere. Everyone will protect their own area. Everyone realizes that if they start a war, they aren't going to get anything out of it."

Nobody wins wars in Lebanon, but unless Syria permanently breaks apart, Yugoslavia-style, one side or another will eventually emerge on top in Damascus. If Assad loses and doesn't manage to take Lebanon with him, Beirut will finally have relief from the cascade of catastrophes that has been ravaging the city for the past 38 years.

Lebanon will still have Hezbollah to deal with, of course, but the so-called Party of God only has two supporters and allies in the world, and one of them is Assad.

Future TV talk-show host Nadim Koteich thinks the fall of Assad will be a catastrophe for Hezbollah. "For decades they've had this huge, stable state behind them, along with a corridor for weapons coming out of Iran. They had this enormous machine and all its tools at their back. It will be a tremendous blow for them when they lose it. I don't know any bully who has a future. A bigger bully will eventually come along and kick their ass, or time will pass by and he'll just realize that he wasted his life pushing people around, while those who were bullied graduated from MIT and Harvard. That's Hezbollah's future."

Beirut looks and feels Middle Eastern when arriving from America, but it still looks and feels startlingly French when arriving from the inland Bekaa Valley, which has more in common with Syria than with the more cosmopolitan Mediterranean parts of the country. It's still a mess, though. I'd love to say Beirut is back. The city has a special place in my heart. It's the only foreign city I've ever lived in, and during the Cedar Revolution in 2005, I felt a rush of incredible optimism. The place looked and felt like I imagine East Germany must have when the Berlin Wall was knocked down.

Beirut, though, isn't back. Beirut, on the contrary, is *on* its back. The economy is in worse shape than I've ever seen it. Tourism is one of the city's primary industries, yet tumbleweeds are blowing through hotel lobbies. Governments all over the world are issuing terrifying travel warnings. Restaurants and nightclubs are closing because they don't have enough foreign customers and the locals don't have enough money.

And yet, paradoxically, the city in some ways looks better than I've ever seen it. It's not Paris—not even close—but it's harder than it used to be to find physical evidence that a terrible war took place there when I was a kid. The amount of reconstruction is simply astounding. While some of it looks like Miami, some of it looks like Dubai and none of it looks even slightly Parisian, all of it is superior to everything built in the city between the end of World War II—when the abundance of cheap materials and a cratering of aesthetic standards ruined architecture all over the world—and the end of the civil war.

All this progress was made despite Syria's military occupation, despite Hezbollah's terrible war against Israel, despite the invasion of Beirut in 2008, despite the global economic downturn that has dragged on for years and despite the civil war next door that is adding yet further insult to Lebanon's already injured economy.

If Beirut can leap ahead into the future while enduring all *that*, it should be able to do even better with the Syrian boot off its neck. When the Iranian regime is eventually overthrown or reformed—it happens to all such regimes in due time—and Hezbollah finds itself with no support whatsoever from anywhere, then Beirut, whether it's the Middle East's Paris or not, might once again become a great city.

Thirteen

Across the Sea of Darkness

Morocco, 2012

The Arab Spring left chaos in its wake. Islamization, renewed state repression and the threat of starvation led to a military coup against Egypt's Muslim Brotherhood President Mohamed Morsi. The Libyan civil war finally put an end to Muammar Qaddafi's Stalinist dungeon state, but terrorism, destabilization, assassination and precarious anarchy followed. Sectarian bloodshed approaching genocidal levels may destroy Syria whether ro not its tyrant Bashar al-Assad survives or the country is taken over by the black-clad head-choppers of ISIS. Internally driven regime changes in the Arab world don't seem to have worked much better than the externally imposed regime change in Iraq.

But on the northwest border of Africa, change is coming to Morocco in a calmer and more gradual way. The ruling regime has been reformed instead of replaced, leaving institutions intact and creating no vacuum for thugs and fanatics to fill. Demonstrations sometimes occur, but they don't degenerate into riots, armed conflict or mob rule. Nobody thinks civil war is coming, nor is there any danger of an Iranian-style revolution.

Morocco has been outperforming its Arab neighbors for years. Now that a political hurricane is battering the rest of the region, it looks better than ever. Morocco evolves instead of explodes, and while incrementalism doesn't offer the instant gratification of uprising and revolution, it's precisely what the Middle East and North Africa need.

After spending more time than was good for my health in Baghdad and Cairo, Morocco's capital, Rabat, struck me as remarkably clean, well ordered, peaceful and civilized. While so much of the region wallows in dreariness, Morocco is awash with startling beauty and aesthetic perfection.

Few people love the largest city, Casablanca. It's a bit chaotic and reminds me of the less fashionable parts of Beirut. But the city center looks and feels like the capital of a European empire, and the reason struck me at once. Unlike most Arab countries outside the Gulf region, Morocco never went through a devastating socialist or Arab nationalist phase. Nor has it suffered revolution or war.

Much of Cairo looks Soviet. Beirut, Baghdad and Damascus chewed themselves to pieces. Soviet-style tyranny and civil war wrecked Algiers. But Morocco passed through the post–World War II era with nary a scratch. It's an astonishing thing to behold, and it's impossible, for me anyway, to ignore why: Morocco has been ruled by a stable monarchy for over 300 years.

Americans instinctively hate monarchy. Our country was forged in revolution against the British Crown, and the nation's founders established one of the most durable and resilient democratic systems in history.

Few Americans, however, are reminded of King George III when they consider the ruling Arab monarchs. The sheikhdoms of the Persian Gulf are run by decadent medievalists at best and terrorist sponsors at worst.

King Abdullah of Jordan looks and is better. He's a modern man who maintains his father Hussein's peace treaty with Israel. Hussein's widow, Queen Noor, is a feminist from America. Abdullah clearly wants to bring his country into the 21st century, but he might not survive the turmoil buffeting the region and his kingdom. Half the country wants him out—and wants him out now. His family isn't even from Jordan.

They come from the Hejaz region of Saudi Arabia and were installed in 1921 by the British.

Monarchies are by definition not democratic. They are, however—aside from Jordan's, perhaps—more stable than anything else in the Middle East and North Africa. Elliott Abrams, in an essay for *Commentary* called "Dictators Go, Monarchs Stay," describes a meeting he had with former Egyptian strongman Hosni Mubarak in 2005, when the Bush administration was pushing for elections in Iraq. "The Iraqis were incapable of democracy, [Mubarak] argued; you don't understand them like I do; they need a general to rule them."

But now the "big men" in the "fake republics," as Abrams described them, have almost all been overthrown, while the monarchs remain. The kings on their thrones have staying power and are not come-latelies. They have tradition on their side, at least.

Morocco's King Mohammad VI is said to be a direct descendent of the Prophet Mohammad. I asked some people in Rabat if that's really true. Everybody said yes. I asked how they know it's true. The answer was always the same. "We just know." Is it true? I have no idea. But everyone seems to think it is, or at least says that it is, and in any case the Alaoui family has ruled the country without interruption for hundreds of years.

The previous king, Mohammad's father Hassan II, ruled more or less as an absolute monarch, and his Ministry of the Interior ran what basically amounted to a police state. The so-called years of lead, from the 1960s to the 1980s, were characterized by heavy state repression against opposition movements from both the left and the right, some of which were heavily armed. I don't know if the word *lead* in that description refers to the use of ammunition or to just the general heaviness of the era. It works either way.

The lead years were rough. The lead years were brutal. The lead years made Morocco a sadly typical country in the Middle East and North Africa at the time.

Then in 2004, Mohammad VI, five years after ascending the throne, established a Truth and Reconciliation Commission—Instance Equité et Réconciliation—the only one in the world I'm aware of that didn't follow on the heels of a regime change. Victims of internal repression by Hassan II were rehabilitated and compensated. The young king encouraged everyone to let it all out, to voice their complaints and their grievances, to do so in public and even to scream if they wanted—and he encouraged them to do so against his own father.

Yet 2 million mourners attended King Hassan's funeral.

"I never even thought that I'd miss him," a Moroccan woman told me, "but every day for a year after he died, I drove to his mausoleum and cried."

One man in Rabat explained the psychology to me this way: "He was a really tough daddy. But he was daddy."

In 2011, after a new constitution was adopted at the behest of both people and king, Morocco was officially transformed into a constitutional monarchy with a democratic parliament and separation of powers. The respected NGO Freedom House raised the country's status from "not free" to "partly free."

"The king hasn't retired from the government," said Nadia Bernoussi, a professor of constitutional law who helped draft the new constitution. "What changed is that the parliament has entered the government. Our intention was not to hobble the monarchy but to clearly set out the responsibilities for each branch of the government. Because the context we were working in was the Arab Spring that's sweeping the region and all of its dangers. We didn't want to hobble the monarchy. We looked to the monarchy to ensure the changes we were making wouldn't get lost."

The changes they made, including sweeping new rights for women, very well could have been lost. Elsewhere in the Arab world, they have been. Egypt was ruled by a calcified military dictatorship the first time I visited in 2005. When I returned during the period between the fall of Mubarak and the election of Morsi, Egypt was a partly free country. At times it felt completely free, a remarkable turnaround from just a few years before. But the new president's power grab and his crude attempts at Islamization made Egypt progressively less free by the month. The army that removed him is no better. It's the same institution that made the state a dictatorship when the self-styled Free Officers, led by Gamal Abdel Nasser, seized power in 1952.

In Morocco, Mohammad VI appointed the council that drafted the new constitution. He wanted representatives from across the political spectrum, but he also wanted a progressive modern document, so he excluded communists and radical Islamists from the process. He achieved liberal results with illiberal means. Such is the paradox of Morocco. Moroccan liberals are generally happy to have the results despite the process. In the Arab world, it seems, you can often get liberal results or liberal means, but not both.

I don't know if Mohammad VI is enacting reforms because he genuinely wants to liberalize the country or because he wants to ride the wave of discontent rather than be swept away by it. I suspect it's a little of both.

What's left of the opposition doesn't agree. A series of protests broke out on February 20, 2011, four months before Morocco adopted constitutional monarchy. The protests were not led by a single movement or party, nor were they particularly organized. They were politically diverse, geographically dispersed and often parochial. In that sense, February 20 was more of a phenomenon than a movement. Whatever we should call it, it was inspired by the mass demonstrations that brought down Egypt's Mubarak and Tunisia's Zine el-Abidine Ben Ali.

In Rabat, tens of thousands took to the streets, shouting "The people want to change the constitution" and "Down with autocracy." They got at least some of what they wanted, and they got it in less than four months. But dozens of them are in prison. Opposition critics say the new constitution's separation of powers is insufficient. They accuse the king of undermining it on the sly.

Whether or not these complaints are fair, all governments—democratic, partially democratic and autocratic—need opposition and critics. What nations usually don't need is revolution.

Americans love revolution. Why shouldn't we? Ours was among the most successful in history. It endures more than 200 years later and was not the result of gradual change. As Thomas Jefferson put it, "The tree of liberty must be refreshed from time to time with the blood of patriots and tyrants."

The French Revolution followed ours, and Jefferson naturally swooned while it was happening. But it didn't end well. Instead of enjoying the blessings of liberty, the French inflicted the Reign of Terror on themselves and later reverted to monarchy. But those lessons are lost to time for all but the most historically minded.

Thanks to the Russians, average Americans looked askance at revolution throughout much of the 20th century. The October Revolution of 1917 installed a totalitarian dictatorship that built a slave empire spanning most of two continents. Then it replicated itself, virus-like, by sponsoring similar revolutions all over the world, creating one ghastly police state after another. But Europe's anticommunist revolutions in 1989 seemed to put everything right. Repressive regime after repressive regime fell to liberal dissidents like Lech Walesa in Poland and Vaclav Havel in Czechoslovakia.

The 1989 revolutions echoed the American Revolution in some ways, and they're fresher in everyone's minds than their botched predecessors. None of us who are old enough to have witnessed it can forget the fall of the Berlin Wall. Freedom was spreading again after the terrible communist detour. The tide of history washed tyrants away, as it should.

The Arab world seemed perfectly capable of replicating what Americans and Eastern Europeans had accomplished. During the Beirut Spring in 2005, the Lebanese evicted Syria's smothering military occupation without firing a shot. The more or less free and fair elections that followed sent the liberal pacifist Fouad Siniora to the prime minister's office. The model for Lebanon's uprising was the revolutions in Eastern Europe. I know because I was there. Surely the same thing could happen in Cairo and Tunis and Tripoli and Damascus. Right?

Apparently not.

Tunisia's revolution was mostly nonviolent and has been at least partly successful, but Egypt's, Libya's and especially Syria's have been much darker affairs. The very name "Arab Spring" evokes the romantic image of the Prague Spring, but we should remember that the 1968 Czech uprising, like the 1956 Hungarian revolution before it, ultimately failed. Soviet troops rolled into Budapest and Prague and crushed both democratic movements under the treads of their tanks.

In celebrating the Arab Spring, too many failed to take into account what was unique about America in 1776, Eastern Europe in 1989 and Beirut in 2005. In all three cases, the people were resisting a tyrannical regime that was imposed from the outside: by the British Crown, Soviet Russia and Syria's Arab Socialist Baath Party, respectively. These revolutions were produced by a more or less democratic political culture that already existed and was being suppressed by force from abroad.

Democratic political cultures aren't created by revolutions. They are created in advance of revolutions and reach their maturity during the aftermath. Lebanon and Tunisia are doing better than Egypt, Libya and Syria because they already had partially democratic and pluralistic political cultures that were being suppressed. But Egypt has never known anything but authoritarian rule, and before rebel fighters lynched Qaddafi outside Tripoli, he treated Libya like a mad scientist's laboratory for longer than I'd been alive.

America was an exceptional place in 1776. So was Eastern Europe in 1989 and, to a lesser extent, Lebanon in 2005.

So is Morocco. It's not exceptional in the same way the American colonies and Eastern Europe were exceptional, but it is exceptional.

Morocco is doing better than most Arab countries because of its system of government, and it's doing better than Arab monarchies because of its history.

That history is unique in large part thanks to geography. I drove from Rabat to Marrakech—a perfect city for tourists—and from there into the towering Atlas Mountains. Morocco is huge. It's rugged and craggy. Much of it is green. Part of it is on the Mediterranean, but most is on the Atlantic.

It doesn't look like anyplace in the Middle East and nothing like the culturally vacuous Persian Gulf emirates. It doesn't look like a Mediterranean country or an African country. Morocco is just Morocco, separated from Europe, the Middle East and sub-Saharan Africa by water, mountains and the hottest desert on earth. Over the centuries, its history and geography have sculpted a culture that's partly Arab, partly Berber, partly European and even partly Jewish. Its government is so stable, it's an anachronism.

The capital is 3,000 miles away from Mecca, the center of the Islamic world, while the city of Tangier is so close to Europe that you can see Spain across the Strait of Gibraltar. A fit enough person could swim there. The Spanish city of Ceuta on the north coast of Africa is actually contiguous with Morocco. It has been free of Muslim rule and either self-governing or Spanish for almost 600 years.

In the past, Morocco ruled parts of Spain. More recently, the Spanish ruled the southern provinces of Morocco, the contested region known today as the Western Sahara. And there is no doubt that the two countries have influenced each other. One of the more striking things about Spain's southern region of Andalusia is how it looks and feels vaguely Moroccan, especially compared with Madrid. No one can visit Morocco without noticing that parts of it look and feel vaguely European, especially compared with the heartland of Arabia.

Moroccan culture is also influenced by sub-Saharan Africa and by Judaism, which has existed there for thousands of years. The new constitution defines Moroccan identity itself as partly Jewish.

What's really striking about Morocco, however, is how much less Arab it is than other Arabic-speaking countries. That's partly because nearly half the people aren't even Arabs. They're Berbers—or Amazigh, as they call themselves—an indigenous people who predated the 7th century Arab invasion by millennia. Morocco is a diverse and polyglot place, but its people have managed to create a coherent and unified culture that is rarely prone to the sectarian and ethnic violence that has torn other Middle Eastern countries apart.

But it's not just the Europeans, Berbers, Jews and black Africans that make Morocco unique. It's also the country's distance from the Arabian Peninsula and the core of the Islamic world.

I met with Dr. Ahmed Abbadi, who holds a Ph.D. in Islamic studies from the University Qaddi Ayaad in Marrakech. Before 1995, he taught comparative history of religions and Islamic thought. Today he teaches sociology in a cooperation program with DePaul University in Chicago. He agrees that Morocco's uniqueness is geographic in origin.

"Morocco used to be called the Far West before America was discovered," he told me. "The Atlantic Ocean was known as the Sea of Darkness. We didn't know if there was anything out there beyond it."

Indeed, when I stood on the beach in Rabat, it felt strange to think that directly across the water lay not Turkey or Iran or Yemen or Pakistan but Myrtle Beach, South Carolina. From the United States, Morocco is closer than most of Europe. Baghdad is as far from Rabat as Canada's Prince Edward Island.

"We're separated from the center of the Middle East by great distances and great mountains," Abbadi said. "Because we are so far away, we have time to analyze everything that comes out before it gets here. Everything emanating from the Middle East arrives on our shores in milder form. To quote Frank Sinatra, we did it our way."

The ancient Phoenicians helped establish the rudiments of civilization in Morocco, but the early Moroccans resisted the Roman Empire. "We also resisted the Umayyads," Abbadi said. "We resisted the Fatimids. We did not accept the Ottomans. We stood at the border of Morocco and Algeria and told the Ottomans no."

Robert D. Kaplan, in his fascinating book *The Revenge of Geography,* notes that mountains are a conservative force. For good or bad, they block the spread of ideas. The Atlas Mountains are a powerful conservative force: not only do the snowcapped peaks slow the progress of ideas and culture coming from the Middle East, but they also create hyperlocal cultures within Morocco itself.

Port cities, moreover, are inherently liberal, and Morocco has lots of them. Because they are hubs for travel and trade, they provide access to foreign people, ideas and culture, and they do it safely because the sea protects them from ground invasion. Morocco's port cities are all right next to Europe.

Morocco's geography, then, is a blessing. Its port cities near Europe tend to bring good ideas in, and its mountains keep some of the Middle East's worst ideas out.

Arab nationalists like to claim that the Arab world is a single nation cruelly divided by European imperialists, but this is a fantasy. The Arab world is coherent as a civilization, but like all civilizations, it's splendidly diverse and tragically fractious. Not even Lebanon can hold itself together as a coherent nation, and it's smaller in population than metropolitan Houston. So of course Morocco is different from other Arab countries. All Arab countries are different from other Arab countries.

When the Prophet Muhammad's armies swept out of the Arabian Peninsula 13 centuries ago, they spread their religion and language, but they didn't exterminate and replace indigenous populations. And the natives often influenced their conquerors as much as vice versa. In Egypt, Arabs became Egyptian even as most Egyptians eventually converted to Islam and learned Arabic. In Tunisia, the conquerors assimilated themselves and their religion into a highly advanced civilization that was Western in orientation. And in Morocco, they mixed with a Berber population linked to both sub-Saharan Africa and southern Europe. This is how it always goes for imperial expansionists. Mexico, for example, is to this day a fusion of European and Aztec cultures.

Religions also change as they spread. Christianity is practiced in strikingly different ways in Norway and Cuba. And both are very different from Christianity as practiced in Jerusalem, its birthplace. In the same way, Islam as practiced in Rabat is very different from how it's practiced in Mecca. Like everything else in Morocco, it's milder.

I asked Abbadi what he thinks of the term *moderate Islam*. Some Muslims don't like it. Some non-Muslims think moderate Islam doesn't exist. Even some Muslims insist that moderate Islam doesn't exist.

"I prefer 'ponderous and reflective' Islam," he said. "The word *moderate* per se doesn't mean anything. Islam should be modern, teleological, clear, contextualized, realistic and feasible."

"The reason I ask," I said, "is because I want to know what you think about something Turkish Prime Minister Recep Tayyip Erdogan once said. Quote, 'There is no moderate or immoderate Islam. Islam is Islam, and that's it.'"

"That's very dangerous," Abbadi said. "Islam is not absolute. It is yoked to the human dimension. It is we humans who understand Islam. It is subjected to my reason, my way of understanding the world and my analysis. Religions encounter previous cultures, previous religions, previous visions and cosmologies. It merges with all of them. No religion falls from the sky onto bare ground."

Moroccan journalist Abderrahman Aadaoui laughed when I asked him if he needs a license from the government to practice his profession. "Of course not," he said, as if my question was bizarre. But journalists in plenty of Arab countries do need a license. They are heavily regulated by the dictators they write about. Not sufficiently toeing the party line? Say goodbye to your license and income, perhaps your family and home, and maybe even your life.

Aadaoui graduated with a degree in English literature from University Mohammad V in 1985, and he works today as the moderator of a weekly political show called *Issues and Opinion* on Moroccan TV.

I asked him about red lines in the media. Surely they must exist. All Arab countries have red lines. They aren't the same everywhere, but they exist everywhere. And of course they exist in Morocco, as well.

The red lines are these: You can't bang on the king. You can't bang on Islam. And you can't question the territorial integrity of Morocco—meaning you can't say that the still-disputed Western Sahara region belongs to the Polisario, a communist guerrilla army backed by Fidel Castro and Muammar Qaddafi that tried to take over the region after the Spanish imperialists left.

Theoretically, Moroccan journalists can say whatever they want about anything else, including the parliament and the Arab-Israeli conflict.

"But Moroccans can even cross those lines now to an extent," Aadaoui said. "They can write about the king and argue about Islam."

"Can you say terrible things about the king?" I said.

He smiled and laughed. "Well, it depends," he said. "What do you mean by terrible? You can talk about his fortune, his wealth. People are talking about that right now. You can talk about his personal life. There used to be a red line, a wall, that has been destroyed. The word *wall* is better than *line*. Like the Berlin Wall, every day someone takes another brick out of it.

"As far as liberty," he continued, "Morocco has recently gone from zero percent to 95 percent. But we don't have total freedom. Once in a while somebody goes to jail. And people ask, How come during the reign of Hassan II nobody went to jail? The reason is because no one wrote about anything controversial. Those were real red lines back in that day. No one had the right to write anything about the king except what was official, the things he was doing. Now people take the initiative and write about the king."

Moroccan journalists do get arrested sometimes, and not only for crossing those red lines. For instance, in 2011, Rachid Niny, a controversial newspaper publisher, was jailed for a year for supposedly publishing "disinformation" about Morocco's intelligence agency.

Because of incidents of that sort, and because of the red lines, Freedom House ranks Morocco's press as "not free" even while listing Morocco as a "partly free" country.

Aadaoui thinks that's grossly unfair.

"Freedom House," he said, "is critical of Moroccan press freedom because they were expecting 100 percent freedom. They shouldn't make judgments about the current era without taking into consideration what we had before. There was enormous oppression. We weren't allowed to say one single word. I left during King Hassan's reign. I went to the United States. And when I came back, Morocco was a different country. You had to have lived in the period before to enjoy what we have now."

I can understand his frustration, but that doesn't make Freedom House wrong. The ranking doesn't by itself reveal that Morocco is more free than it used to be, but it's nevertheless the case that the media isn't yet free. The rating is accurate even if Aadaoui is right that the press is freer than it was.

Aadaoui sees a glass that's half-full while Freedom House sees a glass that's half-empty. They're both right. They even agree with each other. Neither disputes the fact that half the glass is filled with water while the other is nothing but air.

He and I discussed the society as well as the media. Morocco is an inherently conservative place. It's like Japan in some ways. Change occurs gradually and very carefully over long stretches of time. That's how it has always been there. That's one of the reasons Morocco still has a king with actual power long after its European neighbors across the Mediterranean got rid of theirs.

But this is the 21st century, and no culture is static.

"The modern political parties talk about separating religion from government," he said. "This is new. But you should understand something. You see all this modernity around you." I did, indeed, see a modern-looking country around me. "We're modern in the street, but we are conservative when we go home. We have two faces. A man may watch a pornographic movie outside, but if he's home with his wife and he sees a kiss on the TV, he might change the channel. This is Morocco."

"Can you explain that?" I said.

"Modernity is new here," he said. "We got some of it from French and

Spanish colonialism, and from America. After the French and Spanish left, modernity stayed. There will always be a debate between modernity and conservatism, but the new generation can be as modern as they want to be. They're on Facebook and Twitter. They know only one thing. They are separating from the past. In 20 or 30 years, I think, we will no longer have two personalities. The duality we have here will fade. But people my age live in both worlds at the same time. And you find both points of view in the media. Some newspapers are strictly modernist and constantly attack the conservatives. One newspaper has pictures of women on what's called the 'hot page.' It's almost pornographic."

"The women are wearing, what, swimsuits?" I said.

"Not even swimsuits!" he said. "You don't see this in other Arab countries."

"Which side does the king come down on in the argument between the modernists and conservatives?" I said.

"He isn't supposed to take sides because he represents all the people," Aadaoui said, "but he's young and he encourages the modernist current. He says Morocco can't abandon its roots or religion, but he insists all the time on modernity. It is a key word in his speeches."

The United States has precious few allies in the Arab world. Only two Arab governments are genuine friends instead of friends of convenience. One is Jordan. The other is Morocco. Unlike "frenemy" nations like Egypt and Pakistan, Morocco is a real ally of the United States and has been for more than 200 years.

Morocco has never done anything bad to America. Unlike Libya and Algeria, it was not even a belligerent in the early 19th century Barbary Wars. Likewise, America has never done anything bad to Morocco.

Morocco was the first country on earth to recognize America's independence from Britain, and it was one of the first countries the United States liberated from Hitler. (Incidentally, even when it was occupied by the Nazis, the Moroccan government refused to hand over its Jews.) During the Cold War, Morocco stood fast with the United States not only against the Soviet Union but also against Arab nationalism. Today, it stands fast with America against radical Islam.

In 2004, President George W. Bush upgraded Morocco's status to that of a major non-NATO ally, alongside Israel, South Korea and Japan. In 2012, relations between Washington and Rabat were strengthened even further by what's called the Strategic Dialogue.

Our relationship today is partly built on a foundation of past friendship, partly on the fact that Washington and Rabat share the same strategic vision for the region and the world and, to a lesser extent, on shared values.

Youssef Amrani, Morocco's minister-delegate for foreign affairs, put it to me this way: "We have the same values. We have economic and cultural ties. The United States recognizes the commitment of Morocco to human rights and the rule of law. With all the changes in the region, we need to send the message that an Arab country can work with the United States on the basis of shared values."

He overstates things a bit. Moroccan values are not the same as American values. The two nations don't have nearly as much in common as Britain and the United States do. But aligning with Morocco doesn't offend American sensibilities the way buddying up with Pakistan does. Morocco is an island of stability, but it's not calcified like Saudi Arabia or frozen and stagnant like Egypt under Mubarak. The relationship between Washington and Rabat isn't repulsive like America's tactical alliance with Saddam Hussein during the Iran-Iraq war.

American policymakers would have to be out of their minds to suggest a different approach to Morocco. But an alliance with any kind of autocrat, even a benevolent one with limited power, can feel at least a bit awkward for both liberals and conservatives. Speaking for myself, I feel uneasy writing anything about a monarch that isn't disparaging. It doesn't come naturally. It feels wrong on some level. A decade ago, I wouldn't have done it. But if the Middle East has taught me anything, it's that moderation and stability are hard-won and precious.

Human-rights activists have a particularly difficult time praising a monarch, especially one who governs a country that Freedom House still ranks as just "partly free," with a press that's ranked "not free." And that's fine. Human-rights activists are supposed to be critical of Mohammad VI. It's their job.

It's still only fair to point out that Morocco is a lot freer than it used to be. Egypt and Syria certainly aren't. Tunisia and Libya are, but they're also unstable. Freedoms gained can be easily lost.

And let's not forget that human rights depend on stability. One of the most searing things I learned as a foreign correspondent in Baghdad is that human rights mean nothing in war zones. What good is freedom of speech if you'll get killed just for stepping outside your house? What good is freedom of assembly if your city is loaded with car bombs? What good are women's rights on paper if militias can assault women with impunity?

And let's not confuse elections and political liberalism. Mature political liberalism requires elections, but elections held in illiberal countries are often just referendums on who will be the next tyrant. That's exactly what happened in Egypt. Elections are liberal democracy's roof, not its floor.

Morocco has free and fair elections, but not for its head of state. That has to change sooner or later. The Moroccan monarchy will eventually have to sideline itself or face being sidelined by others. Smart Arab kings know this of the institution in general. As Jordan's King Abdullah said to Jeffrey Goldberg of the *Atlantic*, "where are monarchies in 50 years?" In the meantime, Morocco provides a safe space for peaceable coexistence between liberals and Islamists, Muslims and Jews (including Israelis on holiday), Arabs and Berbers, modernists and traditionalists.

The Western press has wasted a lot of words describing the Muslim Brotherhood as moderate. But Mohammad VI is a real moderate. He's a conservative in the sense that he belongs to a very old tradition and order, and he's a liberal insofar as he advances pluralism and women's rights and has willingly abdicated some of his power. He's a Muslim ruler who not only protects Jews but also declares Jewishness a part of Moroccan identity. He pushes for careful and deliberate change without overwhelming the country with too much at once, thus avoiding a hostile and potentially violent reaction from traditionalists.

Morocco is a little like Costa Rica during the Cold War—a calm, friendly, stable, sane, peaceable and essentially civilized oasis in a region that has known precious little of those things.

Morocco remains a conservative Muslim society, but the traditions it is conserving aren't the same as they are everywhere else in the region. The country has a strong moderate Sufi current, and the religion as practiced and understood there has long been influenced by ideas from sub-Saharan Africa and from Europe, which is only 11 miles away. Plenty of uncovered women are out and about in the streets. I didn't see a single woman with her face covered the entire time I was there. Female genital mutilation, with an incidence rate somewhere between 78 percent and 97 percent in Egypt, doesn't even exist in Morocco.

The city of Marrakech elected its first female mayor in 2009. Fatima Zahra Mansouri from the Authenticity and Modernity Party is the first female mayor in the country's history. She speaks perfect French and wouldn't have seemed out of place in the mayor's office in Paris.

She does not wear a headscarf. Every time she meets with local Islamists, they tell her she should cover herself, but she refuses. She has a standard—and I'm sorry to say, unprintable—response to that demand.

I asked her what's the hardest thing about her job, and she knew the answer immediately. "The most difficult thing is making unpopular decisions that are necessary for the city's future. Like making people pay for parking. People hate that, but it's important! And I don't like taxes, but the city needs money."

That's the kind of answer the mayor of a city in a peaceable and fully developed nation might have. The mayors of Benghazi and Baghdad have far bigger problems on their plate at the moment than parking meters. When public anger over such things becomes the biggest source of stress for the mayor of Baghdad, we'll know Iraq has truly and finally changed.

Mansouri and I talked urban issues for a while—I can be a bit of a geek about urban affairs and can talk about cities all day—but she really came to life when I asked my final question.

"What do you wish Americans knew about Morocco that they might not already know?" Most Americans know Morocco is a nice place for tourists, but that's about it. Most who know a little bit more know that Morocco is a Muslim country with a king, but—again—that's about it.

"It may be hard for you to understand Morocco politically," she said. "I often read analyses that are totally wrong, but I can't blame people for not understanding, because this is a hard place to understand."

She leaned forward and spoke in English rather than French to make sure I understood.

"The Moroccan soul is not one of revolution," she said, "but of evolution. It is our specialty. Transitions are easier here than they are in other places. We don't have what they have in Egypt and Syria and Libya today. We have a special system, one with a strong king but one who does not have all the power.

"We had the French protectorate period," she continued, "but after independence we built our own institutions. And now we are building democracy. Democracy isn't something that's just declared. It has to be built. We have the separation of powers. And we will never tolerate radical Islam because our traditions here have been moderate for 10 centuries. Look, Morocco is stable. We have a secular system. We have strong institutions and a growing economy. We are known as the door to Africa. We have so much cultural diversity here, and I think we can turn into a model of human development. You have to live here to fully appreciate it. We can't adopt a Western style of government yet, but we can strike a balance between who and what we are and what we will have to become."

Nadia Bernoussi, the law professor who helped draft the new constitution, grumbled a bit about how some foreigners see Morocco's democratic reforms as a sham.

"Well," I said. "The king wasn't elected."

She was taken aback by my bluntness, and I felt slightly rude saying it, but it's true, and every Westerner in the world who looks at Morocco's political system notices that and takes it into account. It is the most salient feature of her country's government from our point of view.

"It's true that the king isn't elected," she said, "but he has a different kind of legitimacy. He has national, historic and Islamic legitimacy."

That's for damn sure. Morocco's cities are places where the modern and traditional exist side by side, but the hinterlands are all about God, King and Country.

This isn't the sort of political sentiment Americans like me can relate to, but I did hear something I could understand and appreciate easily. When I asked uncovered Moroccan women if they feared the Islamists, all said they did not. (In Tunisia and Egypt, the uncovered women I know absolutely fear the Islamists.) Even the feminists in Morocco aren't afraid of the Islamists.

When I asked why, all of them said, "Because of the king."

Fourteen

On the Desert's Edge

Western Sahara, 2014

On the West Coast of Africa, directly across the Atlantic Ocean from Cuba, is the region known as the Western Sahara, one of the few remaining on earth that isn't recognized as part of a nation-state.

It is administered by Morocco yet claimed by the Polisario, a guerrilla army hatched by Fidel Castro and Muammar Qaddafi that fought to take over from colonial Spain in 1975 and transform it into a communist state. The Polisario lost the shooting part of its war to Morocco, but the fat lady hasn't even made her way to the dressing room yet.

Western Sahara is often (erroneously) compared to the Israeli-Palestinian conflict, but you wouldn't know that by walking around, nor would you see any evidence that the cities, such as they are, were once slums ruled by a police state.

You certainly wouldn't guess, if you didn't already know, that Western Sahara is still darkened by the long shadow of the Cold War or that the place still quietly bleeds from the unhealed wounds cut by Qaddafi and Castro, but foreign correspondents almost never go down there, and governments outside North Africa rarely give the problem more than a single passing thought every couple of years.

Western Sahara's citizens don't know how to suffer in ways that stir activists or make headlines, but they are suffering. Tens of thousands are to this day held in refugee camps—which are really more like

247

concentration camps—across the border in Algeria. They've been living in squalor as hostages in one of the planet's most inhospitable places almost as long as I've been alive.

Hardly anyone on earth has ever heard of them.

I flew down there from the Moroccan capital in early 2014 and could see from the air that I was about to land in a place no closer to anywhere else of significance on land than if I were on Ascension Island in the middle of the Atlantic.

The city of Dakhla, my destination, is a bubble of sorts. It's a seaside town on the edge of the Sahara Desert that is closer to Africa's tropical forests than to the Mediterranean on the continent's north coast, yet the climate is near perfect. The average high temperature in January is room temperature, and even in August it's just 82 degrees Fahrenheit—the same summer high as in the mild Pacific Northwest. The cool waters of the Atlantic create a razor-thin coastal microclimate that spares Dakhla's people from the infernal heat of the desert that broils anyone alive who dares to venture far from the beach.

Few live out in the wasteland. Western Sahara is one of the world's least densely populated areas. It's two-thirds the size of California, but only 800,000 people live in the whole of it, fewer than in metropolitan Omaha.

The area has virtually no resources to speak of. When Spain pulled out in 1975, there was less than 50 miles of paved road and one schoolhouse. Dakhla was little more than an army base with a couple of stores outside the gates surrounded by ocean and sand.

It was a ghastly place until the late 2000s, filled with shantytowns typical of the poorest regions of Africa. People lived in cinder-block houses with no running water or electricity. And it was repressed.

"I went down there in 1998," a retired diplomat said to me in Rabat, "and I counted 35 policemen in four blocks. I couldn't go anywhere without being followed. It wasn't possible to have even a peaceful demonstration without getting beaten up by the police."

The Moroccan government has eased up dramatically in the meantime just as it has up north, and most of Dakhla is brand-new. A huge percentage of Sahrawis—the Berbers, Tuaregs and Arabs of the Northwestern Sahara—were nomads well past the midpoint of the 20th century, but nearly all of them are now urban.

Dakhla during my lifetime has mushroomed from a remote Spanish outpost into a proper city of more than 85,000 people. Most have lived there for only one or two generations. Few are wealthy, but I saw none of the squalor typical of rapid urban migration in so many developing countries. Morocco has invested an enormous amount of money in the Sahara to make Dakhla livable, not just by building infrastructure and housing but also by investing in parks and a new promenade on the waterfront lined with palm trees.

I'd get bored after a while if I lived there—Dakhla is provincial, small and conservative—but I doubt I'd have many other complaints. The city is clean, friendly and aesthetically adequate. Buildings and houses tend to be rectangular and consist of only the simplest ornamentation, but they're painted in various desert hues and that's enough. Everything seems to work. European tourists love the place for its outstanding kitesurfing, desert adventure tourism and film and music festivals, and they bring a hint of cosmopolitan sensibility to the place that it would otherwise lack.

"Why did nomadism disappear now," I asked a local man, "instead of decades earlier or decades in the future?"

"It's the 21st century," he said and shrugged. As good an answer as any, I suppose. Why shouldn't the Sahrawis live in houses with televisions and Internet and drive cars to work like most of the rest of the world?

On weekends, though, families like to return to the desert. Their hearts still reside in the wildness of the Sahara.

Dakhla would be a great place for a day trip from Spain's nearby Canary Islands if it had ferry service, but a deep sadness soaks into its bones. The war with the Polisario is frozen, but it is not over.

The Polisario was founded as a popular movement in 1973 to resist Spain's colonization in what was then known as Spanish Sahara. Its primary sponsors were Fidel Castro, Muammar Qaddafi and Soviet-backed Algeria.

In the fall of 1975, the Moroccan government orchestrated the Green March, a nonviolent yet Godzilla-size demonstration. Hundreds of thousands of citizens crossed the border on foot and walked several miles inside Spanish-occupied territory, demanding that General Franco's forces withdraw. Spain left later that month, Franco died less than a week later, and the war between the Polisario and Morocco was on.

Thousands of refugees fled across the Algerian border and set up a constellation of camps, mostly outside the desert city of Tindouf, but—as expected of the proxies of Castro and Qaddafi—Polisario leaders soon turned those camps into prisons.

The conflict could have escalated into an American-Soviet proxy war, but Moscow was content to let Cuba, Libya and Algeria handle it, and Washington figured correctly that Morocco could win on its own.

Tens of thousands of Sahrawis still live in the camps, some as willing refugees but most as hostages. If they want to go home—and most of them do—they'll have to escape and risk imprisonment, torture and occasionally murder.

The so-called Moroccan Wall—a 10-foot-high barrier in the desert made of sand, stone, fencing and land mines—separates Western Sahara from Polisario territory. Every Moroccan-Algerian border crossing is closed, and the Polisario, in cahoots with the Algerians, hunts down everybody who runs.

Abdelatif Bendahane knows Africa better than just about anyone. He was the director of African Affairs at Morocco's Foreign Ministry and works today as an unofficial adviser to the president of Burkina Faso.

He and I talked politics over coffee.

"Morocco was once an empire from Tangier to Senegal," he said as he leaned back expansively. "The nomadic tribes in the Sahara always had good relations with the sultan in Rabat. Mauritania used to be part of the Moroccan Empire. There was no such entity as Mauritania before 1960. Today it's independent, so some think it's plausible that Western Sahara might also one day become independent."

France ruled what is now Mauritania until 1960, and the French left Morocco in 1956 after 44 years of occupation, but the Spanish held onto their in-between piece of the Sahara until 1975. Morocco has no designs on Mauritania, but it chaps Rabat's hide that its reacquisition of Western Sahara in the wake of the Spanish withdrawal hasn't been recognized internationally, partly because the conflict is a relic of the now long-dead Cold War and also because from Morocco's point of view, the region has been liberated after a long colonial occupation.

The only reason the conflict still simmers is that Algeria won't let it go.

"The problem is between Morocco and Algeria," he said, "not between Morocco and the Polisario. Without Algeria, the Polisario wouldn't exist. Algeria's government used to be leftist and socialist. It's not anymore, but their hegemonic ambitions are exactly the same. To this day there is no settled border between Algeria and Morocco. They want a federation with Western Sahara so they will have an Atlantic seaport. They believe this might actually happen."

But it can't happen unless somebody first forces out the Moroccans. And the Moroccans are no more likely to leave the Sahara than the United States is to leave California. Franco's Spain never considered Western Sahara an integral part of its territory, but Morocco does, right or wrong. "Imagine if Spanish speakers in the U.S. voted to secede," he said. "Washington would never accept it."

But since no country in the world recognizes Moroccan sovereignty over the area, Rabat is making a compromise offer of autonomy under the umbrella of sovereignty. The Sahrawis could run their own affairs, and unlike under Polisario rule, they could do so democratically.

Morocco could hold on to territory. And the stability Western Sahara currently enjoys as an extension of Morocco's wouldn't be lost.

It's the best deal the Polisario is ever going to get.

But Algiers thinks it's all a zero-sum game, that any gain for Morocco comes at the mathematical expense of Algeria. That's nonsense on stilts. All countries are better off with friends and allies as neighbors rather than enemies, but the Algerian regime, reheated Soviet leftover that it is, hasn't figured that out yet.

There was a brief period when Western Sahara might have slipped from Morocco's grasp had things gone a bit differently. The Polisario was once much more popular than it is now, but it's hard to gauge how popular or not the Polisario is today because no vote has ever been held on the question.

The Polisario won't accept a referendum on the status of Western Sahara if everyone who lives there gets to vote, and Morocco won't accept a referendum on the Polisario's terms because it would disenfranchise anybody who didn't live there before 1975, including all the Sahrawis who were forced out of the territory by the Spanish occupation.

The Sahrawis hold their own local elections, however, and they vote for their own representatives in the Moroccan capital, but Polisario Secretary-General Mohamed Abdelaziz writes letters to Ban Ki-moon asking the U.N. to put a stop to it. (The man really does take his opinions and style from Castro and Qaddafi.)

"The Polisario might have won the vote on their terms if it was based on their restricted voter list during the reign of Hassan II," Bendahane said. "Western Sahara was a police state back then. Today it's different. The Polisario would suffer a crushing defeat if everybody could vote. That's why there has not been a vote."

"What do the other North African countries think of all this?" I said.

"Tunisia, Libya, Egypt and Mali are all with Morocco," he said. "Mauritania fears Algerian power and splits the difference, supporting both sides more or less equally."

In some ways the status quo should be fine from Rabat's point of view because Morocco will never leave the Sahara and no one will ever force out Morocco. But the cold war with Algeria makes the creation of a functioning and stable North Africa all but impossible.

Former Moroccan political prisoner Driss el-Yazami says Morocco was in bad shape during the rule of the previous king, Hassan II, and that Western Sahara under his rule was even worse. "In the '60s and '70s," he said when I met him in his office in Rabat, "we had huge tension between leftists and the monarchy. The leftists wanted to kill the king and were armed by Algeria and Qaddafi. We had disappearances, detention centers, secret trials. Socialist newspapers were censored, and I was sentenced to life in prison."

He's out now and is president of Morocco's National Human Rights Council, which was created by the younger and more liberal King Mohammad VI after his father died.

"In the mid-1990s political prisoners were released, and we began the process of democratization," he said. "Sometimes it goes too slow, in my opinion, but we're moving in the right direction."

The Polisario, though, isn't moving in any direction. The organization has apparently junked its ideas about Marxist-Leninist economics—it's hard to build a dictatorship of the proletariat in a refugee camp whose only industry is smuggling—but its totalitarian structure remains intact.

Dakhla native Mohammad Cherif experienced that at its worst. He spent more than a decade with the Polisario—first as a willing recruit, then as a prisoner.

Growing up under Spanish colonialism, he found the Polisario's demands for independence compelling, and he signed on in 1977. "Their propaganda appealed to a lot of people," he told me.

He left Dakhla in 1978. After he went through six months of military training, the Polisario sent him to Libya, where he trained for three more years at a military academy.

But he'd barely even finished when he was arrested in 1981 for criticizing the Polisario leadership and was scurrilously accused of collaborating with Moroccan security. "They use that tactic against people whenever they have trouble in the camps."

The guards tossed him down a hole, slammed a grate over the top and left him there for five years.

"I had no name in the hole," he said. "They called me by a number."

They permitted him no contact whatsoever with the outside world. He used a bucket for a toilet and had his hands tied behind his back at all times. "They wouldn't let me sleep," he said. "For five years I hardly slept. The guards banged on the grate every hour at night and forced me to yell out 'I'm here.'" Whenever they dragged him out, usually to torture and interrogate him, they put a sack over his face so he couldn't see anything or anyone else.

Their questions rarely even made sense.

"They hanged me from the ceiling by my wrists and ankles and whipped me," he said. "I had to make up stories just to get them to stop. They'd leave me alone for a month to let my body heal, then start again."

Pressure from his family, some of whom were senior Polisario members in good standing, *finally* got him out of that hole. He asked if he could rejoin the army, but there was no chance they'd give him a gun, so they sent him instead to the Polisario embassy in Algiers and then on to Spain's Canary Islands, where he managed to escape to the Netherlands.

"The Polisario are not the representatives of the Sahrawi people," he said. "They are the torturers of the Sahrawi people."

.

For decades the Polisario shipped Sahrawi children to Cuba for indoctrination at the primary source. Maghlaha Dlimi was one of them, but she's home now in Dakhla, and she agreed to meet me for coffee and talk about it.

I was keenly interested in what she had to say, partly because I had just returned from Cuba myself, which ties with Qaddafi's Libya as the most repressive country I've ever visited. It says a great deal about the Polisario and its ideological severity that those two countries were its principal backers when it was founded.

"They sent me to Cuba when I was 10 years old," she said. My flawed Spanish is about as good as her flawed English, so we hobbled along in both languages. "First to the Isle of Youth, then to Santa Clara, then to Camaguey. This was in the 1980s. I got there on a Russian boat from Algeria with 3,000 other kids."

She took Spanish lessons in the camps before heading over. Children who struggled with the language went to Algeria, Syria, Libya, Russia or Yugoslavia—all communist or communist-aligned countries.

Ostensibly she went to Cuba for school because better teachers were available than in the refugee camps, but that wasn't really the reason.

"I had no idea until I got there," she said, "but the real purpose was to indoctrinate me with communist ideology. We also received military training, girls as well as boys. None of us wanted to stay. We wanted a real education."

She didn't get one. Nor did the other Sahrawi children. Castro's education of children from across the ocean wasn't a charity mission. He used them as pawns in one of his grand adventures in Africa. Western Sahara was but his latest. Havana's men, including Che Guevara, trained guerrillas in Eritrea, Ethiopia and the Congo. Cuba even sent soldiers into Angola.

"The Polisario wanted to impose a communist structure on nomadic populations," she said. "I don't believe that has changed. The same people are the leaders today as when I was young. There are still Sahrawi children in Cuba right now."

She wanted to study journalism and translation in school, but they wouldn't let her. "I got good grades, but they said no. Only kids who were part of the Polisario cadre could choose what to study. They forced me to study education and teach Spanish."

The leadership eventually sent her to Spain, and she managed to escape through the Moroccan embassy in Madrid.

Her cousins are still there, but her brothers and sisters made it out. Her oldest brother fled first, in 1997, then organized escapes for everyone else.

"It's impossible for an entire family to get out at once," she said. "And when one family member leaves, they keep a close eye on the rest. We don't dare tell anyone we're planning to leave, not even our parents. There is no family intimacy in the camps. You never know if one of your brothers or sisters will rat you out to the guards."

The Polisario is the self-styled representative of the Sahrawis, but Khallihanna Amar has a much stronger case since he was elected to the local community council in Dakhla.

He, too, is one of the Polisario's former prisoners.

They scooped him up the first time he tried to escape from the camps in 1995. "They interrogated me for a month," he told me. "Over and over again they asked why I was trying to leave and where I was going."

Surely, I said, the Polisario has an ass-covering excuse for not letting prisoners leave that makes at least some vague sense ideologically. They still refuse to admit they're holding even a single soul hostage.

"Of course," he said. "If you try to leave, they accuse you of being a counterrevolutionary and a Moroccan agent. My father was accused of collaborating with the Mauritanian resistance and sent to a re-education camp. And for my second escape attempt, I paid a smuggler to take me to the Mali-Mauritanian border. Traffickers there smuggle humanitarian aid, cigarettes and everything else. I worked my way up the coast and walked past a minefield to the Moroccan border. The Moroccan soldiers saw me coming and grabbed me."

Western Sahara is not a police state anymore, but not everyone who followed the conflict in the early days when it made headlines is aware of that yet. Dakhla isn't exactly a hotspot for foreign correspondents. It's more than 1,000 miles down the West African coast from Tangier and pinned in the middle of nowhere by the Atlantic Ocean on one side and a Mars-like desert bigger than the United States on the other. It takes 20 hours to drive there from Rabat, about as long as it takes to drive from Seattle to Los Angeles. Aside from European kitesurfers, hardly anyone ever goes there.

I had to wonder, though, if I was being fooled by cosmetic relaxation that didn't go very far. It happens. My thoughts kept returning to Cuba, not only because the Castro regime backs the Polisario but also because I had recently been in Cuba myself and know all too well how many people visit on holiday and think everything's fine when it's not. It's at least theoretically possible that repression in Western Sahara is simply less obvious than it used to be—as in Cuba—and therefore more insidious.

The lack of men with guns on the streets does not by itself mean it isn't oppressive. I didn't see men with guns in Havana, but Cuba has the worst human-rights record by far in the western hemisphere. I was sitting across the table from a man who had been elected to the local community council in a multiparty election, though, so how bad could it be?

"When I came back," he said, "I found that I still had all my social, political and economic rights. And I got elected to the council. So, no, I'm not being oppressed. No one here is oppressed. But there are young people who know nothing about the camps and who demonstrate against Morocco because the Sahara is not independent. They are like me when I was 14 and Che Guevara was my hero. I didn't listen to anybody back then."

Morocco's government isn't like Cuba's. It holds free and fair elections with a range of parties to choose from across the political spectrum. The Polisario runs an asteroid belt of actual police states in the camps across the border inside Algeria, which itself is smothered by a Soviet-style regime. *That's* where you'll find the Cuban analogue in North Africa, which makes perfect sense because the Polisario is partly a creature of Castro.

"Conditions in the camps are miserable," Amar said. "People are living in tents and mud buildings built by Moroccan slave labor. Food is only available depending on what kind of relations people have with the leadership. There are constant epidemics. And they're out in the middle of nowhere."

Try to imagine living like that in the hottest place in the world. The climate in Dakhla is near perfect, thanks to the cool winds off the Atlantic, but go just a few miles inland and you'll feel like you've stuck your face in front of an open oven on broil.

"What do people *do* all day in the camps?" I said.

"The Polisario gave us a schedule to occupy our time and our minds," he said. "Men get military training. Woman are organized into committees for education, distribution of humanitarian aid and social relations." The disgraceful use of child soldiers in sub-Saharan Africa is well documented, but they're up north, too, out in the desert. "Children begin military training at age 10. They are taught how to take apart an AK-47 and put it back together blindfolded."

Morocco's human-rights record is far from perfect. Freedom House ranks the country as "partly free" rather than "free." But the Polisario's patron states stomp on human faces with boots as a matter of course. It's fine and good to be skeptical of the Moroccan government, its reforms and its claims, but that goes double for Cuba, Algeria and the Polisario.

"We want American guarantees to Morocco so we can fix this," Amar said. "People here have suffered a great deal since the mid-1970s. We want peace and security and to have our families together again. What purpose has been served all these years by keeping our families hostage in those camps?"

North Africa is so close to Europe. The two continents can see each other across the Strait of Gibraltar. Yet they are politically, socially and economically thousands of miles apart.

The entire Sahara-Sahel region is unstable. Egypt is ruled again by a military dictatorship. Libya is on the verge of total disintegration, à la Somalia. Algeria is mired in a Soviet time warp. Northern Mali was taken over by Taliban-style terrorists so vicious they prompted the French to invade. At the time of this writing, U.S. troops are hunting Nigeria's al-Qaeda-linked Boko Haram across the border in Chad.

Tunisia is doing okay, but it's small. Aside from Morocco, the entire northern half of Africa is a disaster. Most of the continent, really, is still a disaster, but North Africa matters more to the West because it's the southern half of the Mediterranean. The region isn't Las Vegas: what happens there doesn't stay there and never has.

The region's potential is obvious to everyone who has seen it at its best. Marrakech in Morocco, Sidi Bou Said in Tunisia, Ghadamis in Libya: these are some of the world's most beautiful places, and they're inhabited by the some of the friendliest and most delightful people I've ever met.

Well into the 21st century, though, there is still more darkness than light, even in the blazing Sahara. Military dictators, Islamist mass murderers, human traffickers, gunrunners, thuggish communist proxy militias and kidnappers run roughshod and wild. The city of Dakhla has managed to keep it all at some distance, but it's fragile. On most maps, Western Sahara is nothing but a geographic abstraction.

That can't possibly last.

Maybe, perhaps even during my lifetime, North Africa will realize its potential and flourish with the freedom and prosperity that exists on the other side of the Mediterranean, but that time is not yet. Not even Morocco—the most stable and civilized state in the region by far—has managed to permanently secure its backyard yet.

"What would happen," I said to Amar, "if the Sahara became independent and the Polisario, one way or another, became the government?"

"An instant civil war," he said, "and an instant failed state."

Turn the page for a special preview of

Michael J. Totten's

Where the West Ends

Published by Belmont Estate Books

Available now from Barnes and Noble
and Amazon.com

"The forced collectivization of agriculture decreed by the Soviet master and his party likely cost the lives of more people than perished in all countries as a result of the First World War."
– Michael Marrus

"They had gone over the country like a swarm of locusts and taken away everything edible; they had shot or exiled thousands of peasants, sometimes whole villages; they had reduced some of the most fertile land in the world to a melancholy desert." – Malcolm Muggeridge

I bought a map of Eastern Europe in an old Oregon bookstore that's as big as a couch when unfolded. The most heavily trafficked roads appear as fat red lines on the paper. Almost all of them lead directly to Moscow. Even as late as the year 2012, the nerve center of the former Soviet Empire looks on my map like a world-devouring octopus capturing less important capitals in its tentacles.

On a cold night in late October I pointed at a thin red line on that map leading across the former Soviet frontier into Ukraine from a remote corner of Poland.

"Hardly anyone will be on this road," I said to my old friend Sean LaFreniere. He had just met up with me in Romania so we could hit the road again. "We shouldn't have to wait long at the border."

That logic seemed sound at the time, but I'm here to tell you: never, ever, choose less-traveled roads in countries that used to be part of Russia. Driving from even the most backward country in the European Union into the remote provinces of Ukraine is like falling off the edge of civilization into a land that was all but destroyed.

Sean and I hadn't learned that yet, though, and we wanted a scenic route. European road trips aren't like road trips in the American West where we live. Outside our major metropolitan areas, huge empty spaces and wide open roads are the norm. Most of Europe is crowded and neither of us wanted to sit in the car for hours in line at the border.

We had no idea what we were in for, but a Polish border guard warned us after stamping our passports.

"It is very *strange* over there," he said. "And nobody speaks English."

Screwing up in the strange parts of the world is never fun and is often miserable, but you learn things by doing it. You see things that governments and ministries of tourism wished you would not. Ukraine is so strange that you can even see these things in the dark. We actually saw more of Ukraine's strangeness *because* we showed up in the dark.

I don't remember what time we crossed the frontier. Eight o'clock in the evening? Anyway, it was dark. When I say it was dark, I mean it was *dark*. The back roads of Western Ukraine are as black at night as the most remote parts of the American West where no humans live in any direction.

Yet Western Ukraine is not empty.

And the roads. Oh God, the roads. I don't care where you've been. You almost certainly have never seen anything like them.

The second worst road I've ever driven on was in Central America in the mid-1990s. It's only ten percent as bad as the road Sean and I took into Ukraine. This one would have been no worse off had it been deliberately shredded to ribbons by air strikes. The damage was so thorough that the surface could not possibly have been repaved or repaired even once since the Stalinist era.

I white-knuckled it behind the wheel while Sean cringed in the passenger seat. I did not dare drive faster than five miles an hour. Even at that speed I had to weave all over the place to avoid the worst of the gaping holes, some of which were as wide as mattresses and deep enough to swallow TV sets.

I saw no cars, no street lights, not even a light from one single house. Ukraine looked depopulated. My maps said there were villages all over the place, but where were they? Did we just drive into an episode of *Life After People*?

"This is exactly like Russia," Sean said. "Exactly."

He had visited Russia two years earlier and will never forget the vast darkness at night on the train between Moscow and St. Petersburg. "We're in Russia!" he said

Then the ghost figures appeared.

They walked on the side of the road in wine-darkness. They did not carry flashlights. They seemed, like us, to be out in the middle of nowhere. It was then that I realized we had entered a town. In the periphery of my headlight beams I could faintly make out a few unlit houses shrouded in shadow away from the road, which was as broken and crumbling as ever. I still hadn't seen any other cars on the road, nor did I see any parked on the side. I don't know if the roads were so bad because nobody drove or if nobody drove because the roads were so bad.

"They should put up a sign on the border," Sean said, "saying *That was Europe. You like that? Now prepare for something completely different.*"

We were on our way to Chernobyl, or at least we thought we were headed there. *City Journal* assigned me to go there and write about the spooky ghost city of Pripyat that, along with the surrounding area in the so-called Exclusion Zone, was struck by a local apocalypse in 1986. The Soviet Union's Chernobyl nuclear reactor number four exploded and showered Pripyat, where 50,000 people lived, and the countryside around it with a storm of deadly radiation. Only 31 people were dead in the immediate aftermath, but the World Health Organization thinks the long-term effects of radiation poisoning will eventually kill another 4,000. More than 350,000 people in Ukraine and nearby Belarus have been permanently displaced. The fire still burns today beneath the crumbling concrete sarcophagus that caps the reactor.

No one should wander around there alone. The Ukrainian military won't let you in anyway if you don't have a guide and a permit. Some of Pripyat's buildings are still lethally radioactive, and there's no way to tell them apart from the relatively "safe" ones without sophisticated instruments. The scrap yard, where fire-fighting equipment was abandoned long ago, is spectacularly dangerous. Even mutant animals are supposedly running around.

Sean and I didn't yet know it, but the Chernobyl administration was about to cancel our permit and refuse to allow anyone entry. They didn't say why, but I assume it was because the zone suddenly became more dangerous than usual.

We would not get to go, but going there was our plan and we didn't yet know we would be re-routed. For a while there, we weren't sure we'd get *anywhere* in Ukraine, let alone hundreds of miles away to Chernobyl.

First we had to get to Lviv, the "capital" of Western Ukraine and the heartland of Ukrainian nationalism. That first stop alone was almost a hundred miles away. The road was so shattered I was barely able to drive any faster than I could walk. And we were lost. We couldn't even figure out how to get to Sambir, a small town that was hardly even inside Ukraine at all.

Sambir was spelled Самбір in Ukrainian and only one sign pointed the way. The Cyrillic letters in that particular name resembled the Latin letters well enough that I could figure it out. Then we came to a four-way junction. Road signs pointed to various towns in every direction, but none said Самбір. And none of the towns the signs *did* point toward appeared on my map—or, if they were on my map, I didn't know how to transliterate their names into Cyrillic. Which way we were supposed to be going?

"Let's go back," Sean said, "and ask one of those people on the side of the road."

I drove back the way we came until I saw two ghostly figures shambling along in the headlights. I pulled over and rolled down the window.

"Excuse me," I said. "Do you speak English?" I doubted they did, but this was a way of preparing them for the fact that they weren't going to hear any Ukrainian or Russian from me.

The two stopped walking and stared. A young man, perhaps 20 years old, held his young girlfriend's hand. He stared at me with wide eyes and slowly stepped between me and his girl as if I were a threat.

"We're trying to get to Sambir," I said and paused. "Sambir," I said again in case he understood nothing else but might at least know I needed directions and that he could point. He looked at me and didn't say anything.

"Sean," I said. "Hand me that map."

Sean handed over the map. I pointed at it. "Sambir." I said. "Which way to Sambir?"

The young man took several of cautious steps back. His girlfriend, terrified, moved behind him and peaked over his shoulder. They backed up another five feet or so, then walked away without saying anything.

"Well, that's just great," I said. We were the first foreigners they'd ever seen? Just a few miles from the Polish frontier?

"Go back and take the road that goes to the left," Sean said. "I'm pretty sure it's that one."

"How can you be pretty sure that it's that one?" I said. I had no idea where we were and wanted someone who lived there to tell us.

"It just feels right," he said. "If we see any more people, we can stop and ask."

I was in no mood to argue, and his guess was as good as mine, so we drove back to the four-way intersection and took a left. And we found ourselves in a forest.

"This doesn't look right at all," I said.

"How do you know what it's supposed to look like?" he said.

"I don't," I said. "It just looks like we're going into the middle of nowhere."

"Everywhere we've been is in the middle of nowhere," he said.

Perhaps he was right. Suddenly the road improved slightly. I could increase our speed, so I did, but then BANG. I ran us into a sink-sized hole in the ground at twenty miles an hour. The car shuddered as though a land mine had blown off a wheel.

Sean had rented this car on his credit card. "Oh my God," he said. "Oh my God, oh my God, oh my God."

"It's okay," I said, though I didn't for one second believe it. "There's still air in the tire."

"Not for long," he said and put his face in his hands.

I drove onward again, slower this time. We passed a dark house. Somebody lived out there in the forest.

"There are some people up ahead," Sean said. "Pull over and ask them where the hell we are."

I pulled the car over next to the two figures. Like the others, they looked ghost-like in the headlights. Like the others, they shuffled along as though they were wandering toward no place in particular for lack of anything better to do in a village at night without light.

This time we encountered not two scared teenagers, but an elderly man and his wife.

They looked startled as though they couldn't believe someone was out and about in a car.

"Excuse me," I said. "Do you speak English?" I was certain they didn't.

The woman flinched and the man said, "eh?"

"We're trying to get to Lviv," I said. Then I pointed at the map. "Lviv."

Not knowing better, I pronounced it "Luh-*viv*."

They had no idea what I was talking about.

"Luh-*viv*," I said again, and pointed at the map.

"Eh?" the woman said. "El-*veev*?"

"Da," I said, Russian for *yes*. Many ethnic Russians live in Eastern Ukraine and even ethnic Ukrainians in the west can speak Russian though they'd rather not. The bits of Russian that Sean and I knew were useful wherever we happened to be.

"Da," I said. "El-*veev*."

She pointed in the direction we were heading. "Poland," she said.

"Unbelievable," I said. We were on our way back to Poland?

"Argh!" Sean said.

"We've been driving around for hours," I said, "and we haven't gone *anywhere*."

So we turned back. I drove five miles an hour. I weaved around giant holes in the road, but still ran into five or six small ones per second. I had no idea where we were or where we were going. The night was almost half over and we had made zero progress. All we had done so far was damage the car and burn half the gas in the tank.

We eventually came to another small town even though we saw no more signs to even Sambir, let alone Lviv or Kiev. This time a few buildings were lit. One was a gas station. Incredibly, it was open.

I pulled in. Sean and I got out. We both inspected the banged-up wheel. It looked okay and apparently was not leaking air. We were lucky.

A man emerged from the office and asked us—I assume—if we needed gas.

"Do you speak English?" I said and chuckled. I knew he wouldn't.

Of course he didn't. A gas station attendant in rural Ukraine is no more likely to speak English than a gas station attendant in rural Kansas is likely to be fluent in Russian. Unlike the others we'd spoken to, though, he didn't seem surprised or alarmed that the wrong language came out of our mouths.

He filled the tank. I pointed at the map and said "Sambir." He gave us complicated directions that neither Sean nor I could make sense of. All we could really glean from him was which direction to start with.

I heard children giggling behind the gas station office. A young boy and a young girl, each no older than five, peeked their heads around the corner. They pointed at us and laughed as though we wore clown suits and squeaky shoes. Sean and I were the evening's entertainment. We spoke an alien language and that made us freaks.

"Good grief," I said. "Are we going to have to put up with this all week?"

I can only imagine how the locals would have reacted if we were black.

We drove in the dark on hideous roads for another hour. The gas station attendant told us we were supposed to turn left at some point, but we had no idea where.

"I hope it's not like this everywhere," Sean said.

"If it's like this everywhere," I said, "we won't even get to Lviv, let alone Kiev and Chernobyl."

"Turn left here," Sean said when we came to a road that looked promising for no apparent reason.

"Sure," I said. "Why not?"

I turned left. After a few minutes we came to a rusting dinosaur of a factory. It was dark and abandoned and clearly had been for decades. After we passed it, the road somehow managed to get worse. I had to slow down to three miles an hour to prevent the car from breaking apart. We'd need an off-road vehicle to keep going.

"This can't be the way to Lviv," I said. "No one can drive on this road."

So we turned back. And eventually we found the town of Sambir. We found it by sheer chance, but we found it. There were a few cars here and there, and some street lights, too. There wasn't much to it, but it was the closest thing we had yet seen to civilization in Ukraine. And we finally knew where we were on the map.

We had been in Ukraine for four hours and had barely made twenty miles of progress. Lviv was sixty more miles away.

I saw a sign on the side of the road pointing to Львів.

"That must be Lviv," I said. "I guess their в is our *v*. And the letter *i* is the same. I can tell by the way they spelled *Sambir* on the other signs." Over the next couple of days, Sean and I would eventually figure out and memorize the entire Cyrillic alphabet this way.

The road *did* improve after we left Sambir and headed toward Lviv.

"We need food," I said, though I wondered if that would be possible in a countryside that hardly even had light.

"Look for a sign that says pectopah," Sean said.

"A sign that says what?" I said.

"Pectopah," he said. "That's Russian for *restaurant*. That's not how they say it, but that's what it looks like when they spell it."

A few moments later we saw a well-lit building on the side of the road that looked like a restaurant. A sign read "Ресторан."

"There we go," Sean said.

"It even looks open," I said.

And it was.

We stepped inside. The place was half full and a few people were still grimly eating.

"Do we wait to be seated or just grab a table?" I said. I had no idea how to behave in this country. Rural Ukraine doesn't have any handles. We were on the European continent, but we sure weren't in the West any more.

Made in the USA
San Bernardino, CA
28 December 2014